007596 KT-485-746

KCWD (gus)

HAROLD BRIDGES LIBRARY
S. MARTIN'S COLLEGE
LANCASTER

Books are to be returned on or before
the last date below.

23. APR 93

- 2 OCT 1996

0805809481

Female Life Careers:
A Pattern Approach

PATHS THROUGH LIFE

A series of volumes edited by David Magnusson

Volume 1
Individual Development from an Interactional
Perspective: A Longitudinal Study

Volume 2
Pubertal Maturation
in Female Development

Volume 3
Female Life Careers:
A Pattern Approach

PATHS THROUGH LIFE
Volume 3

Female Life Careers:
A Pattern Approach

Sigrid B. Gustafson
Virginia Polytechnic Institute and State University

David Magnusson
University of Stockholm

LEA LAWRENCE ERLBAUM ASSOCIATES, PUBLISHERS
1991   Hillsdale, New Jersey   Hove and London

Copyright © 1991 by Lawrence Erlbaum Associates, Inc.
All rights reserved. No part of this book may be reproduced in
any form, by photostat, microform, retrieval system, or any other
means, without the prior written permission of the publisher.

Lawrence Erlbaum Associates, Inc., Publishers
365 Broadway
Hillsdale, New Jersey   07642

Library of Congress Cataloging-in-Publication Data
Gustafson, Sigrid B.
    Female life careers : a pattern approach / Sigrid B. Gustafson,
        p.   cm. — (Paths through life : v. 3)
    Includes index.
    ISBN 0-8058-0948-1
    1. Women—Psychology. 2. Women—Education. 3.
Women—Employment.
    I. Magnusson, David. II. Title. III. Series.
    HQ1206.G87 1991
    305.43—dc20   90-13923
                                                           CIP

Printed in the United States of America
10 9 8 7 6 5 4 3 2 1

To our respective daughters—
Erin Laura Bekowies, Ulla Magnusson, and *Anna Magnusson Sjöberg*

Contents

Preface

This volume illustrates a pattern approach to investigating the career development of women, from early adolescence through early adulthood. Rather than addressing sex differences, the study focuses on individual differences among females. Rather than constructing a general model of female career development, our objective is to use the interplay between theory and observation to build networks of pattern associations, reflecting differential processes that carry differential long-term consequences.

The current volume is the third in a series entitled Paths Through Life. Like the previous volumes, it is based on research conducted within the longitudinal project, Individual Development and Adjustment (IDA), which was initiated by the second author in the mid-1960s, at the Department of Psychology, University of Stockholm. The first volume in the series (Magnusson, 1988) presented the theoretical background of the program, the methodological and research strategy implications of the theoretical foundation, and empirical studies demonstrating the potential of a longitudinal approach to the study of individual development. The second volume (Stattin & Magnusson, 1990) presented a biosocial model of female development in adolescence, as a framework for empirical studies focusing on the short- and long-term consequences of individual variations in female pubertal development.

We offer our thanks to our colleagues in the research group, for the many constructive discussions that accompanied the preparation of this volume. To Professor Lars Bergman, upon whose methodological expertise we especially relied, and to Ola Andersson, the database manager of the IDA project, we would like to extend our particular gratitude for the assistance they have provided. In addition, the first author would like to express her deep appreciation to Professor Magnusson and to the other members of this excellent Swedish research group for the opportunity to participate in the IDA Project over the past 3 years.

The research presented in this volume was made possible through the financial support of the Bank of Sweden Tercentenary Fund, the Wenner-Gren Postdoctoral Fellowship Fund, and the Swedish Institute.

Sigrid B. Gustafson
David Magnusson

Chapter 1

An Interactional Perspective on Female Career Development

This book is about the career development of young women, from early adolescence through early adulthood. It is concerned with individual differences, not sex differences. Its theoretical framework is interactional; its research strategy, the methodological details of which are discussed in the next chapter, is oriented toward patterns.

A LITTLE BACKGROUND MUSIC

Despite several decades of lamentation and exhortation by parents, educators, psychologists, and those in sympathy with the loosely knit movement known as "feminism," girls are still relatively more likely than boys to grow up to be nurses and secretaries rather than physicians and corporate executives. Girls still avoid the mathematics courses required for careers in "nontraditional" professions like science and engineering (Chipman & Thomas, 1985; Eccles, 1983; Eccles, Adler, & Meece, 1984; Ernest, 1976; Pedro, Wolleat, Fennema, & Becker, 1981; Sells, 1982). Young women in the United States, from upper middle-class homes that have encouraged female achievement, still expect that after they marry, their husbands will provide the bulk of the family's income (Camarena, Petersen, & Seidensticker, 1990). And a recent issue of *Newsweek* magazine (April 16, 1990, international edition) reported that, when asked why there were not more men in her field, the director of the human-rights group Helsinki Watch replied

1

(perhaps with more candor than tact), "One reason human rights draws a lot of women is that it doesn't pay well. Women are more willing to make sacrifices" (p. 9).

Given that sex roles seem to be alive and well, it is not too surprising that career development, as a specific area of study, has historically been devoted to models depicting the aspirations and accomplishments of males. Roe (e.g., 1949, 1951, 1956) has concentrated on the careers of eminent scientists. Only 10 females comprised the sample used to shape Ginzberg, Ginsburg, Axelrad, and Herma's (1951) initial theory regarding the compromises between preference and opportunity that constitute their proposed stages of vocational choice. Even Super's (1953, 1963) formulation of age-linked career stages that extend across the life span, although it remains one of the most influential career theories in terms of guiding research, is less relevant to the female life course, which must accommodate childbearing and childrearing, than it is to males.

Although the lack of career development theories applicable to women has certainly not gone unremarked (Betz & Fitzgerald, 1987; Fitzgerald & Crites, 1980; Tittle, 1983), women's career experience may be far more heterogeneous, and therefore less amenable to uniform categorization, than that of men: "The potential career development of women . . . is a great deal more complex, due to that combination of attitudes, role expectations, behaviors, and sanctions known as the socialization process" (Fitzgerald & Crites, 1980, p. 45). In short, men expect a life of full-time, paid employment, regardless of their marital status; women do not—necessarily.

The development of heterogeneity in women's career experience provides the focus of this volume. Rather than attempting to formulate and test a single, unified theory, we concentrate on the differential processes through which individuals embark on differential life paths, including the path of homemaking. Our research strategy is consistent with that proposed by Greenwald, Pratkanis, Leippe, and Baumgardner (1986), who recommended a "condition-seeking" approach, whereby an investigator views the research process as an interplay between theory and empirical results and seeks to establish the limiting or qualifying conditions for observed relationships: "Sustained use of the condition-seeking method generates a progression of research questions that, if pursued empirically, yield increasingly precise conclusions" (p. 224).

We know at the outset of our study that Tinsley and Faunce (1980) found the social stage of women's lives, from the time they married to the time their children left home, to account for fully 32% of their career orientation. We also know that only 33% of Yuen, Tinsley, and Tinsley's (1980) career-oriented women were married, as compared to 82% of their homemaker-oriented sample. Moreover, we know that, at age 26, nearly 70% of the females who constitute the sample for our investigation either had *no* academic education beyond the 9 years of Swedish compulsory school *and* had given birth to at least one child *or* had completed some level of advanced academic education and had no children (Gustafson, Stattin, & Magnusson, 1989).

These summary statistics illustrate the varied texture of the female life experience. Carol Gilligan's (1982) documentation of the interpersonal relatedness that informs women's moral judgments, as well as their worldview, further underscores the proposition that women's "career" decisions are only part of the holistic fabric of their lives (cf. Camarena et al., 1990; Tittle, 1983). Our study is conducted in appreciation of the subtlety of this fabric and of the individual variation in its weave. Across the adolescent period we examine factors that facilitate or hinder girls in realizing their potential for achievement in the occupational arena and in maintaining a maximum number of options for the future; however, we also recognize that adult occupational achievement is not the *sine qua non* of life satisfaction.

AN INTERACTIONAL PERSPECTIVE

Brief Overview

The theoretical perspective of our investigation is grounded in modern interactional psychology. We subscribe to the view that behavior is a multidetermined, stochastic process—expressed through the constant, dynamic, reciprocal interaction between an individual who functions as an intentional agent and that individual's environment (Bandura, 1986; Endler & Magnusson, 1976; Magnusson, 1988; Mischel, 1973). So widely accepted has this theoretical framework become that it currently serves as a "metatheory" for research in numerous, disparate psychological domains (Bergman, 1988).

One recent extension of the interactional paradigm is its emphasis on considering the person-as-totality (Bergman & Magnusson, 1987; Magnusson, 1985, 1988) and the environment-as-totality (Magnusson & Törestad, in press) in addressing questions of individual functioning. Psychological research has traditionally relied on investigating relationships among *variables* in its efforts to understand human behavior. In contrast, the "person approach" delineates the *person* as the appropriate unit of analysis. It is the total individual, embedded in his or her total environment, who, across time, exhibits the change and the stability in behavior that psychologists label *development*. And it is the "lawful continuity" (Magnusson & Törestad, in press) of this change and stability that psychology seeks to explain.

A Rationale for Patterns

Of course, to study *all* facets of individual functioning, from the interaction among microcosmic biological systems to the influence of macrocosmic sociological forces would be an impossible (and an exceedingly arrogant) feat for any single study to attempt. In selecting a level of analysis suitable to the investigation of individual differences in female career development, we have therefore focused on individuals' *patterns* across certain person and environmental variables relevant to educational and occupational achievement. For example, the patterns of ability and school adaptation that form one of our core individual difference constructs include measures of intelligence test performance, of school achievement, and of self-perceived ability, as well as an index of self-perceived adaptation to the academic aspects of the educational environment. By treating individuals' patterns or profiles across these variables as coherent, meaningful wholes, rather than assessing girls' relative standing on a series of group variables and then relating their rank on one variable to their ranks on others, we have defined the *individual-in-the-environment* as the analytic unit.

We believe this conceptualization to be especially meaningful in a study that relies heavily on individuals' interactions with academic demands over time. That individuals select, manipulate, and are affected by the situations in which they engage is a virtual hallmark of the interactionist position (e.g., Magnusson, 1980, 1990; Mischel, 1973). However, for a compulsory 9 years of their lives, our subjects had very little choice regarding whether or not to participate in an environment designed specifically to prepare them for independence in adulthood—namely, school. To be sure, they were afforded an increasingly wide opportunity to select optional curricula after the first 6 years, and the determinants of these choices constitute an integral part of our investigation. But females' adaptation to an environment they cannot avoid and the long-range consequences of their adaptation, which may or may not be consistent with their ability and performance, is an individual difference issue that patterns are particularly helpful in elucidating.

Similarly, for better or worse, adolescents are members of *families* they did not choose. Yet parents' socioeconomic status (SES) and the values they espouse form another, in this case a wholly environmental, pattern that may both influence and, with respect to parental values, be influenced by their daughters' aspiration and achievement. Thus, patterns of girls' home environments and the career-related consequences of these patterns across time also receive considerable attention in our overall investigation.

The use of patterns in the analysis of individuals' interactive behavior in a particular area is a natural outgrowth of the interactional theory summarized earlier (Magnusson & Törestad, in press). In addition, such an approach is becoming paradigmatic in fields of scientific research as diverse as chemistry, ethology, meteorology, biology, psychobiology, and developmental biology. In fact, the initial algorithms for cluster analysis, which constitutes a particularly appropriate methodology for operationalizing our theoretical framework, were originally developed as a classification tool for biologists (e.g., Sokal & Sneath, 1963).

THE CONCEPT OF "DEVELOPMENTAL STREAMS"

At this juncture, the reader might wonder what one *does* with the patterns that describe individuals' functioning within a given domain at a given age. Indeed, defining an optimal number of patterns that characterize, for example, girls' cognitive ability and school adaptation in early adolescence is only the first step. The most important questions are as follows: (a) What might account for the development of the individual differences observed among the patterns derived at a particular age? (b) For which individuals is a "lawful continuity" of development over time expected to result in a substantial *change* in patterns of functioning and for which individuals is pattern *stability* to be expected? (c) What career consequences do these developmental differences carry, across adolescence and into young adulthood?

Our tentative answers to these questions comprise the material presented in the ensuing chapters. Of central concern to the *second* of these issues, that of demonstrating the lawful continuity of developmental patterns, is the concept of "developmental streams." Throughout our study we employ the term *developmental stream* to connote the operation of *expected, differential processes of development over time*. Specifically, we assume that underlying the differential patterns we observe at a given age are individuals' dynamic interactions with environmental demands. If development is lawful, that is, if it can be explained by psychological principles, then the processes captured by a pattern at one time should evolve in a predictable fashion across time. When we can verify that a statistically significant number of individuals develop as we expect, with regard to their being characterized by particular patterns of functioning from one age to another, the evolution observed constitutes a developmental stream.

IN DEFENSE OF "ASSOCIATION"

In the empirical investigations that follow, we often formulate our expectations and interpret our findings in terms of "associations" instead of in terms of "influence" or "effect." In so doing, we are *not* subscribing to the convention that "association" is a "poor cousin" of causality. Rather, we are interested *explicitly* in significant associations for their own sake. We are assuming that, by the very nature of the processes involved, patterns demonstrate a lawful continuity *through their association with other patterns*.

Conversely, if the underlying developmental processes are operating as we suggest, then certain patterns should be thoroughly incompatible with others. To test this assumption, we also posit significant *nonassociations* among patterns when appropriate to a particular issue.

Our goal is to build an ever-widening network of understanding with respect to the phenomena we observe. Demonstrating the associations and nonassociations among patterns of variables, across domains and across time, supplemented by traditional variable-oriented analyses, will, we hope, reveal a somewhat more comprehensive picture of individual differences in female career development than has been illustrated heretofore. The heuristic value of this picture, and of the methodology upon which it rests, is for the reader to judge.

Chapter 2

Research Strategy
and Methods

A LONGITUDINAL DESIGN

The interactional perspective presented in the previous chapter emphasized that individuals' functioning in a given area is expressed through their dynamic, purposeful, and reciprocal interaction with the environment over time. The theoretical framework of interactionism, as we conceptualized it here, is thus inextricably linked to a longitudinal research design. To illustrate the consequences of person–environment interactions, and the manner in which past interactions might influence individuals' future paths, our investigation follows the same young women from early adolescence (age 13) through early adulthood (age 26).

AN INTRODUCTION TO THE SUBJECTS

The girls who comprise our sample are the 557 females who were participating in the longitudinal project, Individual Development and Adjustment (IDA), in 1968. The project was initiated by Magnusson of this volume in the mid-1960s at the University of Stockholm. Data collection for the main group, which is the group of interest for the present investigation, was begun in 1965 when the subjects were in Grade 3 (total $N = 1,025$, females $n = 510$). Our study begins 3 years later when the subjects (total $N = 1,100$, female $n = 557$) were in Grade 6 (age 13). Information from a variety of

7

sources was gathered on a regular basis throughout the subjects' additional 3 years of Swedish compulsory school. An adult data collection, conducted via a questionnaire mailed to all subjects when they were age 26, yielded a 90% return rate by the females who formed the original sample in 1965.

The community selected as a target for the IDA Project is located in the central part of Sweden. It includes both an urban and a rural area and has a well-developed educational system (elementary school to university) and a diversity of industry. At the time of the first data collection, the community had approximately 100,000 inhabitants. Because there are no private schools in this area of Sweden, the students in our study, minus fewer than 1% who were excluded from public education due to severe mental retardation or mental illness, constituted the entire sixth-grade population of the community.

A full description of the entire sample and of the breadth of data collected over the years is provided by Magnusson, Dunér, and Zetterblom (1975) and in the first two volumes of the present series, which is devoted exclusively to research from the IDA Project (Magnusson, 1988; Stattin & Magnusson, 1990). For our purposes, suffice it to say that the girls whose career development we trace here were representative of the greater Swedish population, with respect to both intelligence and family socioeconomic status (Bergman, 1973). This latter point is especially noteworthy because a large number of previous studies regarding career-related issues have relied primarily on data from middle- or upper middle-class subjects.

THE CASE FOR PATTERNS

As discussed in the previous chapter, our theoretical perspective is geared toward considering the person-as-totality and the environment-as-totality in addressing questions of individual differences in female career development. This theoretical position requires that we define a broad range of variables simultaneously, in our effort to capture the most salient aspects of an individual's functioning within a particular domain. A research strategy that focuses on *individuals' patterns or profiles* across theoretically relevant variables is especially appropriate to this task.

However, just as we cannot consider every possible aspect of functioning in our definition of individuals' patterns, so, too, we cannot consider each individual as a separate analytic unit. At a *theoretical* level each person is unique; at a *research strategy* level, we preserve the concept of individuality by combining individuals with similar patterns into homogeneous subgroups.

AN INTRODUCTION TO THE METHODS

Cluster Analysis

Conceptual Background

The methodology we employ for grouping individuals on the basis of pattern similarity is cluster analysis. For those who are unfamiliar with clustering techniques, a brief comparison to moderator analyses may be helpful.

The operationalization of "classic" interactional theory has been virtually synonymous with models that assess "interaction" as statistical moderation (e.g., Bowers, 1973; Ekehammer, 1974; Endler, 1975; Endler & Hunt, 1966, 1968). In the simplest form of moderator analysis, a person variable, a situation variable, and an interaction term are entered into a regression or an analysis of variance equation, with the situation serving as the moderator. The hypothesis is that the relationship between the person variable and some criterion will differ according to the situation in which the person in functioning (e.g., stressful vs. nonstressful). To test this hypothesis, the interaction term is examined to determine whether or not it contributes significantly to the percent of explained variance, over and above the variance explained by the main effects of person and situation.

In contrast, modern interactionism's emphasis on the person and the environment as *interdependent totalities* (cf. Baron & Boudreau, 1987; Magnusson & Endler, 1977) argues for a more differentiated approach. Rather than assessing the statistical interaction between two (or possibly three) variables, to explain the functioning of all individuals in a sample, we first define the *interacting individual*, by her *pattern* or profile across a number of variables. We then employ cluster analytic techniques to combine individuals with similar patterns into *homogeneous subgroups*, each of which yields a profile of mean scores that characterizes the subgroup as a whole. Last, we assess the *differential* functioning of the individuals who comprise different subgroups, either with respect to single criteria or in relation to patterns from another domain.

One very important aspect of cluster analysis is that it is *nonlinear*. The advantage of a nonlinear methodology is that higher order interactions, which may be masked by more traditional methods based on correlations (e.g., regression or factor analysis), are not masked in clustering. Thus, the method reflects our theoretical assumptions that (a) the relationships among the variables we have selected to define individuals in a given domain are not the same for all people; and (b) the differential relationships among variables, represented by the mean profiles of the various subgroups, have theoretical value for the explication of individual differences.

The Procedures

The (Dis)Similarity Matrix and the Need for Standardized Scores.
The procedures used to define homogeneous subgroups of individuals
through cluster analysis are reasonably straightforward. First, each individual is represented by her profile across the variables selected, that is, across
the *pattern indicators*. Because the individuals are to be clustered according
to their similarity, the second step is to construct a (dis)similarity matrix,
based on a measure of the "distances" among all individuals, across all
indicators.

The measure of distance we consistently employ for our (dis)similarity
matrices is squared Euclidian distance (D^2), a distance measure that takes
account of both the *form* and the *level* of a profile (Cronbach & Gleser,
1953). This measure is sensitive to the units in which the indicators have initially been measured: When the indicators have been assessed on different
scales, D^2, like any distance measure, will primarily reflect the contributions
of indicators that have been assessed in large measurement units. However,
standardizing the original scores as z scores, before constructing a (dis)simi-
larity matrix, ensures that all indicators will be represented by the same
scale of measurement; thus, each will contribute equally to the calculated
distances and, finally, to the formation of homogeneous clusters (Anderberg, 1973).

All the cluster analyses conducted in the following investigations were
performed on data standardized as z scores. In addition to the justification
just provided, our decision to standardize the indicators was based on our
desire to make our results easily comprehensible to the reader. Because we
are most interested in differential characteristics, whether a particular subgroup's mean IQ score, for example, ranks above or below the grand mean
(i.e., its standing relative to the means of other subgroups at the same age)
is more important than the subgroup's average IQ score expressed in absolute terms. Furthermore, the comparison of subgroups' *patterns* across indicators (e.g., the girls in the second subgroup are higher than average in
achievement but lower than average in school adaptation, whereas the girls
in the third subgroup display the opposite pattern) is also facilitated by the
use of z scores.

Last, the fact that our measures of such constructs as self-perceived ability or school adaptation were not *identical* at each measurement occasion
also contributed to our decision to standardize the data. In general, the
constructs we measure tended to be more broadly defined as the subjects
grew older and had experienced more interaction with the environment.
Therefore, to avoid confusion as to the *meaning* of individuals' change or
stability over time, as reflected by their patterns across the indicators from
one age to another, we describe individual functioning in relative (i.e.,

standardized) rather than in absolute (i.e., raw score) terms, even when exactly the same girls are being considered.

The Ward Clustering Algorithm.   Once a (dis)similarity matrix was constructed, the Ward (1963) minimum variance clustering algorithm, programmed in CLUSTAN (Wishart, 1982), was used to group similar individuals into homogeneous clusters. The Ward method is an agglomerative, hierarchical clustering technique, so named because it initially considers every individual as a separate "cluster" and ultimately reduces the data set to a single cluster containing all individuals (Anderberg, 1973; Blashfield & Aldenderfer, 1978; Everitt, 1974).

The Ward algorithm iteratively joins those clusters, the fusion of which minimizes an increase in the *within*-cluster or *error* sum of squares (error SS), while maximizing the *between*-cluster sum of squares. (The error sum of squares is defined as the sum of the squared Euclidian distances from each individual to the centroid or mean profile of the individual's "parent" cluster.) This procedure is particularly efficient in extracting known populations from contrived data sets (Blashfield, 1976; Morey, Blashfield, & Skinner, 1983).

Initial Criteria for Optimal Solution.   The optimal solution for the number of clusters to retain in a cluster analysis is based on the substantial *increase* in the error sum of squares associated with a particular number of clusters, compared to the error sum of squares associated with the previous iteration. The decision regarding an optimal solution is somewhat subjective, just as deciding how many factors to retain following a factor analysis requires judgment. "Breaks" in the error SS may occur at several points near the end of the iterations. Thus, the optimal decision may represent a "trade-off" between minimizing error while, at the same time, not retaining an unwieldy number of clusters.

Along with a substantial increase in the error SS, the *percent reduction in error variance* (PR) associated with a given number of clusters also serves as a criterion for determining the descriptive power of a solution. This calculation is made as follows (L. R. Bergman, personal communication, November, 1987):

$$PR = \frac{\text{Total Error SS} - \text{Error SS for the Cluster Solution}}{\text{Total Error SS}} \times 100$$

The *total error SS* can be calculated as:

$$\frac{\text{Sum of the Variance for Each Indicator} \times \text{Sample Size}}{\text{Number of Indicators}}$$

The percent reduction of error variance is somewhat analogous to the "explained variance" associated with a given number of factors in factor analysis. We report this statistic in connection with each cluster solution presented in the following chapters.

Relocation to Correct for Centroid "Drift".   One problem with hierarchical cluster analysis is that once an individual has been assigned to a cluster, the assignment is final. To cope with the "drift" of cluster centroids that might result from hierarchical methods (Zimmerman, Jacobs, & Farr, 1982), we next submitted the selected number of clusters as an input to the RELOCATE procedure (Wishart, 1982) found in CLUSTAN. The relocation procedure considers each individual in turn as a member of each cluster and assigns the individual to the cluster in which her membership will lead to the smallest increase in the error. If the individual is replaced in her original cluster, no "relocation" occurs.

Relocation to Remove a Residual.   The relocation procedure had a second purpose. As Bergman (1988) emphasized, when one performs a cluster analysis, "it is often unreasonable to believe that a small number of typical patterns or clusters can represent *all* kinds of possible configurations . . ., although it may be reasonable to expect that *most* persons fit into a small number of typical patterns" (p. 426). To address this issue, we used the RELOCATE procedure conducted after each Ward analysis to remove a "residual" of individuals whose profiles were not similar to any of the cluster centroids. Any individual whose squared Euclidian distance from the centroid of any possible "parent" cluster was more than 1.00 was removed to the residual. The percent of individuals so removed is presented with the results of each cluster analysis.

Examination of Within-Cluster Statistics.   Finally, with the residual removed, we examined the clusters themselves, to ascertain that they did, indeed, contain individuals who were homogeneous with regard to the indicators selected. First, we examined the "average coefficient" of each cluster, which represents the average squared distance, across all indicators, between each cluster member and the cluster centroid. Although we have not reported this statistic for every cluster, the average coefficients in all our analyses were low, indicating that the clusters were "tight" or homogeneous. The highest coefficient was .48; however, most were less than .20, and many were less than .10.

We also examined the within-cluster variance on each of the indicators. If the cluster members are homogeneous, the variance on an indicator *within* a cluster should, of course, be considerably less than the indicator's variance across the sample as a whole. Again, although we do not report ratios of within-cluster to total variance for single indicators, all our solutions were satisfactory in this respect.

Summary. In summary, we routinely conducted a number of analyses in connection with each clustering solution. These analyses, which reflected the examination of both overall and within-cluster criteria, were designed to ensure that the clusters we derived contained individuals who were homogeneous across the indicators selected to reflect their functioning in a given domain.

An Exact Test of Single Cell Frequencies (EXACON)

Procedure

As discussed in the previous chapter, one of the most important aspects of our investigations concerns the expected associations or nonassociations of individuals' patterns across time, across domains, or across both domains and time. To test for expected associations and nonassociations we use the exact analysis of single cells in a contingency table (EXACON), developed at the University of Stockholm by Bergman and El-Khouri (1987).

Through this procedure we assess whether or not members of a particular subgroup from one category are significantly *over- or underrepresented* among the members of a certain subgroup from another category (e.g., are the individuals who comprise Subgroup 7 of the ability/adaptation subgroups defined at age 13 significantly overrepresented among the individuals who comprise Subgroup 9 of the ability/adaptation subgroups defined at age 16?). In EXACON terminology, a significant overrepresentation is called a *type*; a significant underrepresentation is called an *antitype*.

The EXACON procedure is an extension of Fisher's (1934) exact test of a 2×2 contingency table. EXACON can test the single-cell frequencies of any two-way contingency table that is not larger than 9×9. As we employ it, the test is based on Fisher's fixed margins random model, which assumes that, under the null hypothesis, every possible arrangement of N objects is equally probable. The observed frequency of a cell follows the hypergeometric distribution (Lindgren, 1965). The EXACON program computes the *exact* one-tailed probability of each observed cell frequency; it does *not* rely on a continuous chi-square distribution to obtain approximate probabilities (Bergman & El-Khouri, 1987).

Implications

For our purposes, EXACON carries two main advantages. First, because it considers each cell separately, one can test hypotheses concerning *specific* relationships among individuals' patterns, as represented by their joint membership in two subgroup categories. Second, beyond the limits on power that may be encountered through having an extremely small marginal frequency in either subgroup category, the test is valid even for small cell sizes, a condition under which a chi-square component test, for example, is not appropriate.

Two final points regarding our EXACON analyses deserve emphasis. First, in speaking of "expectations," we signal our consistent reliance on establishing a priori specifications concerning the significance of particular cells in a given EXACON analysis. With a large number of tests which are not independent, spurious significances due to Type I error could be difficult to disentangle from theoretically meaningful results. Our a priori specification of which cells should be significant (and, by extension, which should *not*) reduces this problem considerably.

Second, the tables that depict the results of our EXACON analyses throughout this volume give the number of individuals comprising one subgroup category, the number comprising the other subgroup category, and the number involved in the *overlap*, which is, of course, the observed frequency of a single cell. Thus, we report the *actual number of individuals* for whom our expectations were correct, as well as the statistical significance of the frequency observed. Such information is generally not available in reports based on linear-model-oriented analyses.

CONCLUSION

The statistical portion of this chapter has focused on two methodologies, cluster analysis and EXACON. Although they are central to the material that follows, these procedures are perhaps less familiar to the reader than are the other, more traditional methods we use, such as analysis of variance and discriminant analysis. Having presented a brief overview of the analytic strategies that are most closely allied to our theoretical perspective, which is oriented toward the study of patterns, we are now ready to begin our investigations.

Chapter 3

Girls' Ability and School Adaptation at Ages 13 and 16

The previous discussion has introduced the theoretical and methodological implications of the individual-in-the-environment framework that constitutes the primary focus of this volume. The following chapters examine empirical results based on the application of this approach.

INTRODUCTION

Our first task is to describe girls' functioning in the school environment at age 13 and again at age 16. These descriptions take the forms of *patterns*, each of which reflects the ability and school adaptation of a homogeneous subgroup of individuals. Besides being of interest in their own right, the patterns will provide the basis for testing further expectations concerning (a) the stability or change in individuals' ability and adaptation across time, (b) factors that are associated with individual differences in ability/adaptation at each age, and (c) the educational choices and career aspirations that are associated with individuals' academic functioning in adolescence.

To define patterns of girls' functioning in the school environment requires us, first, to select relevant variables to serve as indicators of the girls' patterns. The indicators chosen to represent the ability/adaptation domain we discuss in this chapter reflect the girls' *intelligence*, academic *achievement*, *perception of their own ability*, and *self-reported adaptation* to the academic aspects of the school environment.

15

The rationale for this configuration is based on the acknowledgment that school performance is a multifaceted phenomenon. For example, despite the ongoing discussion regarding the nature of intelligence (e.g., Flynn, 1987; Sternberg, 1977, 1979; Sternberg & Detterman, 1979; Weinberg, 1989), there is virtually no doubt that the intelligence-related capacity to form and manipulate concepts strongly affects successful academic performance, as measured by school grades and standardized achievement tests. Furthermore, a number of longitudinal investigations in various Western cultures have demonstrated the stability of intelligence from about the age of 10, through late adolescence, and on into adulthood (Anastasi, 1958; Bradway, Thompson, & Cravens, 1958; Conley, 1984; Härnqvist, 1968; Husén, 1951).

Although ability and achievement denote conceptually distinct constructs, the distinction often disappears in practical application (Betz & Fitzgerald, 1987; Green, 1974; Walsh & Betz, 1985). Like achievement tests, most standardized tests of intelligence assess the extent to which individuals have mastered skills taught through the educational curricula (Anastasi, 1982). However, including both intelligence and achievement indicators in our patterns of ability/adaptation enables us to consider the development of individuals whose school performance is either higher or lower than might be expected given their intelligence.

Moreover, Campbell (1976) has observed a decrease in intelligence test scores among adolescent girls who tended to accept the stereotype that intelligence is not a feminine trait. In light of Campbell's results, which suggest that acceptance of certain sex-role stereotypes may influence *actual* performance, a further characteristic that is salient to a description of individual functioning in the school milieu is females' *perception* of their own academic competence. That self-perceived ability may not always be consistent with demonstrated performance is, for example, illustrated by Hollinger's (1983) investigation of career aspirations among a sample of 15-year-old girls, all of whom had been assessed as highly talented in mathematics: The subjects' perceptions of their own career-related abilities significantly discriminated the type of mathematics- or nonmathematics-related career they selected as ideal.

One promising line of research concerning self-perceived ability involves the application of Bandura's (1977, 1989) model of self-efficacy to the career development of women (Betz & Hackett, 1981; Hackett & Betz, 1981). Briefly, Bandura's model states that behavior and behavioral change are mediated by one's expectation that one can successfully perform a given task—that is, by one's view of one's own efficacy. Efficacy expectations vary with the extent to which one's perceived efficacy generalizes across various behavioral domains, the degree of task difficulty one is willing to confront, and the strength with which one perseveres following failure.

With regard to the last two of these dimensions, the self-efficacy model is consistent with the demonstrated positive relationship between self-esteem and achievement motivation (e.g., Weiner, 1978). Specifically, high self-esteem, established through previous success, leads individuals to expect that persistence in difficult tasks will result in future achievement and, thus, in increased self-esteem; conversely, low self-esteem creates a propensity for individuals to cease persisting in difficult tasks and to choose instead tasks in which success is relatively assured, thereby protecting themselves from experiencing further failure (Kuhl, 1978; Revelle & Michaels, 1976; Weiner, 1985).

In a similar vein, Dweck and Leggett (1988) and Dweck and Henderson (1989) have recently shown that, under certain conditions, self-perceived academic competence (i.e., self-efficacy) exerts a moderating influence on the relationship between a child's implicit theory of intelligence and his or her response to experiencing failure in the area of academic problem solving. Pre-adolescent boys and girls who subscribe to an "incremental" theory of intelligence believe intelligence to be a malleable aspect of their personal make-up and, when confronted with failure, attempt to develop new strategies for problem solving, *regardless* of their level of self-perceived ability; in contrast, the performance of children who view intelligence as *non*malleable (the "entity" theorists) deteriorates following failure among children who have low confidence in their own academic ability but does not deteriorate among children who perceive themselves to be highly competent. As was the case for the high self-esteem individuals in the earlier cited research, the "incrementalists" are also more likely than their "entity" counterparts to indicate a preference for difficult rather than easy tasks.

In a more general sense, the literature has consistently demonstrated that individuals' high self-efficacy in the academic arena exerts a positive influence on their performance (e.g., Eccles, Adler, & Meece, 1984, Eccles et al., 1983; Lent, Brown, & Larkin, 1986; Meece, Parsons, Kaczala, Goff, & Futterman, 1982). However, females have been reported to exhibit lower academic self-confidence than do males with the same level of measured ability (Gold, Brush, & Sprotzer, 1980; Maccoby & Jacklin, 1974; Stake, 1979), and female college students have been reported to exhibit significantly higher self-efficacy with respect to traditional, as opposed to nontraditional, occupations (Betz & Hackett, 1981). Thus, in the present context of educational and occupational development, Bandura's model suggests that a female's self-efficacy expectations may expand or constrain her perceived range of available options.

The last indicator included in the patterns of girls' school experience at age 13 and age 16 is a measure of the subjects' general adaptation to the academic aspects of the educational situation. That a match between environmental demands and individuals' predispositions, personalities, or temperaments strongly conditions adaptive behavioral outcomes is, of course, an axiom of the interactional perspective, one that has alternatively been discussed in the context of "individual–environment fit" (Pervin, 1968) and "goodness of fit" (Lerner, 1983). Baron and Boudreau (1987) have even argued that the Personality X Situation interaction cannot be separated into components, that personality is the "key" that "unlocks" the opportunities and constraints available in a situation. Moreover, as discussed in chapter 1, to the extent that they have options, individuals tend to select environments they believe will best facilitate their own adaptation.

The performance requirements students confront through their interaction with the school curricula are, however, less easily avoided than are other situational demands they may encounter later in life. School attendance is compulsory in Sweden from the age of 7 through the age of 16. Thus, consistent with Super's (1980) concept of career, academic/vocational development may be viewed as a continuum in which school constitutes the subjects' first "job". Because Swedish society imposes certain sanctions against quitting this job before age 16, the degree to which individuals, over time, experience a person–environment fit with school may exert a strong influence on whether or not they choose to continue their education beyond the compulsory level. The decision to continue or not will, in turn, affect their long-term career options. McCauley (1989), for example, has found limited support for the proposition that adolescent girls' liking for school mediates the influence of academic achievement on educational aspiration across a 4-year period.

To summarize, five indicators were selected to describe the ability and adaptation patterns of the subjects at age 13 and at age 16: (a) intelligence, (b) verbal achievement, (c) achievement in mathematics or science, (d) self-perceived ability, and (e) adaptation to the academic aspects of school life. Because the indicators for the age-16 patterns are taken from instruments administered across one entire year, certain indicators included in these patterns were actually assessed at age 15. The specific measure of all indicators at both ages is described briefly in the following section and is detailed fully in Appendix A. Further information regarding the instruments from which specific indicators were constructed can be found in Magnusson, Dunér, and Zetterblom (1975).

GROUPING THE GIRLS' ABILITY/ADAPTATION PATTERNS

Methods

Data

Intelligence Indicators. Testing formed a part of the regular school program in both Grade 6 (age 13) and Grade 8 (age 15). At age 13 the subjects' intelligence was measured through the Härnqvist (1961) Differential

Intelligence Analysis (DIA), developed in Sweden. The total score was used as the intelligence indicator for the ability/adaptation patterns in early adolescence.

At age 15 the subjects were administered the Wechsler Intelligence Test III, translated into Swedish by Westrin (1967). The total score comprised the intelligence indicator for the ability/adaptation patterns in mid-adolescence.

Achievement Indicators. Nationally standardized achievement tests were also administered by the various schools as part of the ordinary Swedish educational program in Grade 6 and in Grade 8. At age 13 (Grade 6) the total score on the achievement test in Swedish and the total score on the achievement test in mathematics comprised the two achievement indicators used for the ability/adaptation patterns.

At age 15 (Grade 8) the achievement test in mathematics was not equivalent for all subjects because students had opted for one of two levels of mathematics courses offered in Grade 7. To define a uniform measure of achievement that would reflect subjects' competence in manipulating mathematics-related concepts at age 15–16, a composite score was formed, using students' final eighth-grade marks in chemistry and physics. Each course was graded from 1 (low) to 5 (high).

The subjects who took the achievement test in Swedish at age 15 were fewer in number ($n = 497$) than those for whom eighth-grade marks in Swedish were available ($n = 573$). Because there was a strong correlation between the standardized test scores and the grades ($r = .79$), the final eighth-grade mark in Swedish was selected as the second achievement indicator for the ability/adaptation patterns at age 15–16. As before, the grades were given on a 1–5 scale.

Self-Perceived Ability Indicators. The measure of self-perceived ability at age 13 was taken from the Educational and Vocational Choice Questionnaire administered to all subjects during Grade 6. The measure reflected, on a scale of 1 to 3, the highest level, in terms of an academically oriented *optional* curriculum, that the girl thought she would be capable of handling the following year. The scale was as follows:

1: the two optional combinations that contained no foreign language instruction;
2: the two choices that included three classes in foreign language per week, combined with two classes in other subjects; and
3: the choice of five classes in foreign language per week.

At age 16 the indicator of self-perceived ability was drawn from the Educational and Vocational Choice Questionnaire administered during Grade

9. The measure reflected, on a scale of 1 to 4, the highest level of education, past compulsory school, which the girl was confident of completing successfully:

1: no further education past compulsory school;
2: pursuing a 2-year gymnasium (secondary school) curriculum in any area *except* economics, social studies, or technical studies;
3: pursuing a 2-year gymnasium curriculum in economics, social studies, or technical studies; and
4: pursuing a 3- or a 4-year gymnasium education.

School Adaptation Indicators.   The measure of adaptation to the academic aspects of school life at age 13 constituted the composite score of 10 items taken from the Student Questionnaire administered to subjects during Grade 6. The scale formed from these items, each of which was assessed on a 5-point Likert-type response format, was designed to reflect the extent to which sixth-grade subjects experienced a comfortable "fit" with their current academic environment.

At age 15–16 the same basic procedure was followed in defining a comparable indicator of school adaptation. Six items were drawn from three separate self-report inventories: two items from the Educational and Vocational Choice Questionnaire administered to all subjects during the eighth grade, one item from the Study of Symptoms inventory administered only to females during the eighth grade, and three items from the Student Questionnaire administered to all subjects in the ninth grade. All items were answered on 5-point Likert-type response formats. To minimize the loss of subjects, we included all girls who had responded to at least four of the items.

In accordance with the rationale presented in chapter 2, all 10 indicators were standardized as z scores. Further information regarding the manner in which the indicators were constructed at each age, and their reliability, is presented in Appendix A.

Subjects

The subjects whose ability and school adaptation patterns were analyzed at each age comprised all females in the Individual Development and Adjustment (IDA) project for whom complete data were available at that age. At age 13 there were 418 girls with scores on all five indicators. These girls, who formed the sample for the ability/adaptation patterns in early adolescence, represented 75% of the 557 girls who constituted the entire female sample in the sixth grade (1968).

At age 15, when the subjects were in Grade 8 (1970), 590 girls comprised the female sample investigated. Of these, 505 (86%) had also been represented in the sixth-grade data. Of the potential sample of 590, the 495 females (84%) with complete data on all five of the age 15–16 indicators constituted the sample for the ability/adaptation patterns in midadolescence.

Analyses

At each age, subjects' scores on each of the five indicators formed the individual profiles or patterns. Individuals were grouped into homogeneous clusters on the basis of their pattern similarity, using the cluster analytic techniques described in chapter 2. Prior to clustering, the simple correlations among the indicators were assessed at each age. All relationships were expected to be positive.

Results and Discussion

Correlations Among Indicators

At age 13 the mean correlation among the five ability indicators was .47. As expected, all correlations were positive. Further, in accordance with the relationship traditionally demonstrated between verbal facility and intelligence test performance (Anastasi, 1982), the strongest association was between intelligence and achievement in Swedish ($r = .73$). Conversely, in support of the expectation that intelligence per se would not constitute the overriding determinant of an individual's adjustment to the academic environment, the *lowest* correlation was between intelligence and school adaptation ($r = .23$).

At age 16 the mean correlation among the five ability indicators was .46. As was the case at age 13, all relationships were positive; again, the highest relationship occurred between intelligence and achievement in Swedish ($r = .64$) and the lowest between intelligence and school adaptation ($r = .10$), a somewhat weaker relationship than had been observed between these two indicators at age 13. The relatively low relation of intelligence to adaptation at both ages carried particularly interesting implications for interpreting the higher order interactions reflected in the *patterns* that emerged through the cluster analyses.

Girls' Ability/Adaptation Patterns At Age 13

For the cluster analysis performed with the indicators reflecting ability/adaptation at age 13, a nine-cluster solution was judged optimal, with regard to the criteria discussed in chapter 2. These clusters, depicted in Table 3.1, represented the assignment of each of 403 girls into one of nine characteristic subgroups. As discussed in chapter 2, one important aspect of deriving clusters in which the profiles of all members reflect a "tight fit" to

TABLE 3.1
Ability/Adaptation Patterns at Age 13

Subgroup label	Standardized subgroup means				
	IQ	AM[a]	ASw[b]	PA[c]	SchAd[d]
1-High-Ability, High-Adapted Achievers (n = 65)	.85	.97	1.11	.66	1.07
2-Gifted, Moderately Low-Adapted Achievers (n = 38)	1.33	1.18	1.31	.66	− .34
3-High-Adapted Normals (n = 55)	− .39	− .19	− .27	.66	.96
4-Math-Oriented Verbal Underachievers (n = 24)	.50	1.08	− .30	.66	− .18
5-Ability-Underestimating Normals (n = 41)	.41	.18	.31	− 1.16	.17
6-Moderately Low-Adapted Normals (n = 58)	.27	.01	.38	.66	− .29
7-Low-Adapted, Unrealistic, Low Achievers (n = 35)	− .57	− .63	− .93	.66	− .79
8-Low-Adapted, Realistic, Low Achievers (n = 46)	− .43	− .72	− .74	− 1.11	− .68
9-Low-Adapted, Low-Ability Non-Achievers (n = 41)	− 1.62	− 1.42	− 1.31	− 1.50	− .59

Note: In total 403 subjects were clustered.
[a]Achievement in mathematics.
[b]Achievement in Swedish.
[c]Perceived ability (z score of .66 = raw score of 3.0 on the 3-point scale used).
[d]School adaptation.

the cluster centroid involves removing, as a residual, those subjects whose profiles do not adequately match the centroids of any of the derived clusters (Bergman, 1988). In the present case, this residual comprised 15 subjects (3.59%). The chosen solution, with the residual excluded, accounted for a 60% reduction of within-group (error) variance over considering the entire sample as a single cluster.

Not surprisingly, the nine subgroups discriminated among girls exhibiting high, average, and low levels of ability and achievement. However, the content of each pattern as a coherent whole guided the selection of the label assigned to each subgroup of individuals and provided a basis for further interpretations and hypotheses.

In interpreting these patterns of ability/adaptation it might first be noted that a z score of -2.81 corresponded to a raw score of 1 on the scale constructed to assess self-perceived ability at age 13, whereas a z score of -1.07 corresponded to a raw score of 2, and a z score of .66 corresponded to a raw score of 3. Thus, *all* the individuals in six of the age-13 subgroups perceived themselves as capable of managing the most theoretical group of optional courses available in Grade 7 (five lessons of French or German per week). This result might perhaps be attributable to the fact that, until Grade 7, instruction was geared to encompass all levels of ability, and subjects had had no previous opportunity to select courses or to test themselves against somewhat more rigorous academic requirements.

Nevertheless, it is interesting to consider those individuals who did *not* uniformly express high confidence in their ability, even on a measure that was quite narrowly circumscribed to address only the following year's optional coursework. For two of these subgroups, the Low-Adapted, Realistic, Low Achievers (Subgroup 8) and the Low-Adapted, Low-Ability Non-Achievers (Subgroup 9), a low level of self-perceived ability seemed consistent with the low levels exhibited by these students on the measures of intelligence and achievement. This congruence between demonstrated and self-perceived ability was especially noteworthy for the latter subgroup of individuals, whose mean on all indicators, except school adaptation, was more than one standard deviation below the mean of the sample as a whole.

However, a consistency between low demonstrated and low self-perceived ability was *not* evident among the 41 individuals who comprised the Ability-Underestimating Normals (Subgroup 5), whose level of perceived ability was considerably lower than might have been expected, considering their somewhat higher than average intelligence mean and their average levels of performance. The emergence of this subgroup particularly supported our initial belief that both demonstrated and self-perceived ability would comprise meaningful constructs in describing early adolescent females' experience in the school environment.

In combination with the other indicators, school adaptation also discriminated among the girls at age 13. For example, the lowest adaptation mean characterized the Low-Adapted, Unrealistic, Low Achievers (Subgroup 7), so named because their *high* level of self-perceived ability appeared inconsistent with their *low* levels of intelligence and performance. Below-average school adaptation means also characterized the Low-Adapted, Realistic Low Achievers (Subgroup 8) and the Low-Adapted, Low-Ability Non-Achievers (Subgroup 9), both of which subgroups exhibited *low* levels of self-perceived ability and demonstrated performance.

In contrast, the High-Adapted Normals (Subgroup 3) displayed a *high* adaptation mean, in combination with somewhat *below-average* means on the intelligence and achievement indicators. In fact, the High-Adapted Normals' adaptation was almost as high as that of the High-Ability, High-Adapted Achievers (Subgroup 1), whose adaptation mean was the highest of all the subgroups and whose means on the other indicators were also well above average. Despite their differences in intelligence and achievement in sixth grade, the individuals in both of these subgroups appeared to be extremely well adjusted to academic demands and to perceive themselves capable of pursuing the most theoretical courses in Grade 7.

Finally, school adaptation differentiated strongly between the High-Ability, High-Adapted Achievers (Subgroup 1), discussed earlier, and the Gifted, Moderately Low-Adapted Achievers (Subgroup 2). The latter girls demonstrated the highest means of any of the subgroups on both the intelligence and the achievement indicators. Yet their mean adaptation was one third of a standard deviation *below* the overall mean. That the most intelligent and highest performing individuals in the entire sample should report relatively low school adaptation, whereas individuals characterized by somewhat lower levels of demonstrated ability should report considerably higher adaptation, suggested differential processes that are investigated in some depth as we continue our analyses.

To condense these results, perhaps the most interesting of the nine subgroups, in terms of differential processes that might have generated the patterns we observed in early adolescence were:

1. those girls who scored high on all indicators (the High-Ability, High-Adapted Achievers, Subgroup 1);
2. those girls who were obviously talented and had a high opinion of their own ability but were not particularly well adapted to the school environment (the Gifted, Moderately Low-Adapted Achievers, Subgroup 2);
3. those girls who were extremely well adapted to the academic aspects of student life, despite their low-normal intelligence and achievement levels (the High-Adapted Normals, Subgroup 3); and
4. those girls who had a remarkably low perception of their own academic competence even though their actual intelligence and achievement levels were somewhat above average (the Ability-Underestimating Normals, Subgroup 5).

Because these four subgroups of girls are the targets of further analyses as we move through the chapters ahead, it might be helpful to display their patterns pictorially so that the reader can more easily conceptualize the individual differences we are addressing. The mean profile of each of these four subgroups is shown in Fig. 3.1.

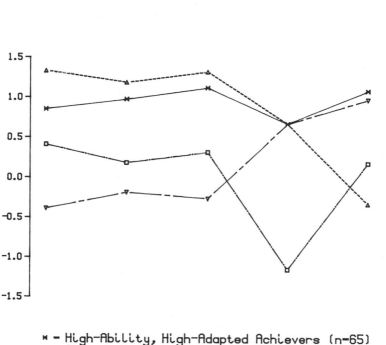

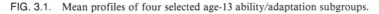

× – High–Ability, High–Adapted Achievers (n=65)
▲ – Gifted, Moderately Low–Adapted Achievers (n=38)
▽ – High–Adapted Normals (n=55)
□ – Ability–Underestimating Normals (n=41)

FIG. 3.1.   Mean profiles of four selected age-13 ability/adaptation subgroups.

Girls' Ability/Adaptation Patterns At Age 16

For the cluster analysis performed with the indicators reflecting ability/ adaptation at age 16, a nine-cluster solution was once again judged optimal. These clusters, depicted in Table 3.2, represented the assignment of each of 485 girls into one of the characteristic subgroups. The nine-cluster solution, excluding a residual of 10 subjects (2.02%) whose profiles did not match the centroids of any of the derived clusters, accounted for a 68% reduction of error variance over considering the entire sample as a single cluster.

The age-16 subgroups also differentiated high, average, and low levels of demonstrated ability and achievement. In addition, presumably because the measure of self-perceived ability at age 16 was designed to encompass a more comprehensive assessment of academic self-confidence than had been employed in the earlier analysis, this indicator discriminated among the ability/adaptation subgroups more at age 16 than it had at age 13. However, as was the case for the earlier set of subgroups, the meaningful coher-

TABLE 3.2
Ability/Adaptation Patterns at Age 16

Subgroup label	Standardized subgroup means				
	IQ	ASc[a]	ASw[b]	PA[c]	SchAd[d]
1-Gifted, High-Adapted Achievers (n = 84)	1.07	1.31	1.26	.85	.76
2-Gifted, Low-Adapted Achievers (n = 40)	1.16	.81	1.10	.65	− .75
3-High-Adapted Overachievers (n = 56)	− .50	.61	.17	.66	.77
4-Low-Adapted, Normal-Ability Underachievers (n = 56)	− .04	− .57	− .50	− .29	− .78
5-Ability-Underestimating, High-Adapted Normals (n = 57)	.17	− .17	− .03	− .32	.70
6-Moderately Able Normals (n = 66)	.56	.25	.32	.65	− .00
7-Moderately Adapted, Unrealistic, Low Achievers (n = 46)	− 1.20	− .86	− .84	.10	.31
8-Moderately Adapted, Realistic, Low Achievers (n = 43)	− 1.06	− .36	− .78	− 1.50	.20
9-Low-Adapted, Low-Ability Non-Achievers (n = 37)	− .73	− 1.34	− 1.03	− 1.92	− 1.98

Note: In total 485 subjects were clustered.
[a]Achievement in science.
[b]Achievement in Swedish.
[c]Perceived ability.
[d]School adaptation.

ence of each pattern, viewed as a whole, determined its descriptive label and provided the basis for further interpretations and hypotheses.

Three subgroups of individuals exhibited low demonstrated ability at age 16. Among these three, the Low-Adapted, Low-Ability Non-Achievers (Subgroup 9) were characterized by the lowest means of any of the subgroups on all indicators, except intelligence. The other two low-ability subgroups, the Moderately Adapted, *Unrealistic*, Low Achievers (Subgroup 7) and the

Moderately Adapted, *Realistic*, Low Achievers (Subgroup 8), differed from one another primarily on the basis of their respective levels of self-perceived ability, hence their differential designation.

Because the individuals comprising the two latter low-ability subgroups differed from one another most markedly in self-perceived ability, these subgroups captured the same distinction that had determined the labels assigned to the "unrealistic" versus the "realistic" low-ability subgroups derived at age 13 (Subgroups 7 and 8 in Table 3.1). However, the two age-16 subgroups were characterized by even *lower* levels of *intelligence* than had been exhibited by the low-ability "realistics" and "unrealistics" at age 13.

The low level of intelligence observed among both the "unrealistic" and the "realistic" low-achieving girls at age 16 was perhaps attributable, at least in part, to the increasingly differentiated curricula offered to students after the sixth grade. The midadolescent intelligence test addressed more complex concepts than were included in the sixth-grade test. Therefore, intelligence test performance, difficult to disentangle from school achievement at any age (as has been discussed earlier), might have been more influenced at age 15–16 than at age 13 by subjects' differential exposure to theoretically oriented coursework. If so, it might be expected that, even given the general stability of intelligence over time, as expressed through *correlational* analyses, intelligence in midadolescence would nevertheless exert a stronger discriminating influence on *patterns* (i.e., in combination with other indicators, the high scores would be higher and the low scores would be lower) than they did at the earlier age. Such, in fact, appeared to be the case: *Four* of the nine ability/adaptation patterns defined at age 16, compared to only *two* of the nine patterns defined at age 13, exhibited an intelligence mean more than one standard deviation above or below the overall average.

One last observation might be made concerning both the "unrealistic" and the "realistic" low-achievers (Subgroups 7 and 8) at age 16. Although their intelligence and achievement levels were low, their school adaptation means were somewhat *above* average. The association between below-average intelligence and moderately positive school adaptation at age 16, a pattern that did not emerge at age 13, suggested the operation of adaptation processes that were perhaps not available at the earlier age. One might surmise, for example, that the normal school adaptation of these girls in midadolescence was associated with their having chosen nonacademically oriented courses as soon as they were allowed to do so, thus selecting themselves out of an environment that placed rigorous demands on their limited capability for academic achievement. This suggestion is tested in chapter 9.

The interaction of school adaptation with demonstrated performance in the age-16 patterns produced three other subgroups of particular interest. The first of these, the High-Adapted Overachievers (Subgroup 3), were characterized by a pattern that was not comparable to any of the patterns that had emerged at age 13. Although their intelligence mean was half a standard deviation below average, their levels of school achievement, especially with respect to the math-related science measure, were above average, as were their self-perceived ability and their adaptation means. Because this overachievement syndrome was not observed earlier, its manifestation in midadolescence suggested the operation of processes that had not exerted their full influence at age 13. These processes are investigated in further analyses.

The age-16 patterns also revealed an *underachievement* syndrome. The Low-Adapted, Normal-Ability Underachievers (Subgroup 4) were characterized by well-below-average scores on all the indicators, except intelligence. These were girls whose school adaptation, achievement, and self-perceived ability levels were all lower than warranted by their seemingly average ability to pursue academic studies successfully. Factors that differentiated these girls from their overachieving counterparts, whose intelligence was below average, also forms the basis for further investigations.

Finally, as was the case among the ability/adaptation subgroups at age 13, two high-ability patterns emerged at age 16. The Gifted, High-Adapted Achievers (Subgroup 1) were characterized by the highest levels of achievement, perceived ability, and school adaptation, whereas the Gifted, Low-Adapted Achievers (Subgroup 2) exhibited the highest intelligence mean, in combination with high levels of achievements and self-perceived ability. However, these latter girls' school adaptation mean was more than half a standard deviation *below* average.

The previous discussion of the age-13 subgroups highlighted the importance of investigating adaptation processes underlying the distinction between the two high-ability subgroups that were derived in the first analysis. The definition of comparable subgroups at age 16 further underscored this distinction. Specifically, it should be noted that *if* the Gifted, *Low*-Adapted Achievers at age 16 were, to a significant extent, the same girls who had been only *moderately low*-adapted 3 years earlier, their adaptation level, relative to that of their classmates at each age, had decreased considerably over the interim; moreover, at age 16 they no longer exhibited the highest performance mean on either of the achievement indicators, although, as stated earlier, their intelligence mean was higher than that of any other age-16 subgroup.

Conversely, if the *high*-adapted achievers were, to a significant extent, the same girls at both ages, these subjects' levels of achievement had increased over time, relative to the achievement means of other subgroups at each age. In fact, at age 16 their levels of school performance were somewhat higher than those of their gifted, but low-adapted, counterparts.

As was the case with the age-13 subgroups, four of these age-16 subgroups were particularly interesting in terms of the differential processes that might be affecting their disparate patterns:

IQ   Ach.Sc.   Ach.Sw.   Per.Ab.   School Adap.

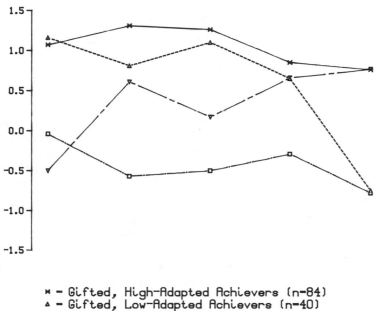

× — Gifted, High-Adapted Achievers (n=84)
▲ — Gifted, Low-Adapted Achievers (n=40)
▼ — High-Adapted Overachievers (n=56)
▫ — Low-Adapted, Normal-Ability Underachievers (n=56)

FIG. 3.2.   Mean profiles of four selected age-16 ability/adaptation subgroups.

1. those girls who were high on all the indicators (the Gifted, High-Adapted Achievers, Subgroup 1);

2. those gifted girls who were remarkably low in school adaptation (the Gifted, Low-Adapted Achievers, Subgroup 2);

3. those girls whose achievement and adaptation levels far exceeded what might be expected given their below-average intelligence (the High-Adapted Overachievers, Subgroup 3); and

4. those girls whose achievement and adaptation means were far *lower* than might be expected given their normal intelligence level (the Low-Adapted, Normal-Ability Underachievers, Subgroup 4).

Because these four subgroups are subjected to in-depth analyses in future chapters, we have presented their mean profiles in Fig. 3.2. In comparison with the age-13 subgroup profiles presented in Fig. 3.1, one observation was especially noteworthy: With respect to the *intelligence* and the two *achievement* indicators, the patterns of the age-13 girls who are represented in Fig. 3.1 differed from one another only in *level*. However, by age 16, the developmental processes that had operated over 3 additional years gave rise to interactive patterns that were differentiated in *shape* across all five indicators.

The Issue of Individual Stability Versus Change

The foregoing discussion concerning the ability/adaptation subgroups at age 13 and at age 16 has implicitly assumed that the patterns that characterized certain subgroups of individuals in early adolescence were, by their very nature, likely to change, because these characteristic patterns implied disparities between environmental demands and the girls' own responses to those demands. For example, a disparity between school adaptation, which was low, and demonstrated ability, which was high, was manifested in the pattern of the Gifted, Moderately Low-Adapted Achievers at age 13. In a similar vein, the age-13 Ability-Underestimating Normals displayed a level of self-perceived ability that was lower than would be expected, given their somewhat-above-average demonstrated ability.

In contrast, the pattern of the age-13 High-Ability, High-Adapted Achievers, with their high means across all indicators, implied a strong individual–environment fit with respect to the school situation. It would be expected that the relationship between these girls' ability and the academic demands they met so easily would stabilize early and demonstrate continued stability across time. Likewise, given their consistency in reflecting a general *lack* of fit with the school environment, in combination with the *lack* of the intellectual resources necessary to perform successfully in the educational arena, the Low-Adapted, Low-Ability Non-Achievers would also be expected to exhibit a stable, albeit a far less successful, ability/adaptation pattern from age 13 to age 16.

When we make predictions about a certain group of individuals' developing in the same way across time, we are hypothesizing a "developmental stream." Our next analysis specifies which developmental streams should emerge with respect to individuals' patterns of ability/adaptation from early adolescence to midadolescence. Such developmental streams, if verified, carry information about differential psychological processes involved in girls' interaction with their first career, that of school.

VERIFICATION OF EXPECTED DEVELOPMENTAL STREAMS

Methodological Considerations

The expected developmental streams were verified statistically through the significant overrepresentation of individuals, compared to a random model, from one ability/adaptation subgroup at age 13 among members of another ability/adaptation subgroup at age 16. Our expectations were tested with EXACON, the exact test of single-cell frequencies (Bergman & El-Khouri, 1987) discussed in chapter 2. In EXACON terminology, a *statistically significant overrepresentation* is designated as a *type*.

It should be emphasized that all expectations concerning the overlap between subgroup membership at the two ages were specified *prior* to conducting the EXACON analysis. This a priori construction of hypothesized developmental streams was crucial to the research design, because the two-way contingency table (Subgroup Membership at Age 13 × Subgroup Membership at Age 16) formed a 9 × 9 matrix, each cell of which was tested individually against an *exact* expected frequency. To unravel spuriously significant overrepresentations that might occur due to Type I error from psychologically meaningful associations reflecting significant differential streams of development would thus be difficult if one relied solely on post hoc interpretations of the results.

Although the ability/adaptation profiles of 403 subjects were clustered at age 13, and the ability/adaptation profiles of 485 subjects were clustered at age 16, the necessary restriction of the EXACON analysis to only those girls who had been included in both previous cluster analyses reduced the number of subjects to 331. These girls comprised the sample on which the following results were based.

Interpretation of Developmental Streams

Nine developmental streams, involving seven of the *age-13* ability subgroups, were expected to be demonstrated through the EXACON analysis. The significance of these hypothesized streams, as well as of other types which emerged through the analysis, are depicted in Table 3.3.

The High-Ability, High-Adapted Achievers (Subgroup 1)

Because of the presumed stability of high intelligence, especially when associated with high performance, high self-perceived ability, and high school adaptation, the High-Ability, High-Adapted Achievers at age 13 were expected to be overrepresented *only* among the Gifted, High-Adapted Achievers at age 16. This highly significant overrepresentation ($p < .0001$), which comprised the sole type involving these particular 13-year-olds, implied the presence of a stable developmental process whereby achievement and self-confidence had reinforced one another over time, through successful adaptation to and increased mastery of environmental demands.

The Gifted, Moderately Low-Adapted Achievers (Subgroup 2)

The Gifted, Moderately Low-Adapted Achievers at age 13 were expected to be overrepresented in two subgroups at age 16. Specifically, given their

TABLE 3.3
Developmental Ability/Adaptation Streams from Age 13 to Age 16

Pattern at 13	Pattern(s) at 16	Overlap n
	Predicted types	
1-High-Ability, High-Adapted Achievers# (n = 55)	1-Gifted, High-Adapted Achievers (n = 59)	29****
2-Gifted, Moderately Low-Adapted Achievers# (n = 31)	2-Gifted, Low-Adapted Achievers (n = 30)	12****
	1-Gifted, High-Adapted Achievers (n = 59)	10*
3-High-Adapted Normals (n = 49)	3-High-Adapted Overachievers (n = 45)	15***
4-Math-Oriented Verbal Underachievers# (n = 17)	6-Moderately Able Normals (n = 44)	7**
5-Ability-Underestimating Normals (n = 34)	4-Low-Adapted, Normal-Ability Underachievers (n = 38)	8*
7-Low-Adapted, Unrealistic, Low Achievers (n = 28)	9-Low-Adapted, Low-Ability Non-Achievers (n = 28)	7**
9-Low-Adapted, Low-Ability Non-Achievers# (n = 35)	8-Moderately Adapted, Realistic, Low Achievers (n = 18)	10****
	9-Low-Adapted, Low-Ability Non-Achievers (n = 28)	8**
	Unpredicted types	
3-High-Adapted Normals (n = 49)	5-Ability-Underestimating, High-Adapted Normals (n = 42)	11*
5-Ability-Underestimating Normals (n − 34)	5-Ability-Underestimating, High-Adapted Normals (n = 42)	9*
6-Moderately Low-Adapted Normals# (n = 48)	1-Gifted, Low-Adapted Achievers (n = 30)	8*
7-Low-Adapted, Unrealistic, Low Achievers (n = 28)	5-Ability-Underestimating, High-Adapted Normals (n = 42)	7*
8-Low-Adapted, Realistic, Low Achievers# (n = 34)	4-Low-Adapted, Normal-Ability Underachievers (n = 38)	9**

Note: Types were derived, from exact tests of the single-cell frequency overlap between the two sets of subgroups, for 331 subjects.

= only significant type(s) observed.

*$p < .05$; **$p < .01$; ***$p \le .001$; ****$p < .0001$.

highest means on the achievement indicators, in combination with their be-low-average school adaptation mean, these subjects were expected, over time, to change in one of two directions, with school adaptation's operating as the fulcrum for this differential development.

First, the Gifted, Moderately Low-Adapted Achievers at age 13 were expected to be overrepresented among the Gifted, Low-Adapted Achievers at age 16. For these girls, who were intellectually gifted but seemingly ill-adapted to the academic environment, the proposed scenario was that although their basic intelligence would facilitate successful performance, the full expression of their ability would be constrained by the "lack of fit" they had continued to experience in connection with adjusting to school demands. Thus, if nothing intervened to interrupt the process before age 16, their adaptation would decrease substantially over time, relative to that of their same-age classmates.

In addition, given the disparity between their intelligence and their adaptation, these girls' past achievements would not be expected to reinforce their future performance to the same extent that past success was assumed to beget future success among their highly able and well-adapted counterparts. Therefore, although they would not perform poorly at age 16, they would, nonetheless, no longer be the highest-achieving subgroup, as they had been at age 13. The validity of this scenario was supported by the high significance ($p < .0001$) of the type formed by the association between these two subgroups.

These girls' decline in adaptation, and to some extent in achievement, over time, is consistent with Dweck's (1986) review of *experimental* results concerning bright girls whose performance debilitates following failure and whose *actual* ability is sometimes *positively* related to their maladaptive learning pattern (Licht & Dweck, 1984; Stipeck & Hoffman, 1980). Furthermore, such girls are more likely than bright boys to subscribe to an "entity" or fixed theory of intelligence and to avoid challenge, instead of viewing intelligence as a malleable quality and seeking challenge (Leggett, 1985).

Second, it was expected that the gifted girls who had "hit their stride," so to speak, over the subsequent years, would be overrepresented among the Gifted, High-Adapted Achievers at age 16 and thus would be indistinguishable from the subjects who had been highly adapted achievers all along. That this developmental stream also emerged as a type ($p < .05$) indicated that somewhat delayed adjustment to the academic environment did not carry negative consequences for these highly able girls, because the achievement and the adaptation means of the Gifted, High-Adapted Achievers were the highest of any of the age-16 subgroups. Moreover, as is demonstrated in further investigations, the results could not be attributed to the moderately low-adapted 13-year-olds' decreasing their school discomfort by avoiding theoretically oriented curricula. Finally, it might be noted that these expected developmental streams were the only two types that were observed with respect to the 13-year-old Gifted, Moderately Low-Adapted Achievers.

The High-Adapted Normals (Subgroup 3)

In light of their high level of school adaptation, combined with their high self-perceived ability mean, the High-Adapted Normals at age 13 were expected to be overrepresented among the age-16 High-Adapted Overachievers. Because both these subgroups displayed below-average intelligence means, a significant developmental stream between them would underscore the powerful influence of self-confidence and individual–environment fit on increased performance over time. This developmental stream did emerge ($p < .001$), although it was not the only type observed.

The Math-Oriented Verbal Underachievers (Subgroup 4)

Although not highlighted in the previous discussion of the age-13 ability/adaptation subgroups, one subgroup of individuals, the Math-Oriented Verbal Underachievers, was characterized by a level of achievement in mathematics that almost matched that of the Gifted, Moderately Low-Adapted Achievers; however, in combination with their *high* level of math performance, the former subgroup also exhibited a *below-average* mean on the Swedish achievement measure, despite their above-average intelligence mean. Because these girls' adaptation mean was about average, not high enough to suggest that they derived any *generalized* reinforcement from their achievement in mathematics, it was expected that, given their intelligence, the difference between their math and their verbal performance would decrease over time, while their adaptation would remain fairly stable. Thus, at age 16 they were hypothesized to be overrepresented among the Moderately Able Normals, a subgroup characterized by means at or somewhat above the overall average on all indicators. This expected developmental stream constituted the only type ($p < .01$) involving the Math-Oriented Verbal Underachievers.

The Ability-Underestimating Normals (Subgroup 5)

As discussed in connection with the age-13 subgroup interpretations, the Ability-Underestimating Normals exhibited a level of self-perceived ability that was markedly lower than would be expected given their somewhat above average demonstrated ability means. This pattern seemed particularly vulnerable to deterioration across time, because self-perceived ability, as discussed in the introduction, is strongly associated with female achievement. Thus, we predicted that these individuals would be overrepresented among the Low-Adapted, Normal-Ability Underachievers at age 16. Our rationale was that, without a sense of self-efficacy regarding their ability to meet academic demands, girls' actual performance and adaptation would decline as academic requirements increased, even though their intelligence remained stable. Although not the only type observed, this developmental stream was significant ($p < .05$).

The Low-Adapted, Unrealistic, Low Achievers (Subgroup 7)

The lowest level of adaptation at age 13, which characterized the Low-Adapted, Unrealistic, Low Achievers, might reflect the frustration these girls experienced in their unsuccessful attempts to meet academic demands, despite their self-perceived ability to do so. If such were the case, the expectation would be that, over time, the Unrealistics' adaptation and academic self-confidence would both diminish, whereas their ability and performance wold continue to be low. Thus, the Low-Adapted, Unrealistic, Low Achievers were expected, at the later age, to be overrepresented among the Low-Adapted, Low-Ability Non-Achievers, whose achievement, self-perceived ability, and school adaptation levels were the lowest of any of the age-16 subgroups. Although not the only type that emerged regarding the Unrealistics, this association was significant ($p < .01$).

The Low-Adapted, Low-Ability Non-Achievers (Subgroup 9)

The final two expectations concerned those subjects who, at age 13, had the lowest self-perceived and demonstrated ability means of any of the subgroups. First, it was expected that, at age 16, these girls would be overrepresented among the Low-Adapted, Low-Ability Non-Achievers, who also displayed the lowest subgroup means on all indicators, except intelligence.

The emergence of this developmental stream ($p < .01$), which reflected little substantive change across time, other than a decrease in adaptation, relative to the means of the other subgroups at each respective age, underscored the proposition advanced in our earlier discussion of individual stability; namely, "development" in a particular domain does not *necessarily* connote relative change. Rather, development may also be expressed through the stability of a pattern that has characterized individuals' functioning at an earlier point in time. This stability may occur through a particularly success-reinforcing series of environmental transactions, as was the case for the 13-year-old High-Ability, High-Adapted Achievers; however, early stability may also occur for individuals who are "locked into" a situation, like school, without the intellectual capacity to meet environmental demands successfully.

Second, one alternative pathway was suggested for this lowest-ability, age-13 subgroup. The adaptation mean of the Low-Adapted, Low-Ability Non-Achievers, although below the overall average, was not as low as that of either the "realistic" or the "unrealistic" low-ability subgroups observed at the same age. If the Non-Achievers' adaptation mean at age 13 reflected that these subjects experienced less frustration and anxiety than might, for example, have accompanied the Unrealistics' failure to assess their academic limitations accurately, then the Non-Achievers' adaptation, although not their demonstrated or self-perceived ability, might actually improve somewhat over time, especially after they were granted the opportunity to select a less academically rigorous curriculum.

Thus, it was expected that the alternative developmental stream involving the Low-Adapted, Low-Ability Non-Achievers would comprise their overrepresentation, at age 16, among the Moderately Adapted, *Realistic*, Low Achievers. The results indicated that this overrepresentation was highly significant ($p < .0001$). Moreover, these two developmental streams were the only types that emerged concerning the 13-year-old Non-Achievers.

Unexpected Types

Considering that with an initially specified alpha of .05, single-cell tests of an 81-cell matrix would theoretically produce four spuriously significant results (Cohen & Cohen, 1983), the four unexpected types that were significant at only the .05 level were not subjected to any further interpretations. However, the remaining unexpected type was briefly considered.

Specifically, the Low-Adapted, Realistic, Low Achievers at age 13 (Subgroup 8) were significantly overrepresented ($p < .01$) among the Low-Adapted, Normal-Ability Underachievers at age 16. No stream had been specified a priori regarding the development of the age-13 Low-Adapted, Realistic, Low Achievers.

Commenting on this result retrospectively, one might note the similarly low achievement and adaptation means of the age-13 Realistics and the age-16 Underachievers; however, the Realistics' intelligence mean was considerably lower than that of the Underachievers. Thus, it appeared that the Realistics' *potential* capability, as measured by intelligence scores, actually increased somewhat over time, relative to the intelligence and self-perceived ability of their classmates at the respective ages; nevertheless, this increase was not reflected in improved *achievement* levels at age 16, perhaps because the school adaptation of these students continued to be quite low.

Moderate support for the importance of adaptation in this scenario might be drawn from the developmental stream that was observed between the High-Adapted Normals at age 13 and the High-Adapted Overachievers at age 16. In this case, high adaptation was associated with levels of achievement that *did* increase substantially over time, relative to the achievement levels of the other subgroups at each age. Moreover, this relative mean increase in achievement occurred among girls who, at age 13, belonged to a subgroup characterized by almost the same level of intelligence as that of the age-13 Low-Adapted, Realistic, Low Achievers.

Summary of EXACON Results

To summarize the overall significance of the EXACON results, nine types, reflecting nine developmental streams linking individuals' patterns of ability/adaptation at age 13 to their patterns of ability/adaptation at age 16, were expected to emerge through the EXACON analysis. The results supported these expectations in all nine cases. Furthermore, the significance of seven of these nine expected types exceeded the .01 level of probability; in three cases the probability of the particular type's occurring by chance was less than .0001.

The viability of our interpretations regarding the differential processes that might underlie these streams of development was further supported by the fact that, among the five *unexpected* types that were also observed, four were significant at only the .05 level of probability, and none reached the $p \leq .001$ level of significance. Moreover, it should be noted that 67 of the cells for which the expectation was that there would be *no* significant over-representation between patterns at the two ages indeed yielded no type.

CONCLUDING REMARKS

In conclusion, this chapter has demonstrated that patterns of variables reflecting girls' intelligence, their achievement, their self-perceived academic competence, and their own assessments of the extent to which they "fit" an academic environment can yield psychologically meaningful descriptions of individuals' ability and school adaptation during adolescence. The interpretations of individual differences in *patterns* at two separate ages have illustrated that the pattern approach reveals information and suggests differential developmental processes that may be masked by more traditional, linear-model-based methodology.

Moreover, developmental streams from early adolescence to midadolescence have generally supported our predictions regarding the stability or change of individuals' patterns across time. Our next step is to explore further the differential processes underlying these developmental streams.

Chapter **4**

A Closer Investigation of Particular "Developmental Streams"

The discussion of "developmental streams" in chapter 3 concerned the predicted stability or change in particular individuals' patterns of ability and school adaptation over time. This stability or change was tested in terms of associations between the patterns of intelligence, achievement, self-perceived ability, and school adaptation that characterized girls in early adolescence and the patterns that characterized them 3 years later.

This chapter examines a few of these developmental streams more precisely, to identify factors that might underlie the individual differences already observed. The analyses focus on the characteristics of certain groups of individuals whose patterns of ability and school adaptation *changed* over time.

INTRODUCTION

The first question is whether or not the inferences we have drawn from the movement of a significant *number* of individuals from one subgroup at age 13 to another at age 16 are supported when we examine *only* those individuals who constituted the developmental stream. To answer this question we selected four developmental streams, the closer investigation of which might allow us to specify conditions under which girls' interaction with school develops in a manner consistent or inconsistent with their intelligence. The four groups of individuals involved in these developmental streams are described in Table 4.1.

TABLE 4.1
Four Developmental Streams Investigated in Detail

Pattern at 13	Patterns at 16	n
2-Gifted, Moderately Low-Adapted Achievers	2-Gifted, Low-Adapted Achievers	12****
	1-Gifted, High-Adapted Achievers	10*
3-High-Adapted Normals	3-High-Adpated Overachievers	15***
	5-Ability-Underestimating, High-Adapted Normals	11*

$*p < .05$; $***p < .001$; $****p < .0001$.

The first two groups are as follows:

1. the group of highly intelligent and high-achieving girls whose school adaptation *decreased* markedly across time (i.e., the Gifted, Moderately Low-Adapted Achievers—Subgroup 2—at age 13 who were Gifted, Low-Adapted Achievers—Subgroup 2—at age 16) and

2. the group of highly intelligent and high-achieving girls whose school adaptation *increased* markedly across time (i.e., the Gifted, Moderately Low-Adapted Achievers—Subgroup 2—at age 13 who were Gifted, High-Adapted Achievers—Subgroup 1—at age 16).

Our analyses of these two groups are concerned with what might account for the substantial *mean decrease* in school adaptation among one subset of gifted girls from age 13 to age 16 versus the substantial *mean increase* in school adaptation among another subset of the same initial age-13 subgroup. The overall ability/adaptation patterns of the subgroups to which these individuals belonged at ages 13 and 16 are shown in Fig. 3.1 and Fig. 3.2.

The third and fourth groups are:

3. the highly adapted group of low-normal intelligence girls who became overachievers by age 16 (i.e., the High-Adapted Normals—Subgroup 3—at age 13 who were High-Adapted Overachievers—Subgroup 3—at age 16; and

4. the highly adapted group of low-normal intelligence girls whose perception of their own ability decreased across time (i.e., the High-Adapted Normals—Subgroup 3—at age 13 who were Ability-Underestimating, High-Adapted Normals—Subgroup 5—at age 16).[1]

---

[1]Technically speaking, these individuals' changes across time did not constitute a "developmental stream" because, although a statistically significant number of girls were involved, we had not hypothesized their development a priori. However, because this group provided a meaningful contrast to the girls who became overachievers, we included them in the analyses.

Our analyses of these last two developmental streams focuses on the substantial *mean increase* versus *no substantial mean increase* in *achievement* among two subsets of high-adapted girls who, at age 13, were characterized by the same low-normal intelligence and achievement means. We are also interested in factors which might be associated with a *decrease in self-perceived ability* among the girls whose achievement levels remained near average. Except for the pattern of the Ability-Underestimating, High-Adapted Normals, the overall ability/adaptation patterns of the subgroups to which these individuals belonged at ages 13 and 16 are shown in Fig. 3.1 and Fig. 3.2.

It should be stressed at this point that our interpretations of individuals' "increases" or "decreases" on certain pattern indicators over time *always* connote a mean increase or a mean decrease *relative to the means of the other ability/adaptation subgroups at each age*. The indicators comprising the ability/adaptation patterns do not *necessarily* carry the same meaning at age 13 as they do at age 16.

For example, as discussed in the previous chapter, the measure of self-perceived ability in Grade 6 (at age 13) was constrained to which level of optional courses the girl perceived herself as capable of completing successfully in Grade 7. At age 16, when the girls were finishing their last year of compulsory school and had had 3 years' additional opportunity to form judgments of their own academic competence, the measure of self-perceived ability encompassed a broader self-assessment. Thus, comparisons of mean score differences between the two measures across time must be viewed in relative rather than in absolute terms, even when exactly the same individuals are involved.

Of course, the relative nature of the mean increases or decreases is further underscored by our consistent use of *standardized* means. Given the differences among the scales on which the various indicators were assessed, one reason we adopted this strategy was to highlight the important differential characteristics of the various subgroups at each age in a manner that would be easily comprehended by the reader.

ESTABLISHING REPRESENTATIVENESS

Inherent in our concern with the differential developmental processes underlying particular developmental streams is the issue of whether or not the *specific individuals* who constituted the four developmental streams selected for further analysis did, in fact, represent the various subgroups of which they were members at each age. Suppose, for example, that we were to discover that the *particular* high-ability, somewhat low-adapted girls whose school adaptation appeared to increase over time were not as *low*-adapted as their age-13 subgroup mean would suggest and/or were not as *high*-adapted as their age-16 subgroup mean would indicate (i.e., that these 10 girls were *not* representative of their respective cluster centroids, composed of the subgroup means across the pattern indicators at each age). If such were the case, we would hardly be justified in inferring a developmental process through which these girls' adaptation level had increased over the 3-year period, much less in attempting to identify factors associated with such an increase.

Similarly, unless the *specific* high-adapted girls with low-normal levels of intelligence and achievement whose achievement, but not their intelligence, increased over 3 years were representative of their respective subgroups at each age, the "developmental stream" from low-normal achievement to overachievement would be an illusion. Assessing this general principle of representativeness, which applies to all four of the developmental streams being investigated, therefore constituted the first step of our analyses.

Methods

Evaluations of Centroid Similarity

To assess their representativeness the four groups of individuals that constituted the developmental streams were designated as "target" groups. The first strategy used was to calculate the average squared Euclidian distance (average D^2) between each target group's centroid (defined as its means across the indicators from which the patterns were derived) and the centroid (or means) that defined the *entire* subgroup to which the target group belonged at age 13 and at age 16. The rationale for such a strategy is that the *less* the average squared distance between a target group's centroid and the centroid of the subgroup in its entirety, the more the target group can be said to represent the subgroup from which it is drawn. The formula employed for these calculations was:

$$\frac{(x_{\text{tar1}} - x_1)^2 + (x_{\text{tar2}} - x_2)^2 + \ldots + (x_{\text{tarj}} - x_j)^2}{J}$$

where x_{tar1} = the mean of the target group on the first profile indicator,

x_{tarj} = the mean of the target group on profile indicator j,

x_1 = the mean of the entire subgroup, including the target group, on the first profile indicator, and

J = the total number of indicators.

The guiding principle in interpreting "similarity" for the purpose of representativeness is that the average squared distance between the target group's centroid and that of the overall cluster *should not exceed* the average squared distance of the cluster as a whole, expressed as the "average coefficient." The average coefficient is defined as the average squared distance, across all indicators, between each member of the cluster, including the members of the target group, and the centroid of the entire cluster in question. (This concept is explained more completely in Appendix B.)

Thus, if the four target groups that were the focus of the present analyses were indeed representative of the clusters to which they belonged at the two points in time, the average squared distance between these groups and the overall cluster centroid should not exceed the average coefficient of the cluster as a whole. This criterion formed the basis of our first evaluations of representativeness.

Discriminant Analyses

The second strategy used to assess representativeness involved a discriminant analysis. The discriminant function was composed of the pattern indicators on which there were differences between a target group and the rest of the subgroup to which it belonged at a given age. The subjects in these analyses were the same individuals who had comprised the sample for the EXACON test of developmental streams in the previous chapter (see Table 3.3). If the target group drawn from a particular subgroup could *not* be differentiated from the rest of the subgroup members (i.e., if the discriminant function were nonsignificant), the target group's representativeness would be supported. (It might be noted that because all the age-13 Gifted Moderately Low-Adapted Achievers and High-Adapted Normals had the same score on perceived ability, this indicator was not included in discriminant functions involving members of the age-13 subgroups).

On the other hand, if the target group differed significantly from the remainder of the subgroup members, indicating a lack of representativeness, the result could be interpreted in one of two ways, depending on the direction of the mean difference(s). For example, suppose that we were to find that the highly intelligent and high-achieving girls whose school adaptation appeared to *decrease* markedly across time were significantly discriminable from the rest of their subgroup at age 13 and that this early discriminability could be attributed (through univariate analyses) to their displaying a significantly *higher* adaptation mean than did the other age-13 Gifted, Moderately Low-Adapted Achievers. As long as the target group's school adaptation was representative of the *low* adaptation mean exhibited by the Gifted, Low-Adapted Achievers 3 years later, this earlier difference would not invalidate our inference regarding the existence of a developmental stream whereby the school adaptation of these high-ability girls had decreased substantially over time. If, however, the school adaptation mean of this target group at age 13 were *already* to be significantly lower than that of their counterparts, the target group's lack of representativeness on this crucial variable would invalidate the meaningfulness of a developmental path that presumed a mean decrease in adaptation.

TABLE 4.2
Centroid Representativeness of the "Decreasers" and the "Increasers"

Group	IQ	AM^a or ASc^b	ASw^c	PA^d	SchAd^e	Avg. coeff. of cluster as a whole	Avg. D^2 from clus. centroid
			Standardized group means				
			At age 13				
Entire subgroup 2 (n = 38)	1.33	1.18	1.31	.66	− .34	.19	
Decreasers (n = 12)	1.54	1.33	1.51	.66	− .33		.02
Increasers (n = 10)	1.27	1.16	1.45	.66	− .20		.01
			At age 16				
Entire subgroup 2 (n = 40)	1.16	.81	1.10	.65	− .75	.28	
Decreasers (n = 12)	1.40	.94	1.28	.76	− .71		.02
Entire subgroup 1 (n = 84)	1.07	1.31	1.26	.85	.76	.23	
Increasers (n = 10)	1.34	1.63	1.60	.92	.63		.06

^{a}Achievement in mathematics at age 13.
^{b}Achievement in science at age 16.
^{c}Achievement in Swedish.
^{d}Perceived ability.
^{e}School adaptation.

Results and Discussion of Representativeness Assessments

Streams Involving the Gifted, Moderately Low-Adapted Achievers

The first two target groups were the age-13 Gifted, Moderately Low-Adapted Achievers (Subgroup 2) who were Gifted, *Low-Adapted* Achievers (Subgroup 2) at age 16 and the age-13 Gifted, Moderately Low-Adapted Achievers (Subgroup 2) who were Gifted, *High-Adapted* Achievers (Subgroup 1) at age 16.

The results of the centroid evaluation analyses concerning these two target groups are depicted in Table 4.2. To characterize the differential mean change in the two groups' school adaptation from age 13 to age 16, the first group were called *Decreasers* (n = 12) and the second group were called *Increasers* (n = 10).

Results of Age-13 Analyses.   At age 13 both the Decreasers and the Increasers were representative of the Gifted, Moderately Low-Adapted
Achievers (Subgroup 2). The average squared distance between each of
these target groups and the overall subgroup centroid was substantially
lower than the average coefficient of the entire subgroup, indicating that
the centroids of both target groups represented a "tight fit" to the overall
cluster centroid. Moreover, because the average coefficient of the age-13
Gifted, Moderately Low-Adapted Achievers was already quite low (.19), the
further reductions reflected in the means of the Decreasers and the Increasers (.02 and .01, respectively) showed these individuals to be extremely close
to the mean profile on which our initial expectations regarding developmental streams were based. Moreover, the discriminant function between
these two target groups was nonsignificant.

Finally, we considered the 31 Gifted, Moderately Low-Adapted Achievers
who, at age 13, had constituted the sample of the EXACON analysis that
tested for the developmental streams (see Table 3.3). When the 12 Decreasers and the 10 Increasers were combined into one group, a significant
discriminant function ($p < .05$) was obtained between these 22 girls, whose
subgroup membership at age *16* had matched our a priori predictions, and
the nine remaining girls, who had not been not *significantly* represented in
any of the age-16 ability subgroups.

This result lent further support to the validity of the hypothesized developmental streams. An examination of the mean differences between the
two groups revealed that the nine age-13 subgroup members who were not
part of *any* developmental stream had lower mean values on all the indicators defining the function (and were significantly lower on achievement in
Swedish), compared to the means of the 22 more gifted subgroup members
whose scores most strongly influenced our initial interpretation of the
Gifted, Moderately Low-Adapted subgroup and whose mean changes over
3 years reflected our expectations.

Results of Age-16 Analyses.   As shown in Table 4.2, the Decreasers became Gifted, Low-Adapted Achievers (Subgroup 2) at age 16. Given that
the average coefficient for the entire subgroup was .28 and the average
squared distance between the target group and the cluster centroid was only
.02, the Decreasers were representative of the subgroup as a whole. This
target group's representativeness was further supported by the nonsignificant discriminant function between the Decreasers ($n = 12$) and the remainder ($n = 18$) of the 30 Gifted, Low-Adapted Achievers who had comprised
the age-16 sample for the EXACON test (see Table 3.3).

A similar situation was manifested in the results of the representativeness
tests involving the Increasers. The average coefficient for the Gifted, High-
Adapted Achiever subgroup (Subgroup 1), to which the Increasers belonged
at age 16, was .23. That the .06 average squared distance between the In-

creasers and the cluster centroid was considerably less than this value indicated that the Increasers were representative of the subgroup of which they were members.

Unlike the result of the parallel test involving the Decreasers, the discriminant function between the Increasers ($n = 10$) and the remainder ($n = 49$) of the 59 Gifted, High-Adapted Achievers who comprised the age-16 EXACON sample (see Table 3.3) was significant ($p < .05$). However, an examination of the mean differences between the Increasers and the other Gifted, High-Adapted Achievers showed that the observed differences did *not* invalidate the meaningfulness of a developmental stream through which the average level of school adaptation among certain high-ability girls increased substantially from age 13 to age 16.

Specifically, the Increasers' school adaptation mean did *not* differ significantly from that of the remaining Gifted, High-Adapted Achievers comprising the EXACON sample. Furthermore, with respect to ability, the Increasers' intelligence, science achievement, and Swedish achievement means were all *higher* than those of the remaining subgroup members. For the science achievement and Swedish achievement indicators, these mean differences were significant ($p < .05$ and $p < .01$, respectively), thereby accounting for the significant discriminant function between the two groups.

Thus, the characteristics of *only* those individuals who formed the two developmental streams we had hypothesized and observed concerning the age-13 Gifted, Moderately Low-Adapted Achievers yielded strong support for the meaningfulness of these streams. Although we have yet to identify specific factors associated with the differential development of high versus low school adaptation among these highly able students, we can at least be confident that two distinct processes took place.

Streams Involving the High-Adapted Normals

The second two target groups were the age-13 High-Adapted Normals (Subgroup 3) who became High-Adapted Overachievers (Subgroup 3) at age 16 and the age-13 High-Adapted Normals (Subgroup 3) who became Ability-Underestimating, High-Adapted Normals (Subgroup 5) at age 16.

The results of the centroid evaluation analyses concerning these two target groups are depicted in Table 4.3. To characterize the differential mean changes in the two groups' achievement and perceived ability from age 13 to age 16, the first group were called *Overs* ($n = 15$) and the second group were called *Unders* ($n = 11$).

Results of Age-13 Analyses. At age 13 both the Overs (average $D^2 = .002$) and the Unders (average $D^2 = .03$) were representative of the High-Adapted Normals (Subgroup 3, average coefficient = .28). In addition, the discriminant function between these two target groups was nonsignificant.

The last representativeness analysis concerning these two target groups

TABLE 4.3
Centroid Representativeness of the "Overs" and the "Unders"

Group	IQ	AM[a] or ASc[b]	ASw[c]	PA[d]	SchAd[e]	Avg. coeff. of cluster as a whole	Avg. D^2 from clus. centroid
			At age 13				
Entire subgroup 3 ($n = 55$)	− .39	− .19	− .27	.66	.96	.28	
Overs ($n = 15$)	− .46	− .26	− .27	.66	.91		.002
Unders ($n = 11$)	− .14	− .25	− .11	.66	1.15		.03
			At age 16				
Entire subgroup 3 ($n = 56$)	− .50	.61	.17	.66	.77	.25	
Overs ($n = 15$)	− .68	.46	.03	.66	.87		.02
Entire subgroup 5 ($n = 57$)	.17	− .17	− .03	− .32	.70	.21	
Unders ($n = 11$)	.11	− .21	− .23	− .17	.90		.02

Note: At age 13 a perceived ability mean of .66 meant that all the individuals in a given group had the same score. However, at age 16 the .66 perceived ability means of Subgroup 3 and of the Overs do *not* imply that all of these girls had the same score.
[a]Achievement in mathematics at age 13.
[b]Achievement in science at age 16.
[c]Achievement in Swedish.
[d]Perceived ability.
[e]School adaptation.

considered the 49 High-Adapted Normals who had comprised the sample of the EXACON analysis (see Table 3.3). When the 15 Overs and the 11 Unders were combined into one group, the discriminant function between these 26 girls and the 23 remaining girls was nonsignificant.

Results of Age-16 Analyses.   As shown in Table 4.3, the Overs (average $D^2 = .02$) were representative of the High-Adapted Overachiever subgroup (Subgroup 3) into which they streamed at age 16. This target group's representativeness was further supported by the nonsignificant discriminant function between the Overs ($n = 15$) and the remainder ($n = 30$) of the 45 High-Adapted Overachievers who had comprised the sample for the EX-ACON test (see Table 3.3).

Similarly, the Unders (average $D^2 = .02$) were representative of the age-16

Ability-Underestimating, High-Adapted Normal subgroup (Subgroup 5) to which they belonged. Again, the target group's representativeness was further supported by the nonsignificant discriminant function between the Unders ($n = 11$) and the remainder ($n = 31$) of the 42 Ability-Underestimating, High-Adapted Normals who had formed the sample for the EXACON test (see Table 3.3).

In conclusion, the characteristics of *only* those individuals who formed the two developmental streams emerging from the age-13 High-Adapted Normals yielded strong support for the meaningfulness of these streams. The next step is to identify specific factors associated with the development of a strong overachievement syndrome among certain of these girls versus continued average achievement, but decreased self-perceived ability, among others.

FACTORS ASSOCIATED WITH THE DIFFERENTIAL DEVELOPMENTAL STREAMS

Having ascertained that all four of the developmental streams targeted for further examination in this chapter were meaningful, the following analyses concerned factors associated with the differential developmental processes reflected in these streams. Factors associated with individuals' differential expression of achievement in and adaptation to the school environment at age 16 form the subject of future chapters. Because we know that the four target groups were representative of the subgroups to which they belonged at age 16, these future analyses of among-subgroup differences will, by definition, apply to the target groups in midadolescence.

Therefore, our concern in the present analyses was to identify relevant differences at the age of *13* between the high-ability, high-achieving girls whose *school adaptation* decreased over time (the Decreasers) and the high-ability, high-achieving girls whose adaptation increased over time (the Increasers). Similarly, we sought to identify relevant differences at the age of 13 between the low-normal-ability, high-adapted girls whose *achievement* increased markedly over time (the Overs) and the low-normal-ability, high-adapted girls who continued to achieve at normal levels, but whose *self-perceived ability* was relatively lower at age 16 than it had been at age 13 (the Unders).

Factors Associated With Changes in Adaptation

Family Background

The first question we addressed concerning possible differences at age 13 between high-ability, high-achieving girls whose school adaptation decreased over time and those whose adaptation increased was whether or not

TABLE 4.4
Family Background Patterns at Age 13 of High-Ability, High-Achieving
Girls Whose School Adaptation Decreased Versus Increased Over Time
("Decreasers" vs. "Increasers")

| | Standardized group means | | | | |
Group name	Family income	Fathers' educ.	Mothers' educ.	Parents' aspiration	Parents' evaluation
Decreasers (n = 11)	1.02*	1.07	1.10	—	—
Increasers (n = 8)	.04	.43	.29	—	—

Note: All parents of both groups aspired to their daughters' enrolling in an academic education after compulsory school, and all parents of both groups evaluated their daughters as capable of pursuing academic studies.
*p < .05.

these girls came from different family backgrounds. To address this issue we once again turned to patterns. Table 4.4 displays the pattern of each group's means across several indicators of family background. The indicators selected were family income, fathers' and mothers' education, parents' aspiration concerning their daughter's educational future, and parents' evaluation of their daughter's academic capability.

Because, in the next chapter, these same indicators are used in defining the family background patterns characteristic of all our subjects, the description of the measures is detailed at that time. For present purposes, suffice it to say that the indicators were taken from a Parents' Questionnaire administered to the parents of all subjects when the subjects were 13 years of age. The indicators presented here were standardized across the entire sample. For example, the family income of the Decreasers was about one standard deviation above the average income of all families, whereas the family income of the Increasers was about average for the sample as a whole.

As related to desires and expectations for their daughters' educational achievement, there were *no* differences between the parental values characterizing the Decreasers and those characterizing the Increasers. All the parents of both groups expressed educationally oriented values concerning their daughter's school achievement. Specifically, all aspired to their daughter's enrolling in an academic or "theoretical" education following compulsory school, and all evaluated their daughter as capable of pursuing academic studies.

Moreover, with respect to significant differences in parental SES, a discriminant function composed of family income and fathers' and mothers' education did not significantly discriminate between the family backgrounds of the Decreasers and those of the Increasers. Univariate tests revealed, however, that the family income mean of the Decreasers was significantly higher ($p < .05$) than that of the Increasers.

Although the mean difference in income was the only *statistically* significant result arising from the comparison of the two groups' family backgrounds, the power of our tests might well have been constrained by the small sizes of the groups involved. When one simply observes the pattern of family SES across the two groups, it is obvious that the socioeconomic status of the high-ability girls whose adaptation had *decreased* over time was *higher* than the SES of their highly able counterparts whose adaptation had *increased* by midadolescence.

This result is interesting. Given the general assumption throughout the literature concerning the *positive influence* of family SES on girls' achievement and aspiration, it is even somewhat counterintuitive. As is thoroughly discussed in the next chapter, high SES is often used as an implicit, indirect reflection of the high value parents place on education. Yet here we see that among certain parents, *all* of whom placed a high value on education, the parents of high-ability, high-achieving girls whose adaptation to school *decreased* over a 3-year-period had a higher socioeconomic status than did the parents of high-ability, high-achieving girls whose adaptation *increased* over time. With this result in mind, we pay close attention to the possible connections between high SES and differences observed between these two groups of girls at age *16*, when each group was characterized by a different pattern of ability and adaptation.

Relations With Parents

We also considered it possible that because all the parents of both groups wanted their daughters to continue an academic education following compulsory school and all parents believed their daughters to be academically capable, the parents of the Decreasers might experience more conflicted relations with their daughters than did those of the Increasers, especially in terms of worrying about their daughters' general obedience or worrying about their homework. Two additional items from the Parents' Questionnaire addressed these issues by asking parents, on a 5-point, Likert-type scale, the extent to which they worried about their daughters in these two areas. "Not at all" was coded at 5, and "very much" was coded at 1.

Contrary to our expectations, the two groups did not differ significantly on these items. The parents of the Decreasers ($M = 4.75$) were slightly *less* concerned than those of the Increasers ($M = 4.33$) over their daughters' obedience [$t (19) = 1.29$, ns], and all parents of both groups expressed *no* worry ($M = 5.00$ for both groups) concerning their daughters' homework.

Educational Aspiration

Another area in which we expected that the high-ability girls whose adaptation decreased over time and the high-ability girls whose adaptation increased over time might have differed from one another in early adolescence was that the Increasers might already have aspired to a higher education than that desired by the Decreasers. To investigate this issue, the difference between the two groups was assessed on an item drawn from the Vocational Questionnaire given to the subjects at age 13. Quite simply, the item asked respondents, "How many years can you accept going to school after compulsory school to get an occupation you like?" The response format was coded from 1 ("no studies whatsoever") to 5 (more than 5 years"). The two groups did not differ significantly [t (20) = .32, ns], although the Increasers' mean (4.20) exceeded that of the Decreasers (4.08) in the hypothesized direction.

Interests

The last domain in which we expected that the Decreasers and the Increasers might already differ at age 13 concerned their interests. Specifically, we expected that the girls whose school adaptation increased over time might, in early adolescence, have had higher technical and verbal interests than their counterparts whose adaptation decreased. To test this hypothesis, we compared the means of the two groups on their composite scores across the 20 items comprising the Verbal scale and across the 20 items comprising the Technical scale of the Interest Inventory administered to all subjects in Grade 6 (age 13).

For each item on each scale, respondents were asked to indicate the extent to which they enjoyed engaging in a particular activity. All responses were scored on a 4-point, Likert-type response format, from "Really boring to do" (coded as 1) to "Really fun to do" (coded as 4). Sample items in the verbal domain were "learning foreign languages" and "writing a short story." Sample items in the technical domain were "using a microscope" and "solving mathematical problems."

The results showed no significant differences between the two groups of girls in either verbal or technical interests at age 13. Thus, other than the differences in family SES which were discussed earlier, these two groups, who were characterized by the same pattern of ability/adaptation at age 13 and by different patterns at age 16, appeared to be quite similar in early adolescence, with respect to the aspects studied here. As mentioned earlier, factors associated with the differential patterns of ability and school adaptation they had developed by age 16 constitute the subject of future analyses.

Factors Associated With Changes in Achievement

Our next investigation addressed the differences between the high-adapted, low-normal-ability girls whose achievement levels rose substantially from age 13 to age 16 (the Overs) and the high-adapted, low-normal-ability girls

TABLE 4.5
Family Background Patterns at Age 13 of High-Adapted
Low-Normal-Ability Girls Whose Achievement Increased Versus Did Not
Increase Over Time ("Overs" vs. "Unders")

| | Standardized group means | | | | |
Group name	Family income	Fathers' educ.	Mothers' educ.	Parents' aspiration	Parents' evaluation
Overs (n = 13)	.39	.93*	.30	.59	.58
Unders (n = 9)	– .33	– .35	– .20	.34	.74

*$p < .01$.

whose achievement levels remained in a normal range, but whose self-perceived ability diminished over time (the Unders). Our procedure was analogous to that followed in the previous analyses.

Family Background

We first examined the means of these two groups across the same indicators of family background just described. The results are depicted in Table 4.5.

As was the case in the previous analysis, the means presented in Table 4.5 were computed from indicators derived from the Parents' Questionnaire completed by parents when the girls were 13 years old. The means were standardized across the entire sample. To interpret these means with respect to the parental values they reflect, it is helpful to know that a mean z score of .59 on parental aspiration indicated that *all* the parents in that group aspired to their daughters' receiving an academic education after compulsory school. Such was the case for the parents of the Overs. Similarly, a mean z score of .74 on parents' evaluation indicated that all the parents of that group believed their daughters capable of pursuing academic studies. Such was the case for the parents of the Unders. The *alternative* outcome (i.e., that parents in a given group did *not* unanimously want their daughters to follow an academic course of study and did *not* unanimously think them capable) would have been reflected in a mean z score of -1.68 on parents' aspiration and a mean z score of -1.35 on parents' evaluation.

Thus, the family backgrounds of the girls in the two groups appeared to be virtually the same in terms of parents' aspiration for their daughters and parents' evaluation of their daughters' capability. For the most part, the parents of the high-adapted, low-normal-ability girls whose achievement improved markedly over time (the Overs) held the same educationally oriented values as those of the girls who manifested normal achievement levels and decreased self-perceived ability at age 16 (the Unders).

The discriminant function composed of all five family pattern indicators was not significant at the .05 level ($p = .06$). However, univariate analyses showed the fathers' education mean among the girls whose achievement improved over time (the Overs) to be significantly higher ($p < .01$) than that of the girls who maintained average achievement levels but experienced lowered academic self-confidence (the Unders).

Once again, the power of our tests might well have been constrained by the small sizes of the groups involved. Observing the pattern of the parental SES measures across the two groups, it seems clear that although the parental *values* reflected in the families of the two groups did not differ meaningfully, the *socioeconomic status* of the Overs was consistently higher than that of the Unders.

Nevertheless, the most salient difference was indeed in the two levels of fathers' education. Possible connections between fathers' education and girls' achieving at a level substantially higher than might be expected given their intelligence are investigated further when we consider factors associated with the overachievement subgroup that emerged in midadolescence. It is recalled from the initial analyses in this chapter that the Overs in the present analyses were highly representative of the pattern that characterized the overachievement syndrome at age 16.

Educational Aspiration

We also investigated the difference between the Overs and the Unders in early adolescence with respect to the extent to which each group aspired to higher education. The measure of aspiration, taken from the Vocational Questionnaire given when the girls were 13, was described earlier. Our hypothesis was that the girls whose achievement improved markedly from age 13 to age 16 would have reported higher aspiration at the earlier age than had their lower achieving and less academically confident counterparts. The mean difference in aspiration between the Overs and the Unders at age 13 was in the expected direction ($M = 3.93$ and 3.36, respectively), but it was not significant [$t (24) = 1.45$, ns]

Interests

The final area in which we expected that the Overs and the Unders might already differ at age 13 concerned their interests. Specifically, we expected that the low-normal-ability, highly adapted girls whose achievement increased over time might, in early adolescence, have had higher technical and verbal interests than their counterparts whose achievement levels remained essentially the same. To test this expectation, we compared the means of these two groups on their composite scores across the 20 items comprising the Verbal scale and across the 20 items comprising the Technical scale of the Interest Inventory administered to all subjects at age 13. A description of these scales was provided in the foregoing section.

In both cases the results were significant. At age 13 the technical interest mean of the high-adapted, normal-ability girls who became overachievers at age 16 was significantly higher [t (24) = 2.88, $p < .01$] than that of their counterparts whose achievement did not change much over time and whose self-perceived ability declined. The Overs' mean was also significantly higher [t (24) = 2.70, $p = .01$] than that of the Unders on verbal interests. These differences suggested that the development of overachievement among the Overs might, at least in part, have been associated with their relatively greater interest, compared to that of the Unders, in areas that would become increasingly important to successful academic achievement over time. The lower *interest* in academically relevant activities, reported by Unders, may also have contributed to this group's perception, at age 16, that they were less academically *capable* than they had been at age 13, relative to the self-perceived ability of other girls at each age.

CONCLUDING REMARKS

This chapter first demonstrated, through a series of representativeness analyses, that certain developmental streams observed from the results presented in the previous chapter reflected genuine differential processes of development from early adolescence to midadolescence. Specifically, we have established that among a group of girls who, at age 13, exhibited the *same* pattern of high intelligence, high achievement, and moderately low school adaptation, two *separate* patterns emerged at age 16: Although school adaptation decreased markedly over time for certain of these girls, it increased substantially for others.

Similarly, we have demonstrated that among another group of girls who, at age 13, exhibited the same pattern of low-normal intelligence and achievement, high adaptation to school, and high self-perceived ability, two separate patterns also emerged at age 16: For certain of these girls achievement increased substantially, to levels that would not be expected given their stable below-average intelligence (i.e., they became overachievers). A second group maintained normal levels of achievement, consistent with their intelligence. However, the self-perceived ability mean of this second group decreased over time, relative to the means of other girls at each age.

Our investigation of factors that might already differentiate among these groups at age *13* revealed all four groups to have come from families with educationally oriented values. However, the socioeconomic status of the high-ability girls whose adaptation level *decreased* was *higher* than the socioeconomic status of the high-ability girls whose adaptation *increased*. Similarly, the socioeconomic status of the high-adapted, low-normal-ability girls who became overachievers was higher, especially with respect to fathers' educational level, than was the socioeconomic status of the high-adapted, low-normal-ability girls who did not become overachievers. We pursue the possible ramifications of both these findings in following chapters.

One other factor, namely interests, differentiated the overachievers from their low-normal-ability, high-adapted counterparts whose achievement at age 16 was consistent with their intelligence. At age 13, the future overachievers were already more interested than their counterparts in technical and verbal activities which might be relevant to successful academic performance.

Thus, even though each pair of groups discussed here was characterized by the same ability/adaptation pattern in early adolescence, it was possible to suggest certain differences between the pairs at age 13. We expect these differences to become more salient when we investigate the factors associated with the various ability/adaptation patterns that characterized our subjects at age 16.

Chapter 5

The Relation of Family Backgound to Girls' Ability and School Adaptation in Early Adolescence

In chapter 3 we described girls' functioning in the school environment, in terms of patterns that characterized their intelligence, their self-perceived ability, and their self-reported adaptation to academic demands. The chapter also illustrated the stability or change of individuals' patterns across a 3-year period. Chapter 4 examined several of these developmental streams in more detail.

This chapter is concerned with the relation of family background to girls' ability and adaptation in early adolescence. Through this investigation we are considering individuals' functioning in a second environmental domain, that of the home.

INTRODUCTION

A plethora of previous studies has addressed the influence of various aspects of family background on females' scholastic and occupational goals and achievements (see Betz & Fitzgerald, 1987, for a review). Several observations regarding this body of literature may be particularly relevant to this investigation.

First, previous studies have frequently assessed family background variables, alone or in combination with other variables from the same or different domains, in an attempt to determine which *single* aspects of the home environment emerge as most "predictive" of females' aspirations or achievement, a sort of "variable competition" approach. This strategy, regardless of whether the research design has incorporated linear or nonlinear methodology, has lead to conflicting results concerning the salience of specific variables, depending, at least in part, on what other variables were included in the analyses.

For example, considering first those variables which reflect socioeconomic status (SES), Marini's (1978) review cites numerous studies, based primarily on simple correlations or on multiple regression, which have demonstrated a positive relationship between adolescent females' educational aspirations (and, to a lesser extent, their occupational aspirations) and their family's socioeconomic status level, whether SES has been represented by father's education, father's occupation, mother's education, or a composite index. Burlin (1976), using chi-squared analyses, also found female adolescents' moderately nontraditional occupational aspirations to be significantly associated with fathers' having college degrees and with mothers' holding nontraditional jobs, although mothers' educational level was unrelated to daughters' aspirations.

In contrast to Burlin's study, the results of Zuckerman's (1980) regression analyses showed that mothers' educational level did significantly predict college women's nontraditional career goals, whereas fathers' education and parents' occupation did not. Further, using a nonlinear, nonparametric design, Falkowski and Falk (1983) found that having a nonemployed mother, a low occupational status father, and a rural background was significantly associated with adolescent girls' reporting that they expected to be homemakers, not professionally or nonprofessionally employed, when they were age 30. The family background dimensions associated with homemaking were established through three separate analyses, however, and thus did not constitute a pattern characterizing one subgroup of individuals. Finally, in a less purely exploratory vein, Smith's (1980) log-linear analysis of the determinants of adolescent girls' desiring and expecting to work in adulthood demonstrated that girls whose mothers were employed in white-collar occupations wanted to work more than did girls whose mothers were employed in blue-collar jobs, even though the daughters of blue-collar workers *expected* to work more than did their higher SES counterparts.

In addition to not delineating precisely which aspects of a family's socioeconomic situation are most consistently related to adolescent females' achievement aspirations, investigations concentrating solely on the influence of SES variables such as parental education and/or occupation are perhaps of limited *psychological* value because they provide little useful information for researchers interested in the *processes* through which parents' influence is transmitted to and evaluated by their children and offer no realistic avenue for intervention by practitioners. One might surely argue, instead, that the important psychological issue may be, not a family's socioeconomic status per se, but, rather, differential *patterns* of interaction between parents' own socioeconomic level and the aspirations they express regarding their offsprings' achievement. It is, most often, parents' *values* concerning their children's future that assessments of SES are *implicitly* assumed to reflect, although perhaps because the assumption is rarely made *explicit*, socioeconomic variables have tended to become reified in their own right.

The underlying (and understated) model seems to have been that high parental education will go hand in hand with high levels of parental occupation and income and, moreover, that this "privileged" family environment, with its *assumed* parental emphasis on offspring education, will provide the ideal background for children's high achievement. The model further presumes, although perhaps more covertly, that *low*-educated parents in *low*-status jobs will *not* adequately reinforce children's academic success. Although such a model is not entirely without statistical support, especially if one considers extreme cases at both ends of the SES continuum, the interpretation of moderate, statistically significant relationships between parents' SES and offsprings' aspirations or achievements can be misleading, particularly because such relationships are usually demonstrated on large samples.

For example, such results do not address the upward-mobility phenomenon, whereby parents want and expect their children to accomplish more than they themselves have done, nor do they address the question of whether parental values are more or less likely to influence individuals' achievement if these values are expressed in an upper class rather than a middle- or a lower class home. Berry (1981) has observed, for instance, that Nobel laureates in the sciences have tended to emerge from stable, upwardly mobile backgrounds, a finding that Silver (1983) has attributed to the upwardly mobile value system, which, like the scientific environment, is geared toward risk-taking.

Direct assessments of the influence of parental values on children's goals or accomplishments have, of course, been conducted, although interpreting the findings in this area also poses certain difficulties. Among female or male individuals whose achievements have been judged as creative, family environments that foster intellectual values and provide intellectual stimulation consistently appear to have contributed to the expression of such creativity (Eiduson, 1962; MacKinnon, 1962; Roe, 1951, 1953). Outside of the creativity literature, the results become less clear-cut.

For example, fathers' encouragement of their daughters' plans to enroll in college was predictive of females' orientation toward a professional career 5 years after high school, according to the study conducted by Astin and Myint (1971). However, because this particular result was based on a discriminant analysis that comprised 49 predictors (predicting membership in 1 of 10 professional and nonprofessional job categories), it underscores the problem of assessing the simultaneous influence of numerous variables from disparate domains.

Nevertheless, using a discriminant analyses with 23 predictors and only three criterion groups, Rooney (1983) also found that, for both males and females, parental encouragement discriminated full-time students (who might be assumed to be pursuing careers) from full-time homemakers or full-time workers. In contrast, Farmer (1980), utilizing step-wise multiple regression with 11 predictors, found that "community support," which included but was not limited to parental support, significantly predicted career motivation, whereas the more *specific* measure of parental encouragement of achievement was unrelated to the criterion.

Other studies have also failed to provide unambiguous support for the role of parental encouragement in children's educational goals or achievement. Through a series of correlations, Crandall, Dewey, Katkovsky, and Preston (1964) found that mothers', but not fathers', evaluation of their offsprings' ability showed a significant positive relationship to elementary school children's achievement test performance. However, the value mothers placed on their children's educational attainment was not significantly correlated with test performance for children of either sex, although the value *fathers* ascribed to scholastic achievement was significantly *negatively* related to their daughters' test performance in reading and unrelated to any other performance dimension for either sex. Lest these results be dismissed too hastily on the basis of methodological primitivism, Fassinger (1985), in a more sophisticated causal analysis employing structural equation modeling, reported similar results for predicting career choice among female university students: Perceived encouragement from mother and father was eliminated as a parameter in the modified models, several iterations before the final, theory-trimmed model was confirmed.

Finally, Schiamberg (1989) has conducted a 14-year longitudinal path analyses of family influence on the educational and occupational achievement of low-income White versus low-income Black adolescents. Among the variables included in the study were value-laden constructs such as assessments of mothers' expectations regarding their children's eventual level of educational and occupational attainment. The results demonstrated that family background exerted a stronger influence on outcomes for Black than for White youths. Nevertheless, because the path-analytic approach is linear, it cannot reflect the higher order interactions that may be observed through pattern analysis.

In summary, two noteworthy limitations seem inherent in previous research concerning the influence of the home environment on females' educational and occupational development. First, these studies direct insufficient attention toward the *interactions* among family background variables themselves, in terms of these interactions' defining an overall pattern that characterizes the home environment. Second, researchers have generally assumed that the processes believed to underlie the variables under consideration will operate in the same manner for all individuals (or for all individuals within large groups, like Blacks or Whites, males or females), with the consequence that family background indicators are used as nomothetic variables in statistical analyses.

To our knowledge, virtually no research has previously asked which *family background patterns* of SES and parental values may or may not be associated with certain *individuals' patterns* of educational achievement in and adaptation to the school environment. Attempting to answer this question is the main goal of this chapter. We should emphasize at the outset that in the analyses that follow, we define parental *values* as the values parents hold concerning their *daughter's* achievement—that is, their *aspiration for her future education* and their *evaluation of her academic capability*.

Five indicators were selected to define the patterns that characterized the girls' family backgrounds when they were 13 years of age:

1. parents' income;
2. father's educational level;
3. mother's educational level;
4. parents' aspirations regarding their daughter's continuing her education past compulsory school; and
5. parents' evaluation of their daughter's academic capability.

Further information concerning the instruments from which these indicators were drawn is provided in Magnusson et al. (1975).

PATTERNS OF FAMILY BACKGROUNDS

Methods

Data

All five family background indicators were drawn from a Parents' Questionnaire completed by the subjects' parents when the girls were in the sixth grade (age 13). The measure of the three SES variables, which were recoded as z scores, was as follows:

1. Family income was assessed, on a 5-point scale, as the combined gross income of both parents.
2. Level of education for father was measured on a 7-point scale, ranging from no education past compulsory school (coded as 1) to at least 4 years of university (coded as 7).
3. Level of education for mother was measured on the same 7-point scale.

Two indicators were selected to assess parental values, as defined earlier:

1. The indicator reflecting *parental aspiration* concerning their daughter's education was an item that asked parents whether, after their daughter's completion of compulsory school, they wished her to pursue a "theoretical" (academic) education, which would involve a somewhat lengthy occupational preparation, or a "practical" (vocational) training program, which would prepare her to begin her working life relatively quickly. Technically, CLUSTAN cannot accommodate continuous and categorical variables in the same profile. Therefore, to allow us to use both SES and values measures, we conceptualized this indicator as a "continuity" of the expression of *theoretical* aspirations on the part of the parents, with the "practical" option's being coded as 1 and the "theoretical" option's being coded as 2. The score thus derived was then transformed into a z score.

2. The measure of *parents' evaluation* of their daughter's academic capability was taken from an identically coded item that asked parents whether they considered their daughter to be better "suited" to a practical or to a theoretical education. Once again, a continuity was defined, wherein parents' perception that their daughter was better suited for a practical education was inferred as an expression of less confidence in her academic capability (and was coded as 1), as compared to the confidence expressed by parents who judged their daughter better suited to a theoretical education (which was coded as 2). As was the case with the other indicators, this measure was recoded as a z score.

It should perhaps be mentioned here that the parents' assessment of their daughter's "capability," in terms of what "suited" her, was a summary judgment that may well have reflected more than the parents' evaluation of their daughter's intelligence. Thus, we are using the term *capability* in its broadest possible context. Finally, it should be stated that for both the parental aspiration and the parental evaluation items, we could not determine whether the response represented the judgment of the mother, of the father, or of both parents, because we had no way of knowing who had actually completed the form or whether or not the parents had discussed it. However, the questionnaire was accompanied by a letter of instruction that strongly urged the cooperation of both parents.

Subjects and Analyses

The subjects for whom a family background pattern was defined were the 463 sixth-grade girls whose parents had completed all of the five relevant items on the Parents' Questionnaire. This sample constituted 81% of the 557 girls who comprised the total female sample in 1968.

The simple correlations among the five indicators were assessed before the individual profiles were clustered. All correlations were expected to be positive. In addition, the raw-score mean of the fathers' educational level

TABLE 5.1
Correlations Among Age-13 Family Background Pattern Indicators

Indicator	1	2	3	4	5
1-Family income	—	.67	.46	.36	.36
2-Fathers' education		—	.55	.34	.38
3-Mothers' education			—	.28	.31
4-Parents' aspiration				—	.76
5-Parents' evaluation					—

Note: N = 463. All correlations significant (p < .001).

was compared to that of the mothers' educational level to verify that the fathers would exhibit a higher level of education than that attained by their wives, an issue of some importance with regard to the direct comparability of fathers' and mothers' education within a given subgroup.

Results and Discussion

Results of Preliminary Analyses

The correlation among the indicators is displayed in Table 5.1. As expected, all correlations were positive, and, perhaps due to the large size of the sample, all were significant ($p < .001$).

The pattern of correlations illustrated that the implicit model so prevalent in previous research, that parental socioeconomic status mirrors parental values, was only moderately supported. The correlations *among* the three SES indicators and *between* the two values indicators were consistently higher than were *any* of the correlations between a values measure and a SES measure. The highest correlation was between the two values indicators, parents' aspiration concerning their daughter's future education and parents' evaluation of their daughter's capability ($r = .76$). The lowest correlation was between parents' aspirations and mother's educational level ($r = .28$).

As also expected, the fathers' raw-score education mean was significantly higher than that of the mothers [$t(924) = 6.51$, $p < .001$]. The fathers' mean of 2.68 corresponded to having completed more than a 1- to 2-year program of relatively low-level training for a trade or a profession (coded as 2) but less than a 4- to 5-year preparation for gymnasium (coded as 3). Because compulsory school was 6 rather than 9 years when the parents were educated, these levels were not relevant markers of the Swedish educational system in which their daughters were participating.

In contrast, the mothers' raw-score mean (1.95) fell a little short of the 1- to 2-year program of relatively low-level training for a trade or a profession. Because of this difference, the following discussion, for the most part, compared mothers' and fathers' educational levels, within a given subgroup, to the overall education means of women and men, respectively.

TABLE 5.2
Family Background Patterns at Age 13

Subgroup label	Standardized subgroup means				
	Inc[a]	FEd[b]	MEd[c]	PAs[d]	PEv[e]
1-High SES Brahmin (n = 27)	1.39	2.07	2.58	.59	.74
2-High SES, High-Educated Fathers (n = 60)	1.21	1.32	.32	.59	.74
3-Middle-Class, High-Educated Mothers (n = 51)	.22	.08	1.24	.59	.74
4-Middle-Class Upwardly Mobiles (n = 83)	.34	−.10	−.51	.59	.74
5-Middle-Class Pushers (n = 11)	.83	.79	−.16	.59	−1.35
6-Low SES Upwardly Mobiles (n = 74)	−.90	−.62	−.51	.59	.74
7-Low SES Pushers (n = 34)	−.55	−.66	−.42	.59	−1.35
8 Low SES Status Quos (n = 116)	−.63	−.62	−.50	−1.68	−1.29

Note: In total, the family backgrounds of 456 subjects were clustered.
[a]Family income.
[b]Fathers' educational level.
[c]Mothers' educational level.
[d]Parents' aspiration for daughter's education (z score of −1.68 = raw score of 1.0, and z score of .59 = raw score of 2.0).
[e]Parents' evaluation of daughter's capability (z score of −1.35 = raw score of 1.0, and z score of .74 = raw score of 2.0).

Interpretation of Family Background Patterns

For the cluster analysis of the girls' family background patterns at age 13, an eight-cluster solution was judged optimal according to the criteria discussed in chapter 2. These clusters, depicted in Table 5.2, represented the assignment of each of 456 girls' home environments into one of eight characteristic subgroups. The eight-cluster solution, excluding a residual of seven subjects (1.51%) whose profiles did not match the centroids of any of the derived clusters, accounted for a 79% reduction of error variance over considering the entire sample as a single cluster.

Initial examination of these subgroups revealed that they discriminated among high, middle, and low socioeconomic status as defined according to family income, although, within an SES level, there was considerable variability in the mean levels of education achieved by the parents. For example, the 27 families who constituted the High SES "Brahmin" pattern (Subgroup 1) were so-named, not only because they exhibited the highest income mean, but also because the educational level of both fathers and mothers in this subgroup was more than two standard deviations above the overall average. In contrast, the High SES, High-Educated Fathers (Subgroup 2), although characterized by almost as high an income mean as that of the previous subgroup and by a high level of fathers' education, exhibited a level of mothers' education that was only one third of a standard deviation above the overall average for the women.

The same variability in educational levels was evident in the middle-class income patterns. The mothers' education mean in the Middle-Class, High-Educated Mothers subgroup (Subgroup 3) was well above the mean for all mothers. In fact, in this subgroup alone, the mothers were, on the average, more highly educated than their husbands, whose educational level essentially reflected the overall average for the men. The opposite pattern was obtained for the Middle-Class "Pushers" (Subgroup 5), whose profile was characterized by relatively high levels of family income and of fathers' education, in combination with a below-average level of mothers' education.

We derived the designation of "Pushers," applied to the aforementioned subgroup and to one subgroup among the low-income patterns (Subgroup 7), from the combination of *high* parental aspiration for their daughter's educational future and *low* evaluation of her capability to pursue such an aspiration. This disparity between aspiration and evaluation, which was not evident in any of the other subgroups, might have connoted a possible "mixed message" to the daughters of these parents.

In the main, however, *regardless* of their own SES level, the parents of the 13-year-old girls both aspired to their daughter's pursuing an academic curriculum following compulsory school and believed her capable of fulfilling their aspiration. A z score of .59 represented a raw score of 2.0, reflecting the parents' aspiration that their daughter pursue a theoretical, or academic, education, whereas a z score of -1.68 represented a raw score of 1.0, reflecting the parents' desire that their daughter pursue a vocational education. Thus, the parents of all but the last of the subgroups in Table 5.2 unanimously expressed the desire that their daughters enroll in an academic education following compulsory school.

On the measure of parental evaluation, a z score of .74 represented a raw score of 2.0, reflecting the parents' belief that their daughter was better suited for an academic education, and a z score of -1.35 represented a raw score of 1.0, reflecting the parents' belief that their daughter was better suited for a vocational education. Therefore, the parents in the subgroups not characterized by the "pusher" syndrome discussed earlier were, with one exception, in unanimous agreement that their daughters were *capable* of pursuing an academic education. Subgroups 4 and 6, in which these educationally oriented aspirations and evaluations appeared to contrast with the parents' own relatively low levels of educational and/or financial attainment, were designated as "upwardly mobile."

The sole exception to this general optimism concerning their daughter's academic future was found in the last subgroup, the Low SES Status Quos (Subgroup 8). Among these parents, low income and education means were combined with a uniform *lack* of aspiration regarding an academic education for their daughter and an almost unanimous belief that she was better suited for vocational school.

Of the eight subgroups that emerged from the analysis, three were of special interest in terms of their demonstrating particularly striking combinations of SES and parental values: The High SES Brahmin (Subgroup 1), the Low SES Upwardly Mobiles (Subgroup 6), and the Low SES Status Quos (Subgroup 8). The mean profiles of these three subgroups are depicted in Fig. 5.1.

ASSOCIATIONS BETWEEN FAMILY BACKGROUND AND ABILITY/ADAPTATION PATTERNS AT AGE 13

Methodological Considerations

The patterns that characterized the girls' home environments at age 13 suggested implications regarding the relation of family background to girls' expression of ability and adaptation to school in early adolescence. These implications, formed as hypotheses, were the core of the next analysis, which used the EXACON exact test of single-cell frequencies (Bergman & El-Khouri, 1987) described in chapter 2.

One purpose of the EXACON analysis was to test whether or not subjects who comprised the membership of a particular family background subgroup were overrepresented in the membership of a specific ability/adaptation subgroup (i.e., in EXACON terminology, whether or not the specified subjects constituted a *type*). However, because the existence of certain family patterns could also be presupposed not to be associated with individuals characterized by certain ability/adaptation patterns, our predictions were expanded to include the specification of *under*representations (or *antitypes*) as well.

Once again, it should be emphasized that all expectations concerning the associations or nonassociations between subgroups in the two domains were established prior to conducting the EXACON analysis. As before, this a priori construction of expectations was crucial to the research design since the two-way contingency table (Family Background Subgroup Membership X Ability Subgroup Membership) formed an 8×9 matrix, each cell of which was tested individually. To unravel spuriously significant over- and underrepresentations that might occur due to Type I error from psychologi-

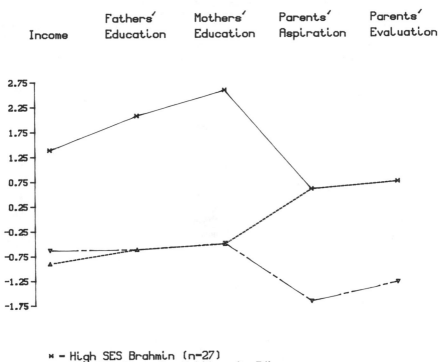

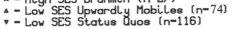

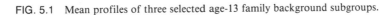

м - High SES Brahmin (n-27)
▲ - Low SES Upwardly Mobiles (n-74)
▼ - Low SES Status Quos (n-116)

FIG. 5.1   Mean profiles of three selected age-13 family background subgroups.

cally meaningful results would be quite difficult if one relied solely on post hoc analyses.

The abilities of 403 subjects and the home environments of 456 subjects were clustered at age 13. However, the necessary restriction of the EX-ACON analysis to only those girls who had subgroup membership in both domains reduced the number of subjects in the EXACON sample to 330.

Verification of Expected Types and Antitypes

In total, we generated 21 expectations concerning the association or the nonassociation between a specific home environment pattern and particular patterns of ability/adaptation expressed at age 13. (The age-13 ability/adaptation subgroups are shown in Table 3.1.) These expectations are discussed here. The significance levels of the hypothesized types and antitypes, as well as those of the types and antitypes that we did not expect, are depicted in Table 5.3.

TABLE 5.3
Associations and Nonassociations Between Family Background Patterns
and Ability/Adaptation Patterns at Age 13

Family pattern at age 13	Ability pattern(s) at age 13	Overlap n
	Predicted types	
1-High SES Brahmin#	1-High-Ability, High-Adapted	
(n = 20)	Achievers	
	(n = 58)	7*
	2-Gifted, Moderately	
	Low-Adapted Achievers	
	(n = 34)	4
2-High SES,	1-High-Ability, High-Adapted	
High-Educated Fathers#	Achievers	
(n = 50)	(n = 58)	14*
	2-Gifted, Moderately	
	Low-Adapted Achievers	
	(n = 34)	10*
3-Middle-Class,	1-High-Ability, High-Adapted	
High-Educated Mothers	Achievers	
(n = 32)	(n = 58)	8
4-Middle-Class	1-High-Ability, High-Adapted	
Upwardly Mobiles	Achievers	
(n = 67)	(n = 58)	12
5-Middle-Class Pushers#	8-Low-Adapted, Realistic,	
(n = 7)	Low Achievers	
	(n = 42)	3*
6-Low SES	1-High-Ability, High-Adapted	
Upwardly Mobiles#	Achievers	
(n = 58)	(n = 58)	17**
7-Low SES Pushers#	7-Low-Adapted, Unrealistic,	
(n = 24)	Low Achievers	
	(n = 26)	5*
	9-Low-Adapted, Low-Ability	
	Non-Achievers	
	(n = 28)	6**
8-Low SES Status Quos#	5-Ability-Underestimating Normals	
(n = 72)	(n = 36)	14**
	6-Moderately Low-Adapted	
	Normals	
	(n = 48)	5*
	8-Low-Adapted, Realistic,	
	Low Achievers	
	(n = 42)	23****
	9-Low-Adapted, Low-Ability	
	Non-Achievers	
	(n = 28)	16****
	Unpredicted types	
3-Middle-Class,	4-Math-Oriented Verbal	
High-Educated Mothers#	Underachievers	
(n = 32)	(n = 14)	4*

(Continued)

TABLE 5.3 (Continued)

Family pattern at age 13	Ability pattern(s) at age 13	Overlap n
4-Middle-Class, Upwardly Mobiles# (n = 67)	3-High-Adapted Normals (n = 44)	15*
	6-Moderately Low-Adapted Normals (n = 48)	17**
	Predicted antitypes	
1-High SES Brahmin (n = 20)	8-Low-Adapted, Realistic, Low Achievers (n = 42)	0
	9-Low-Adapted, Low-Ability Non-Achievers (n = 28)	0
2-High SES, High-Educated Fathers (n = 50)	8-Low-Adapted, Realistic, Low Achievers (n = 42)	0***
7-Low SES Pushers# (n = 24)	1-High-Ability, High-Adapted Achievers (n = 58)	0**
8-Low SES Status Quos# (n – 72)	1-High-Ability, High-Adapted Achievers (n = 58)	0****
	2-Gifted, Moderately Low-Adapted Achievers (n = 34)	2**
	3-High-Adapted Underachievers (n = 44)	4*
	Unpredicted antitypes	
3-Middle-Class, High-Educated Mothers# (n = 32)	9-Low-Adapted, Low-Ability Non-Achievers (n = 28)	0*
4-Middle-Class Upwardly Mobiles# (n = 67)	8-Low-Adapted, Realistic, Low Achievers (n = 42)	4*
	9-Low-Adapted, Low-Ability Non-Achievers (n = 28)	1**

Note: Types and antitypes were derived, from exact tests of the single-call frequency overlap between the two sets of subgroups, for a total of 330 subjects.

= only significant type(s) or antitype(s) observed.

*$p \leq .05$. **$p < .01$. ***$p < .001$. ****$p < .0001$.

The High SES Brahmin (Subgroup 1)

Association With High Achievers.   Considering their exceedingly high level of both parental education and income, in addition to their uniform expression of academic aspiration for their daughter and belief in her academic capability, the High SES Brahmin were expected to be significantly overrepresented among the two age-13 ability/adaptation subgroups whose members displayed the highest levels of achievement: the High-Ability, High-Adapted Achievers and the Gifted, Moderately Low-Adapted Achievers (Subgroups 1 and 2). The High SES Brahmin fathers were characterized by having achieved between a college and a university education ($M = 6.63$ on the 7-point raw-score scale), whereas the mothers' raw-score mean (5.67) corresponded to having completed between a gymnasium and a college education.

It was assumed that this particular background would constitute a condition, at one extreme of the socioeconomic continuum, in which SES, in combination with the parents' value system, might exert a pronounced influence on girls' expression of ability. One might even surmise that, given two academically able parents, the effect of heredity on intelligence would be likely to influence high academic performance among subjects from this family pattern. Heredity aside, it was expected that, within this subgroup, the values espoused by the parents, and reflected in their own achievement, would be associated with sustaining high performance in their daughter, even if the daughter was not all that well-adapted to the school environment, as was the case for the Gifted, Moderately Low-Adapted Achievers.

As Table 5.3 demonstrates, these hypotheses were partially supported: The High SES Brahmin were significantly overrepresented among the High-Ability, *High-Adapted* Achievers ($p < .05$). However, this overrepresentation constituted the only type observed for the Brahmin subgroup. Although the frequencies of the next largest cell did reflect the overrepresentation of the Brahmin among the Gifted, Moderately Low-Adapted Achievers, the association was not significant.

Nevertheless, it might be worth recalling chapter 4's results here: the *specific* age-13 Gifted, Moderately Low-Adapted Achievers whose school adaptation had *decreased* by age 16 were, in fact, characterized by *higher* SES family backgrounds than those characterizing the gifted, high-performing 13-year-olds whose adaptation had *increased* over time. Thus, the notion of high SES, in combination with educationally oriented parental values, exerting a particularly strong influence on the achievement of high-ability girls who do not "fit" the school environment is examined again in mid-adolescence.

Nonassociation With Low Achievers.   We also expected that the Brahmin background would be *under*represented among subgroups whose ability/adaptation patterns were characterized by both a low level of school adaptation and low intelligence and achievement means. Thus, although there were only a few families to test (27 in the initial cluster analysis), we expected that at least one antitype would emerge, in the form of a significant underrepresentation between the Brahmin and the Low-Adapted, Unrealistic, Low Achievers; the Low-Adapted, Realistic, Low Achievers; and/or the Low-Adapted, Low-Ability Non-Achievers (Subgroups 7, 8, and 9, respectively). Although the overlap was *literally nonexistent* between the Brahmin and Subgroups 8 and 9, and although these nonassociations constituted the only zero-frequency cells involving the Brahmin, they were not significant. In fact, perhaps because of the small number of Brahmin families involved in the marginal frequencies, no antitypes were observed. We might nonetheless point out that, regardless of its significance level, an empty cell is an empty cell.

The High-SES, High-Educated Fathers (Subgroup 2)

Association With High Achievers.   Following the same basic logic that directed the previous set of expectations although eliminating any conjectures regarding hereditary influences on intelligence, the same overrepresentations were hypothesized concerning the High-SES, High-Educated Fathers. Specifically, due to the combination of high fathers' education, high family income, and academically oriented parental values, this family background pattern was also expected to be significantly associated with the High-Ability, High-Adapted Achievers and with the Gifted, Moderately Low-Adapted Achievers (Subgroups 1 and 2). Both of these associations were significant at a probability level of less than .05, and they were the only types observed.

Nonassociation With Low Achievers.   Further, as was the case for the Brahmin, the High SES, High-Educated Fathers were expected to be *under-*represented in at least one of the three low-adapted and low- or nonachieving ability/adaptation subgroups (Subgroups 7, 8, and 9). In support of this expectation, the results revealed no overlap between the High SES, High-Educated Fathers and the Low-Adapted, Realistic, Low Achievers (Subgroup 8). The probability of observing an empty cell was highly significant ($p < .001$). This significant nonassociation was the only antitype that emerged in connection with the High SES, High-Educated Fathers.

The Middle-Class, High-Educated Mothers (Subgroup 3)

Association With High Achievers.   Because a mother whose education exceeded the norm for her time was also expected to exert a positive influence on her daughter's adaptation to school, as well as to reinforce her daughter's achievement, the Middle-Class, High-Educated Mothers (Subgroup 3) were hypothesized to be overrepresented among the High-Ability, High-Adapted Achievers (Subgroup 1). This type was not observed.

The only type that emerged concerning the High-Educated Mothers was their significant ($p < .05$) overrepresentation among the Math-Oriented Verbal Underachievers (Subgroup 4). Quite frankly, this association defied interpretation. One would expect the daughters of educated mothers to lack neither verbal competence, in which females are traditionally adept, nor an adaptation to the school environment, given that they have sufficient intelligence to perform satisfactorily, which this ability/adaptation subgroup did.

A Possible Caveat. The family background pattern characterized by mothers who were more educated, on the average, than other women, and even more educated than their own husbands, thus failed to demonstrate a *meaningful* association with any of the ability/adaptation subgroups. This result was in contrast to previous research, cited earlier in this chapter, which has suggested that through her own educational attainment a mother provides an example for her daughter. However, one limitation of the present investigation might have been that the mothers comprising this particular family background subgroup were not actually all that well-educated if one considers their educational level in absolute rather than in relative terms.

The raw-score mean for mothers' education in this subgroup was 3.74, which corresponded to having completed a level between preparation for the gymnasium (coded as 3) and approximately 3 years of professional, but not academic or "theoretical," education beyond the compulsory 6 years of schooling (coded as 4). The raw-score education mean for the fathers in this subgroup was 2.83, which corresponded to not quite a preparation for gymnasium. Thus, although these mothers were well-educated in comparison to the overall mean of the women sampled and had, on the whole, attained a higher educational level than had their husbands, they had not received the extensive, academically oriented education that, for example, characterized the High SES Brahmin mothers.

Therefore, the Middle-Class, High-Educated Mothers could perhaps not, technically speaking, be regarded as setting a personal example for the academic aspirations they held concerning their daughters' post-compulsory school education. Had a subgroup emerged in which mothers as educated as the Brahmin mothers had been married to men with no academic education, the influence of the mothers' achievements might have been more pronounced. Such unions, however, were not characteristic of the patterns that comprised the structure of the data.

Observed Nonassociation. No hypotheses were formulated concerning the High-Educated Mothers' *non*association with the age-13 ability/adaptation patterns. The single antitype that emerged, the High-Educated Mothers' being significantly underrepresented ($p = .05$) among the Low-Adapted, Low-Ability Non-Achievers (Subgroup 9), seemed reasonable, considering the overall disinterest in academic success that this ability/adaptation subgroup manifested.

The Middle-Class Upwardly Mobiles (Subgroup 4)

Association With High Achievers. The Middle-Class Upwardly Mobiles were also expected to be significantly overrepresented among the High-Ability, High-Adapted Achievers (Subgroup 1). This expectation was based on the presumed positive influence on girls' school achievement/adaptation of a family structure that combined a moderate level of income, average (for fathers) and less than average (for mothers) levels of parental education, and parental values oriented toward their daughters' receiving a theoretical education. Although it was hypothesized that such an overrepresentation would characterize a typical syndrome of parents' motivating their daughter to achieve more than they themselves had accomplished, this type did not emerge.

Observed Associations. The two types that did emerge involving the Middle-Class Upwardly Mobiles were the significant associations between this family background and both the High-Adapted Normals (Subgroup 3; $p < .05$) and the Moderately Low-Adapted Normals (Subgroup 6; $p < .01$). With respect to the first of these overrepresentations, the high adaptation mean of the High-Adapted Normals, along with their high level of perceived ability, might have reflected, at least in part, the parental values to which they were exposed at age 13, even though their achievement levels were somewhat below average in early adolescence. In this context, it might also be remembered that the High-Adapted Normals at age 13 were overrepresented among the *Overachievers* at age 16 (see chapter 3); therefore, it is conceivable that a positive parental influence on actual achievement occurred over time.

On the other hand, the association between the Middle-Class Upwardly Mobiles and the Moderately Low-Adapted Normals might indicate that the aspirations experienced by these upwardly mobile parents had not been internalized by their daughters, despite the daughters' average levels of intelligence and achievement. If such were the case, the low school adaptation of these girls would be reasonable, especially if they were enrolled in an academically oriented curriculum. The aspiration and choices of these girls are examined directly in chapter 7.

Observed Nonassociations. Although no underrepresentations were specified a priori concerning the Middle-Class Upwardly Mobiles, the two significant antitypes that were observed supported the general thesis, developed earlier, that the upwardly mobile syndrome should be associated with positive school adaptation, a strong sense of self-efficacy, and high achievement. The Middle-Class Upwardly Mobiles formed an *antitype* with the Low-Adapted, Realistic, Low Achievers (Subgroup 8; $p < .05$) and with the Low-Adapted, Low-Ability Non-Achievers (Subgroup 9; $p = .01$). These ability/adaptation subgroups were characterized, not only by low achievement and adaptation means, but also by the lowest levels of self-perceived ability.

The Middle-Class Pushers (Subgroup 5)

Although the Middle-Class Pushers comprised only 11 families in the initial cluster analysis (and only 7 families in the EXACON analysis), it was hypothesized that this background might be significantly associated with the Low-Adapted, Realistic, Low Achievers (Subgroup 8). The Middle-Class Pushers were characterized by relatively high income and fathers' education, as well as by parental aspiration toward their daughter's pursuing a theoretical education; however, *none* of these parents believed such an education suited their daughter's capability.

In light of this disparity, the assumption was that the daughter in question (who might not be an apt pupil) would have incorporated her parents' negative evaluation into her own perception of her academic ability. This incorporation of negative parental beliefs was assumed to be especially likely given a family environment in which educational achievement, or the lack thereof, was a salient issue for the parents, as might be assumed in the present case, considering the high level of fathers' education among the Middle-Class Pushers. Thus, not only might the daughter in such families perform poorly and exhibit low adaptation to the school environment, but she might also demonstrate a "realistic" (as opposed to an "unrealistic") assessment of her own low competence. This type ($p < .05$), the only one to emerge with respect to the Middle-Class Pushers, was observed.

The Low SES Upwardly Mobiles (Subgroup 6)

Association With High Achievers. The suggested upwardly mobile syndrome described earlier in relation to the Middle-Class Upwardly Mobiles also served as the basis for our expectations regarding the Low SES Upwardly Mobiles. We expected these families to be overrepresented among the High-Ability, High-Adapted Achievers (Subgroup 1). The Low SES Upwardly Mobiles were characterized by the lowest family income mean exhibited by any of the family background subgroups. In addition, the mothers' education mean was exactly the same as that of the Middle-Class Upwardly Mobile mothers.

Like their middle-class counterparts, the Low SES Upwardly Mobile parents unanimously expressed a desire for their daughter to pursue a theoretical education and a belief that such an education matched her capabilities. It was thus assumed that this family background, with its pronounced lack of economic advantage, combined with its parental value system oriented toward achievement, would provide a strong motivating force toward the high performance and high adaptation characteristic of the High-Ability, High-Adapted Achievers.

The association between the Low SES Upwardly Mobiles and the High-Ability, High-Adapted Achievers was significant ($p = .01$). Furthermore, this association was the only type (or antitype) observed for these families.

Advantage of the Pattern Versus the Variable Approach.   This result underscored the point made earlier concerning the limitations of the variable approach. Had the influence of mothers' education been assessed, in isolation from parental values, the strength of the *linear* relationship between mothers' education and daughters' achievement would have been reduced due to the *low* level of education attained by the Low SES Upwardly Mobile mothers, compared to the *high* level achieved by the High SES Brahmin mothers, whose daughters were *also* significantly overrepresented among the High-Ability, High-Adapted Achievers. The same restriction due to nonlinearity would have occurred if the effect of family income alone had been assessed.

Similarly, had only parental values been considered in a variable-oriented design, the influence of the Low SES Upwardly Mobiles would have been indistinguishable from that of either the High SES Brahmin or the High SES, High-Educated Fathers, because all three backgrounds shared the same values concerning their daughter's future and all three were significantly associated with the High-Ability, High-Adapted Achievers. The pattern approach, however, allowed the definition of three *different* family configurations which, through influential processes assumed to be differential with respect to the source of motivation they might represent (e.g., setting an example and maintaining status among the high-SES patterns vs. motivation to improve status on the part of the Low SES Upwardly Mobiles), nevertheless were associated with the same pattern of achievement/adaptation expressed by their daughters at age 13.

The Low SES Pushers (Subgroup 7)

Association With Low Achievers.   In contrast to their middle-class counterparts, the Low SES Pushers were characterized by a low family income mean and by the lowest level of fathers' education. Like the Middle-

Class Pushers, however, these families expressed a unanimous desire for their daughter to pursue a theoretical education, even though they did not, also unanimously, believe that such an education suited her. Again, considering that most parents expressed confidence in their daughter's capabilities, the expectation was that this particular background reflected an acknowledgment that the daughter in question was not an academically able student. Thus, it was expected that the Low SES Pusher profile would be significantly overrepresented among low- rather than high-ability subgroups.

However, it also seemed possible that, whereas the high level of education found among the fathers in the Middle-Class Pusher subgroup might make these fathers particularly attuned to and disappointed by the academic limitations of their daughters, thus influencing the daughters' negative perception of their own competence (a suggestion that was supported earlier), educational achievement might not be as salient a concern among the parents comprising the Low SES Pushers, judging from the low levels of parental education involved. If the two "pusher" syndromes differed with respect to the *priority* they placed on educational achievement, in spite of the fact that both subgroups, when asked, favored a theoretical education for their daughters, then it might be suspected that the Low SES Pushers, compared to the Middle-Class Pushers, manifested less disappointment in or disapproval of their daughters' low achievements.

Therefore, bearing in mind that the indicator of perceived ability in the age-13 ability/adaptation patterns was circumscribed to the issue of successfully completing optional coursework in the following grade, it might be the case that some daughters of Low SES Pushers had not yet incorporated the negative evaluations of their academic capability expressed by their parents. Thus, the Low SES Pushers were hypothesized, first, to be significantly overrepresented among the Low-Adapted, *Unrealistic*, Low Achievers (Subgroup 7), rather than among the Low-Adapted, *Realistic*, Low Achievers (Subgroup 8), as was expected and demonstrated with regard to the Middle-Class Pushers. The association between the Low SES Pushers and the Low-Adapted, Unrealistic, Low Achievers was, indeed, significant ($p < .05$).

Second, considering the overall low level of parental education and income characterizing the Low SES Pushers, *combined with* their low evaluation of their daughters' abilities and leaving aside any subtleties concerning the salience of education in this environment, it was also expected that the Low SES Pushers would be significantly overrepresented among the Low-Adapted, Low-Ability Non-Achievers (Subgroup 9), who, considering their extremely low levels of intelligence and academic achievement, seemed especially unlikely to succeed in a theoretical education. This type also emerged ($p < .01$). These two expected associations were the only types observed for the Low SES Pushers.

Nonassociation With High Achievers.   In line with the general arguments presented here, one antitype was also hypothesized concerning this family background. Specifically, given the general interpretation of the Low SES Pushers' pattern, it was expected that they would be significantly *under*represented among the High-Ability, High-Adapted Achievers (Subgroup 1). This antitype ($p < .01$), which reflected no overlap whatsoever between the two subgroups, was the only antitype observed with regard to the Low SES Pushers.

The Low SES Status Quos (Subgroup 8)

The last subgroup to consider were the Low SES Status Quos. In a sense, these families might be viewed as the mirror-opposites of the High SES Brahmin. The Low SES Status Quos not only exhibited almost the lowest levels of education for *both* parents, but they also neither desired their daughter to pursue academic education past compulsory school nor thought her capable of doing so. In short, as their name connotes, the Low SES Status Quos seemed as committed as the Brahmin to a particular way of life.

Association With Low Adaptation and/or Low Achievement.   Given its overall negation of an educationally oriented value system, in terms of providing either a personal example of or parental support for educational achievement, this family background was expected to be significantly associated with all of the ability/adaptation subgroups whose patterns reflected academic adjustment problems, as well as with certain subgroups whose patterns reflected low performance per se. In other words, this specific background was assumed to exert such a deleterious influence on school achievement and adaptation that it was hypothesized to be overrepresented *even* among ability/adaptation subgroups that were not characterized by below-average intelligence and achievement.

Specifically, it was expected that the Low SES Status Quos would be significantly associated with the Ability-Underestimating Normals (Subgroup 5), who, despite their above-average intelligence mean and their average achievement levels, exhibited a low level of self-perceived ability. It was also expected that these families would be significantly associated with the Moderately Low-Adapted Normals (Subgroup 6), whose relatively low level of school adaptation appeared to be inconsistent with their means on the performance indicators. That these types were both significant ($p = .01$ and $p < .05$, respectively) supported the suggestion that family environments reflecting the Low SES Status Quo syndrome were not conducive to females' developing a realistic sense of their own efficacy regarding academic achievement or an adaptation to the academic requirements of school life.

Of course, as was argued for the "pusher" syndromes, it was also possible that certain Low SES Status Quos' evaluations of their daughter's capability represented an accurate assessment of her potential. If such were the case, the expectation would be that these families would be overrepresented among those low-ability, low-adapted subgroups that *also* exhibited low self-perceived ability—that is, among the Low-Adapted, *Realistic*, Low Achievers and the Low-Adapted, Low-Ability Non-Achievers (Subgroups 8 and 9). In support of this expectation, both associations were highly significant ($p < .0001$). Moreover, these four hypothesized overrepresentations were the only types observed with respect to the Low SES Status Quos.

Nonassociation With High Adaptation and/or High Achievement. Finally, given the foregoing discussion concerning the proposed negative influence of this home environment pattern on girls' realizing their academic potential, three antitypes were expected to emerge in connection with the Low SES Status Quos. In an exact reversal of what was expected for the High SES Brahmin, the Low SES Status Quos were expected to be significantly *under*represented among, first, the High-Ability, High-Adapted Achievers (Subgroup 1) and, second, the Gifted, Moderately Low-Adapted Achievers (Subgroup 2). Both these underrepresentations constituted antitypes ($p < .0001$ and $p < .01$, respectively).

Third, considering that this background was assumed to be incompatible with girls' adaptation to the school environment, regardless of their achievement levels, the Low SES Status Quos were expected to be significantly underrepresented among the High-Adapted Normals (Subgroup 3), whose adaptation mean was almost as high as that of the High-Ability, High-Adapted Achievers. This nonassociation also emerged as an antitype ($p < .05$). These three expected underrepresentations were the only antitypes observed for the Low SES Status Quos.

It is noteworthy that we were able, for the Low SES Status Quos, to specify in advance significant associations and nonassociations between these families and seven of the nine ability/adaptation patterns derived at age 13. Moreover, these seven hypothesized types and antitypes were the only significant over- and underrepresentations in which the Low SES Status Quos were involved. Thus, this final (and largest) family background subgroup allowed us to test a rather stringent series of expectations.

Concluding Remarks

Methodological Significance of Results

In conclusion, of the 21 expectations specified a priori concerning the associations or nonassociations between particular family background patterns and particular ability/adaptation patterns at age 13, fully 16 were supported by the results of the EXACON analysis. Furthermore, the only two hypothesized *non*associations that did not form an antitype (those involving the High SES Brahmin), did, nevertheless, yield empty cells. That these underrepresentations failed to reach significance was, in all likelihood, due to the small number of High SES Brahmin families in the analysis.

Fifty-one cells were predicted to yield no significant results, and only 6 unexpected types and antitypes were observed. Of these, 4 seemed consistent with the overall theoretical framework that guided our hypotheses and interpretations, whereas 2 appeared to constitute anomalies. Among the remaining 45 cells no types or antitypes were observed.

Theoretical Significance of Results

From a theoretical point of view, the results of the EXACON analysis depicted an overall picture indicating that parents' values exerted a substantial influence on their daughters' school performance and adaptation, regardless of the parents' own economic and educational levels. Girls' high ability, high achievement, and high adaptation, for example, were significantly associated with one low SES environment that might be assumed to reinforce educational achievement as well as with two high SES backgrounds, both of which also reflected an educationally oriented value system.

The processes through which such influence was transmitted, however, would appear to have been somewhat different. For example, the low SES parents could not have served as personal examples for their daughters, whereas *both* parents in the High SES "Brahmin" subgroup and the fathers in the high SES subgroup in which only the fathers were well-educated might well have provided personal examples for educational achievement, in addition to motivating their daughters through other means.

Furthermore, it is important to emphasize that in the one family pattern that was characterized by *low* parental aspiration for their daughters, in addition to a low evaluation of the daughters' academic competence, the parents' assessment of their daughters' capability was *not* always accurate. That is, even though this low parental evaluation was indeed associated with ability/adaptation subgroups demonstrating low intelligence and low achievement, as would be expected given that parents had observed their daughters' performance for some time, this low-aspiration, low-evaluation family background pattern was *also* associated with ability/adaptation subgroups that exhibited normal or even above-normal levels of intelligence and/or achievement.

In these cases, however, the associated ability/adaptation subgroups all manifested some form of maladjustment to the school environment, either a poor adaptation to the academic aspects of school life or a low perception of their own academic competence. With respect to self-perceived ability, it might also be noted that even within the two "pusher" subgroups, in which the negative parental evaluation appeared to be justified despite the parents' desire that their daughters pursue academic educations, it was possible to specify conditions under which this parental evaluation would or would not influence girls "realistic" perception of their own low competence.

In summary, the results appeared to support the existence of differential processes through which parents transmitted positive or negative expectations to their daughters, expectations which may be assumed to be modified over time by their daughters' demonstrated potential for academic achievement. The *reciprocal* nature of the influence process, stressed recently by Jacklin (1989), is considered more fully in chapter 8.

However, the results also strongly supported the existence of a particularly pernicious form of parental influence affecting normal-ability girls whose parents' values were not oriented toward educational achievement. At least at age 13, such girls appeared to experience low school adaptation or unrealistically low perceptions of their own ability.

Finally, it was interesting to note that the negative influence associated with a combination of low parental aspiration concerning their daughters' educational futures and a low evaluation of the daughters' capabilities occurred *only* among one subgroup of *low* SES families. Thus, although SES considered in isolation from parental values might provide incomplete or even misleading information concerning parental influence processes, as was discussed at some length in this chapter, there nevertheless appeared to be one condition under which SES was associated with certain values that exerted a powerful, and in this case negative, impact on females' interaction with the school environment during early adolescence. Whether a low emphasis on their daughters' educational attainment continues, over time, to be characteristic only of certain low SES parents is a question we investigate further in chapter 8.

Chapter 6

A Closer Look at Parents' Values and Their Daughters' Achievements

HAROLD BRIDGES LIBRARY
S. MARTIN'S COLLEGE
LANCASTER

The previous chapter addressed the overall associations, in early adolescence, between girls' family background and their expression of ability and school adaptation. This chapter investigates some of these associations more closely.

PARENTAL VALUES IN RELATION TO GIRLS' HIGH ACHIEVEMENT

We demonstrated in chapter 5 that, at age 13, high-achieving girls who were well-adapted to the school environment were significantly overrepresented among families in which the parents, regardless of their own socioeconomic status, wanted their daughters to pursue academic studies and thought them capable of doing so, that is, among families in which the parents expressed educationally oriented *values* for their daughters. Here we examine only the individuals who were involved in these significant overrepresentations between family background subgroups and ability/adaptation subgroups.

Our expectation, once again, was that parents' SES would not be related to their daughters' high achievement in early adolescence, *as long as* parents' values were oriented toward their daughters' pursuing an academic education and the girls themselves exhibited high adaptation to academic demands. In other words, given the same parental value system, the overall pattern of ability and adaptation exhibited by the High-Ability, High-

Adapted Achievers (Subgroup 1 in Table 3.1) from high SES families would not differ from the overall pattern of the High-Ability, High-Adapted Achievers from low SES families.

Assuring That High Achievers Came From Disparate Levels of Family SES

Our strategy in assessing the association between educationally oriented parental values and high achievement among high-adapted girls, *independent* of parental SES, was to conduct a series of representativeness analyses similar to those used in chapter 4. The issue of representativeness, along with definitions of relevant terms, is fully discussed in chapter 4 and in Appendix B.

Representativeness Tests

We first examined the *specific* High-Ability, High-Adapted Achievers whose parents were *High SES* Brahmin, *High SES*, High-Educated Fathers, and *Low SES* Upwardly Mobiles (Subgroups 1, 2, and 6, respectively, in Table 5.2) to ascertain that the girls were representative of the *family backgrounds* with which they were significantly associated at age 13. All of the families in these family background subgroups exhibited the same educationally oriented parental values; not only was there no variance *among* the three subgroups on parents' aspiration for their daughters or on parents' evaluation of daughter capability, but there was no variance *within* any of these subgroups on either of the values indicators. However, the socioeconomic status of the first two subgroups was considerably higher than that of the last subgroup.

Because there were no differences in parental values, establishing representativeness involved demonstrating that the High-Ability, High-Adapted Achievers involved in the significant overrepresentations were characteristic of their respective family background subgroups on the SES indicators. There were 27 families that were High SES Brahmin, 60 families comprised the High SES, High-Educated Fathers, and 74 Families were Low SES Upwardly Mobiles.

Results

The results of the first representativeness tests, depicted in Table 6.1, showed that the mean profile (or cluster centroid) of each selected group of High-Ability, High-Adapted Achievers was close to the cluster centroid of its respective family background subgroup. (See discussion in chapter 4 and Appendix B for further explanation.) Thus, the results indicated that the High-Ability, High-Adapted Achievers were characterized by disparate levels of parental SES.

TABLE 6.1
Representativeness of High-Ability, High-Adapted Achievers to High
and Low SES Family Backgrounds With Which They Were Associated at Age 13

Group	Inc.[a]	FEd[b]	MEd[c]	PAs[d]	PEv[e]	Avg. coeff. of cluster as a whole	Avg. D^2 from clus. centroid
			High SES families				
Entire "Brahmin" subgroup (n = 27)	1.39	2.07	2.58	.59	.74	.14	
High-Ability, High-Adapted Achievers from "Brahmin" families (n = 7)	1.33	2.04	2.51	.59	.74		.002
Entire High-Ed. Fathers subgroup (n = 60)	1.21	1.32	.32	.59	.74	.22	
High-Ability, High-Adapted Achievers from High-Ed. Fathers families (n = 14)	1.28	1.52	.28	.59	.74		.009
			Low SES families				
Entire Low SES Upwardly Mobile subgroup (n = 74)	− .90	− .62	− .51	.59	.74	.21	
High-Ability, High-Adapted Achievers from Low SES Upwardly Mobile families (n = 17)	− .73	− .63	− .42	.59	.74		.02

Note: All means were calculated from scores standardized across the entire sample of subjects included in the age-13 family background clusters.
[a]Parents' income.
[b]Fathers' education.
[c]Mothers' education.
[d]Parents' aspiration for daughters.
[e]Parents' evaluation of daughters' abilities.

Assuring That The Disparate Levels of Family SES Were All Associated With High Achievement

Discriminant Analysis

A discriminant analysis was then conducted to verify that an overall pattern of *high achievement* was just as representative of High-Ability, High-

Adapted Achievers from low SES backgrounds as it was of High-Ability, High-Adapted Achievers from high SES backgrounds. Based on the previous results, the High-Ability, High-Adapted Achievers from the High SES Brahmin families were combined with their counterparts from the High SES, High-Educated Father families, to form a single high SES group for comparison with the High-Ability, High-Adapted Achievers from the low SES families. The discriminant function was composed of all the age-13 ability/adaptation pattern indicators (except perceived ability, which was the same in both groups).

Results

The discriminant function just defined was significant ($p < .01$). However, an investigation of the univariate analyses revealed that the two groups differed significantly only in school adaptation ($p < .05$), with the High-Ability, High-Adapted Achievers from the high SES backgrounds' exhibiting a higher standardized adaptation mean than that of the High-Ability, High-Adapted Achievers from the low SES families (1.60 vs. .88). Because both groups' adaptation means were well above average and because neither their intelligence nor their achievement means differed significantly (or even systematically) from one another, the results supported our hypothesis that SES was not related to high *achievement* among high-adapted girls.

Comment

Although the result did not affect our hypothesis regarding achievement, it was interesting to note that the school adaptation of the high-ability, high-achieving girls from high SES backgrounds was *extremely* high in early adolescence. However, lest this result be viewed as unequivocally extolling the benefits of high SES on school adaptation among high-ability girls, it should be remembered that *another* group of girls with high ability and high achievement (the Gifted, Moderately Low-Adapted Achievers, Subgroup 2 in Table 3.1) were also significantly overrepresented among one of the high SES family patterns discussed here (the High SES, High-Educated Fathers) and that this second group was characterized by lower than average adaptation at age 13. Moreover, among this second group, the specific girls whose school adaptation decreased substantially from age 13 to age 16 were characterized, at age 13, by families whose overall SES was somewhat higher than that of the girls whose adaptation increased over time. (See discussion of Increasers vs. Decreasers in chapter 4.)

PARENTAL VALUES IN RELATION TO GIRLS' LOW SELF-PERCEIVED ABILITY AND UNDERACHIEVEMENT

The analysis just given again demonstrated the association between parents' educationally oriented values, independent of their SES, and high-adapted girls' high achievement. Our next investigation addressed the presumed *negative* influence that *non*educationally oriented parental values may exert on girls' perception of their own academic ability at age 13 and, over time, on their actual school performance.

Parents' Underestimation of Their Daughters' Capability in Early Adolescence

Previous research has demonstrated that a tendency for mothers to *overestimate* their children's academic ability is more characteristic of Western cultures (e.g., the United States) than of Eastern cultures (e.g., Taiwan and Japan) (Stevenson, Lee, & Stigler, 1986; Uttal, 1986; Uttal, Miller, & Stevenson, 1985). However, in chapter 5 we found evidence that parents who neither wanted their early adolescent daughters to pursue an academic education following compulsory school nor believed them capable of doing so (i.e., the Low SES Status Quos, Subgroup 8 in Table 5.2) were *underestimating* their daughters' capabilities in certain cases.

Specifically, normal-intelligence, normal-achieving, normally adapted girls who exhibited *low self-perceived ability* (i.e., the Ability-Underestimating Normals, Subgroup 5 in Table 3.1) were significantly overrepresented among Low SES Status Quo families. The same family background was also significantly associated with low-intelligence, low-achieving girls who, in addition, exhibited both low self-perceived ability and low school adaptation (i.e., the Low-Adapted, Low-Ability Non-Achievers, Subgroup 9 in Table 3.1). For the former girls, parents' low evaluations of their daughters' capabilities appeared to be unwarranted, whereas for the latter girls, parents' low evaluations seemed to be justified by the girls' low achievement.

Assessment of Differential Ability

Analyses. We first wanted to verify, quite simply, that the Ability-Underestimating Normals from Low SES Status Quo environments did, in fact, have higher ability and achievement in early adolescence than did the Low-Adapted, Low-Ability Non-Achievers from the same family background. For ease of presentation, the girls who came from Low SES Status Quo families and were characterized by *normal* intelligence, achievement, and adaptation (and by low self-perceived ability) were called *Inaccurates*. Conversely, the girls who came from Low SES Status Quo families and were characterized by *low* means across all five ability/adaptation indicators were labeled *Accurates*.

We then conducted representativeness analyses: The mean profile of the *Inaccurates* was compared to the cluster centroid of the entire subgroup of Ability-Underestimating Normals, whereas the mean profile of the *Accurates* was compared to the cluster centroid of the Low-Adapted, Low-Ability Non-

TABLE 6.2
Representativeness of the "Inaccurates" and the "Accurates" in Terms of
the Respective Ability/Adaptation Subgroups to Which They Belonged at Age 13

Group	Standardized group means					Avg. coeff. of cluster as a whole	Avg. D^2 from clus. centroid
	IQ	AM[a]	ASw[b]	PA[c]	SchAd[d]		
Entire Ability-Under-estimating Normal subgroup ($n = 41$)	.41	.18	.31	−1.16	.17	.33	
Inaccurates ($n = 14$)	.29	.24	.10	−1.08	.31		.02
Entire Low-Adapted, Low-Ability Non-Achiever subgroup ($n = 41$)	−1.62	−1.42	−1.31	−1.50	−.59	.39	
Accurates ($n = 16$)	−1.71	−1.47	−1.20	−1.83	−.47		.03

Note: All means were calculated from scores standardized across the entire sample of subjects included in the age-13 ability clusters.
[a]Achievement in mathematics.
[b]Achievement in Swedish.
[c]Perceived ability.
[d]School adaptation.

Achievers. (See chapter 4 and Appendix B for a full discussion of representativeness.) Finally, the mean ability/adaptation profiles of these two groups were compared directly to one another, using a discriminant analysis.

Results.   As shown in Table 6.2, both the Inaccurates (average $D^2 = .02$) and the Accurates (average $D^2 = .03$) were representative of their respective age-13 ability/adaptation subgroups. Specifically, the Inaccurates were representative of the Ability-Underestimating Normals, and the Accurates were representative of the Low-Adapted, Low-Ability Non-Achievers.

Moreover, as depicted in Table 6.3, the Inaccurates were significantly different from the Accurates across their respective age-13 ability/adaptation patterns. Not only did the discriminant function composed of all five ability/adaptation indicators discriminate the two groups at a high level of significance ($p < .0001$), but univariate analyses revealed that the standardized means of the Inaccurates were significantly higher than those of the Accurates on every single indicator in the pattern.

Assessment of Family Background Similarity

Having demonstrated that the Inaccurates and the Accurates *differed* in academic capability, we next made absolutely sure that both groups were

TABLE 6.3
Comparison of "Inaccurates' " and "Accurates' " Ability/Adaptation
Pattern at Age 13

Group	IQ	Standardized group means			
		Math achieve.	Swedish achieve.	Perceived ability	School adaptation
Inaccurates (n = 14)	.29**	.24**	.10**	− 1.08*	.31*
Accurates (n = 16)	− 1.71	− 1.47	− 1.20	− 1.83	− .47

Note: All means were calculated from scores standardized across the entire sample of subjects included in the age-13 ability clusters. Discriminant function composed of ability/adaptation pattern means significantly discriminated between the two groups ($p < .0001$). Asterisks reflect the significance of univariate differences between the groups.
$**p \leq 0001$; $*p \leq .01$.

equally representative of the same *family background subgroup* to which they belonged at age 13 (i.e., the Low SES Status Quos). Table 6.4 compares the Inaccurates' and the Accurates' family background profiles to the cluster centroid of the Low SES Status Quos as a whole.

It might be recalled from chapter 5 that a mean z score of − 1.68 on parents' aspiration indicated that *all* parents comprising the subgroup in question reported that they did not aspire to an academic education for

TABLE 6.4
Representativeness of the "Inaccurates" and the "Accurates" in Terms
of Their Belonging to the Same Family Background Subgroup at Age 13

Group	Standardized group means					Avg. coeff. of cluster as a whole	Avg. D^2 from clus. centroid
	Inc.[a]	FEd[b]	MEd[c]	PAs[d]	PEv[e]		
Entire Low SES Status Quos subgroup (n = 116)	− .63	− .62	− .50	− 1.68	− 1.29	.24	
Inaccurates (n = 14)	− .47	− .65	− .61	− 1.68	− 1.35		.008
Accurates (n = 16)	− .57	− .72	− .66	− 1.68	− 1.22		.009

Note: All means were calculated from scores standardized across the entire sample of subjects included in the age-13 family background clusters.
[a]Parents' income.
[b]Fathers' education.
[c]Mothers' education.
[d]Parents' aspiration for daughters.
[e]Parents' evaluation of daughters' abilities.

HAROLD BRIDGES LIBRARY
S. MARTIN'S COLLEGE
LANCASTER

their daughters and that a mean z score of -1.35 on parents' evaluation of their daughters' capabilities indicated that all parents in the group believed their daughters *not* to be suited for an academic curriculum. The parents of the Inaccurates *unanimously* expressed these low aspirations and low evaluations.

Furthermore, the extremely low average D^2 values observed for both the Inaccurates (.008) and the Accurates (.009) demonstrated that both groups were representative of the Low SES Status Quos as a whole. Finally, a discriminant function composed of the four family background indicators on which there were between-group differences (parental aspiration was a constant in both groups) did not significantly discriminate the family background pattern of the Inaccurates from that of the Accurates.

Conclusion

These results provided strong support for the proposition that, in early adolescence, parents' *underestimation* of their daughters' academic capabilities, coupled with their low aspiration for the educational future of their daughters, was indeed associated with *low self-perceived* ability among girls who exhibited average levels of intelligence, achievement, and school adaptation (i.e., the Inaccurates). Whereas the Inaccurates' intelligence, achievement, and adaptation means were all average or slightly above, compared to the respective means of the entire sample, their level of self-perceived ability was fully one standard deviation *below* the overall average. Thus, even though the Inaccurates' self-perceived ability was significantly higher at age 13 than that of the *genuinely* low-ability girls from the same type of family (i.e., the Accurates), their academic self-confidence was considerably lower than warranted.

Long-Term Effects of Parental Misjudgment

Our last investigation predicted that the normal-ability, normal-achieving, and normally adapted girls whose parents underestimated their academic capability would, to a significant extent, be the same girls who, 3 years later, combined the low academic self-confidence they had expressed at age 13 with low school adaptation and low achievement. In other words, we expected that low self-perceived ability among normal-ability girls whose parents had underestimated their capability in early adolescence would be associated with *underachievement* in midadolescence. This final hypothesis represented a rather stringent test of the deleterious effects of a noneducationally oriented parental value system on adolescent females' overall school experience, at least when such a value system is not consistent with the daughter's actual potential.

Analysis

We have already verified a developmental stream between the age-13 Ability-Underestimating Normals and the age-16 Low-Adapted, Normal-Ability Underachievers (see Table 3.3). For our prediction to be supported, we needed to demonstrate that the Ability-Underestimating Normals *from Low SES Status Quo backgrounds* (i.e., the Inaccurates from the previous analyses) would be overrepresented among the eight girls who defined this developmental stream.

The EXACON test of this hypothesis employed, as a sample, the 273 girls who were represented among

1. the family background subgroups at age 13,
2. the ability/adaptation subgroups at age 13, and
3. the ability/adaptation subgroups at age 16.

The requirement that all subjects be represented in three domains meant that the number of Inaccurates was reduced from 14 to 13 (because one girl lacked ability/adaptation data at age 16) and that the number of girls comprising the developmental stream from low self-perceived ability to underachievement was reduced from eight to five (because three girls lacked family background data at age 13).

The EXACON procedure tested whether or not the observed frequency of the age-13 *Inaccurates* who had become *Low-Adapted, Normal-Ability Underachievers* by age 16 significantly exceeded the exact expected frequency. Because our hypothesis was limited to only one cell of a 2×2 contingency table, the lack of independence among the four cells was not problematic. (For a further description of the hypergeometric probability model underlying the EXACON test of single-cell frequencies, see Bergman & El-Khouri, 1987).

Results

As predicted, the results demonstrated that the normally able girls who underestimated their own ability *and came from Low SES Status Quo environments* (i.e., the Inaccurates) were significantly overrepresented among the five age-13 Ability-Underestimating Normals who became Underachievers 3 years later ($p = .02$). The observed frequency was two persons. Although a cell frequency of two may not, at first blush, seem especially impressive, the observed frequency was 10 times higher than the expected frequency of .2.

We do not wish to overemphasize the meaningfulness of any single result. Nevertheless, we might note that the outcome of this test supported a stringent hypothesis, formulated at an extremely precise level of analysis, concerning the increasingly detrimental effects of noneducationally oriented parental values on adolescent females' overall school experience, *under the condition* that such a value system is not consistent with the daughter's actual academic potential. As further support, we might also note that, at age 16, nearly *half* of the Low-Adapted, Normal-Ability Underachievers came from the Low SES Status Quo families defined at age 13 ($p < .01$). (See chapter 8, Table 8.1)

CONCLUDING REMARKS

The results of this last analysis suggest that normal-ability girls may be more vulnerable than high-ability girls to the judgments of significant others who exercise control over them. A similar notion has been expressed in an *organizational* context by Feldman (1986). Feldman has argued that supervisors evaluate employees on the basis of their own cognitive schemas, which may or may not accurately reflect their subordinates' actual performance. Once a schema is in operation, incidents that fit it are remembered, while disconfirming evidence is not encoded in the first place or is forgotten at the time of performance appraisal.

Furthermore, as Feldman noted, these schemas often determine who is afforded the opportunity to improve his or her skills, for example through advanced training, and who is not. The best performers are not likely to suffer from this process, because the supervisor will award them ample opportunity for advancement. However, the average employee, whose ability the supervisor may consistently underestimate because of early impressions, may be denied the chance to improve. If so, the gap between high-ability incumbents and their normal-ability counterparts may widen over time.

Considering parents as "job supervisors" (and certainly they have the power to grant or withhold rewards), one might apply Feldman's scenario to our female Swedish adolescents. Parents' underestimation of their normal-ability daughters was first related only to girls inaccurately low *self-evaluations*. However, across a 3-year period, achievement in and adaptation to the "job environment" decreased substantially among a significant proportion of these individuals. Thus, normal-ability girls whose parents underestimate their academic capability may constitute a special risk group, in terms of not reaching the educational level of which they are capable. We address this issue further in chapter 11.

The next chapter deals with the effect of factors *other* than family background on the differential expression of ability and school adaptation in early adolescence. For these analyses we return to all nine of our age-13 ability/adaptation subgroups.

Chapter 7

Aspiration and Choice as Related to Girls' Ability/Adaptation Patterns in Early Adolescence

This chapter focuses again on early adolescence. Our goal is to identify factors, other than the characteristics of the family environment, which are associated with individual differences in ability and school adaptation among 13-year-old girls.

EDUCATIONAL ASPIRATION AS A SINGLE VARIABLE

To begin with a brief reprise, we might remind the reader that our age-13 subjects' intelligence, achievement, self-perceived ability, and adaptation to the academic aspects of the school environment were first described according to each individual's pattern across five variables. Similar patterns were then combined into homogeneous subgroups (the nine ability/adaptation subgroups defined in chapter 3), using cluster analytic techniques. The mean profile of each of these subgroups defined the subgroup's characteristic pattern (see Table 3.1).

Because the ability/adaptation patterns were based on indicators that reflected the girls' *current* achievements in and adaptation to the school environment, they did not include any measure of long-range "educational aspiration" per se. However, the assumption that aspiration and achievement are closely related underlies much of the female career literature cited throughout our investigation. It might even be argued that career development research has been interested in educational or occupational "aspiration" primarily *because* it provides a prognosis of future achievement in the educational/vocational domain (Astin & Myint, 1971; Gustafson et al., 1989; Marini, 1978; Mulvey, 1963; Mumford & Owens, 1984).

It was our hypothesis that the individuals comprising the age-13 ability/ adaptation subgroups, whose characteristic patterns were based on their *current* educational experience, would be strongly differentiated with respect to their aspiration toward *future* schooling. We expected, first, that girls with high ability, high achievement, and high adaptation to school would have high aspiration to continue school beyond the compulsory 9 years, especially because we knew from our previous analyses (see chapter 5) that such girls came from families in which the parents valued academic achievement. Conversely, low-ability, low-achieving, and low-adapted girls, a significant number of whom came from homes that did not reflect academically oriented values, were expected to exhibit low aspiration with respect to post-compulsory schooling.

Method

Data and Subjects

The measure of educational aspiration was taken from the Vocational Questionnaire administered to the subjects at age 13 (Grade 6). The measure consisted of a single item: "How many years of education can you accept, past compulsory school, in order to enter an occupation you would like?" The responses, given on a 5-point scale, ranged from "No studies whatsoever" (1) to "More than five years" (5). Of the 403 subjects who comprised the nine age-13 ability subgroups, 402 had completed this item.

Analysis

A one-way analysis of variance was employed to test whether or not the means of the age-13 ability/adaptation subgroups differed significantly on educational aspiration. Post host analyses were assessed using Duncan multiple range tests of the significant differences between all pairs of means (Kirk, 1968)

Results

The results of the one-way ANOVA manifested significant individual differences, as shown in Table 7.1 [$F(8,393) = 24.24$, $p < .0001$]. In addition, the results of the post hoc tests were generally in line with our expectations.

The educational aspiration mean of the High-Ability, High-Adapted Achievers (Subgroup 1), which reflected these girls' aspirations to educate themselves a little more than 4 to 5 years beyond compulsory school, was significantly higher than the aspiration mean of *every other* ability/adap-

TABLE 7.1
Individual Differences in Aspiration at Age 13

Ability/adaptation subgroup	Mean	Post hoc tests[a]
1-High-Ability, High-Adapted Achievers	4.21	1 > 9, 8, 7, 5, 6, 3, 4
2-Gifted, Moderately Low-Adapted Achievers	3.97	2 > 9, 8, 7
4-Math-Oriented Verbal Underachievers	3.67	4 > 9, 8, 7
3-High-Adapted Normals	3.58	3 > 9, 8, 7
6-Moderately Low-Adapted Normals	3.55	6 > 9, 8, 7
5-Ability-Underestimating Normals	3.51	5 > 9, 8, 7
7-Low-Adapted, Unrealistic Low-Achievers	2.82	7 > 9
8-Low-Adapted, Realistic, Low Achievers	2.52	
9-Low-Adapted, Low-Ability Non-Achevers	2.12	

Note: Grand $M = 3.33$. $F(8, 393) = 24.24$ ($p < .0001$).
[a]$p \leq .05$.

tation subgroup, except that of the Gifted, Moderately Low-Adapted Achievers (Subgroup 2). Furthermore, the aspiration means of the high- and normal-ability subgroups (Subgroups 2–6) were significantly higher than the means of the low-ability subgroups (Subgroups 7–9).

Thus, a single variable, long-range educational aspiration was differentially associated with individuals' *patterns* of school achievement and adaptation at age 13. However, in *early* adolescence, intelligence and achievement seemed to be the pattern indicators that were *most* responsible for the differences observed. High intelligence and achievement were associated with higher levels of aspiration—except for the High-Adapted Normals, who were somewhat below-average in both areas. The high aspiration of *these* girls, a significant number of whom became overachievers 3 years later, led us to expect that school adaptation might play an increasingly important role in aspiration as academic demands increased over time. We consider this issue further in chapter 9.

EDUCATIONAL ASPIRATION IN INTERACTION WITH GIRLS' ACTUAL CHOICES

Method

To examine educational aspiration in terms of its interaction with *actual choices* the girls made at their first opportunity to choose optional courses, we returned to a pattern analysis. Specifically, we used the clustering techniques described in chapter 2 to characterize subgroups of girls according to their similarity in terms of a profile of four measures that included, as one pattern indicator, the single variable of aspiration defined earlier.

Three measures of educational choice constituted the other three pattern indicators. The choice measures, taken from the age-13 Vocational Questionnaire (Grade 6), were:

1. the "theoretical" or academic level of the *optional* courses the girl had selected for Grade 7, scored as a continuum from 1 (least theoretical, no classes in French or German) to 3 (most theoretical, five classes per week of French or German);
2. whether the girl had chosen to enroll in the high- (scored as 2) or the low- (scored as 1) level English course in Grade 7; and
3. whether the girl had chosen to enroll in the high- (scored as 2) or the low- (scored as 1) level math course in Grade 7.

(To create a "continuous" variable that could be entered into the clustering algorithm, we considered the selection of high English and/or high math to be a "more theoretical" choice than the selection of low English and/or low math.)

A total of 495 sixth-grade girls (89% of the full 13-year-old sample) had complete data on these four indicators. All indicators were re-coded as z scores before being entered into the clustering algorithm.

Results

Statistical Overview

In accordance with the criteria discussed in chapter 2, the results of the cluster analysis showed a seven-cluster solution to be optimal. These clusters, depicted in Table 7.2, represented the assignment of each of 464 girls into one of the characteristic subgroups. The seven-cluster solution, excluding a residual of 31 subjects (6.26%) whose profiles did not match the centroids of any of the derived clusters, accounted for an 84% reduction of error variance over considering the entire sample as a single cluster.

Substantive Overview

Initial examination of these clusters revealed that they discriminated among students on the basis of their selection of the most, the second most, or the least theoretically oriented group of optional subjects for the following grade. Nevertheless, there was considerable variability within the three subgroups of "theoreticals" who also selected high English and high math (Subgroups 1, 2, and 3), in terms of their long-range educational as-

TABLE 7.2
Educational Choices/Aspiration Patterns at Age 13

Subgroup label	Standardized subgroup means			
	Optional courses[a]	Hi/Lo Eng.[b]	Hi/Lo math[c]	Ed. Aspir.
1-High-Aspiring "Theoreticals" (n = 178)	.67	.71	.51	1.00
2-Moderately Low-Aspiring "Theoreticals" (n = 89)	.67	.71	.51	−.28
3-Unaspiring "Theoreticals" (n = 14)	.46	.71	.51	−1.34
4-Lo Eng./Hi Math, Low-Aspiring "Theoreticals" (n = 72)	−.23	−1.40	.51	−.56
5-Hi Eng./Math, Moderately Low-Aspiring "Mid-Theoreticals" (n = 24)	−1.03	.71	.51	−.24
6-Lo Eng./Math, Low-Aspiring "Mid-Theoreticals" (n = 50)	−.78	−1.10	−1.97	−.46
7-Unaspiring "Non-Theoreticals" (n = 37)	−1.95	−1.40	−1.97	−1.36

Note: In total 464 subjects were clustered.

[a]Courses selected for Grade 7, scored on a 3-point scale according to the degree of "theoretical" or academic orientation each reflected (z score of -2.36 = raw score of 1, z score of -.84 = raw score of 2, and z score of .67 = raw score of 3).

[b]High-level versus low-level English course selected for Grade 7. A z score of .71 = raw score of 2 (more theoretical). A z score of -1.40 = raw score of 1 (less theoretical).

[c]High-level versus low-level math course selected for Grade 7. A z score of .51 = raw score of 2 (more theoretical). A z score of -1.97 = raw score of 1 (less theoretical).

piration. Moreover, although most students chose both the high-level English course and the high-level math course for Grade 7, not doing so was characteristic only of patterns that also reflected below-average levels of aspiration and selection of less than the most demanding academic curriculum offered in seventh grade.

Thus, for Subgroups 4, 6, and 7, avoidance of the high-level math and/or English course at age 13 might be viewed as circumscribing the choices available to these individuals at a later time. By "opting out" of the preparation offered by the higher level courses, it would appear that these girls had, in effect, already decided against pursuing an academically oriented curriculum in gymnasium or a university-level education. This assumption is further examined in chapter 9.

ASSOCIATIONS BETWEEN PATTERNS OF EDUCATIONAL CHOICES/ASPIRATION AND PATTERNS OF ABILITY/ADAPTATION

The next logical question with regard to girls' patterns of educational choices and aspiration was how these patterns related to the patterns of ability and school adaptation we defined in chapter 3. The following analysis addressed this issue.

Method

An EXACON analysis identical to those described in previous chapters was used to assess the significant associations (types) between individuals' patterns of ability/adaptation and their patterns of choices/aspiration. In contrast to previous EXACON tests, however, no specific a priori hypotheses were set forth. Because we were interested in this analysis primarily as an illustration of the most *salient* relationships between ability/adaptation and choices/aspiration patterns, our only expectation was that the associations observed would be consistent with the pattern of results presented in earlier chapters. For example, we assumed that high achievers would be overrepresented among individuals whose choices/aspiration pattern combined high aspiration with the highest level of academically oriented ("theoretical") courses available.

To avoid spurious interpretations based on Type 1 errors, we set as a criterion that no type would be reported unless the probability of its occurring by chance were less than or equal to .001. The 364 subjects who were represented among both sets of subgroups comprised the EXACON sample.

Results

The overrepresentations (types) that met the criterion are displayed in Table 7.3. The ability/adaptation subgroup numbers correspond to those used in Table 3.1.

The High-Ability, High-Adapted Achievers and the Gifted, Moderately Low-Adapted Achievers (Subgroups 1 and 2)

As might be expected, the highest achievers (Subgroups 1 and 2) were significantly overrepresented among the students who chose the highest

TABLE 7.3
Associations Between Ability/Adaptation Patterns and
Choices/Aspiration Patterns at Age 13

Ability pattern at age 13	Choices/Aspiration pattern(s) at age 13	Overlap n
1-High-Ability, High- Adapted Achievers (n = 63)	1-High-Aspiring "Theoreticals" (n = 155)	50****
2-Gifted, Moderately Low-Adapted Achievers (n = 38)	1-High-Aspiring "Theoreticals" (n = 155)	27***
5-Ability-Under- estimating Normals (n = 37)	5-Hi Eng./Math, Moderately Low-Aspiring "Mid-Theoreticals" (n = 37)	7***
6-Moderately Low- Adapted Normals (n = 54)	2-Moderately Low-Aspiring "Theoreticals" (n = 75)	21***
8-Low-Adapted, Realistic, Low Achievers (n = 42)	6-Lo Eng./Math, Low-Aspiring "Mid-Theoreticals" (n = 35)	15****
9-Low-Adapted, Low-Ability Non-Achievers (n = 28)	6-Lo Eng./Math, Low-Aspiring "Mid-Theoreticals" (n = 35) 7-Unaspiring "Non-Theoreticals" (n = 17)	9*** 8****

Note: Types were deived, from exact tests of the single-cell frequency overlap between the two sets of subgroups, for a total of 364 subjects.
   ***$p \leq .001$. ****$p \leq .0001$.

level of available courses and, additionally, displayed the highest degree of motivation toward advanced schooling (the High-Aspiring Theoreticals). Lest this result be considered incompatible with the moderately low school adaptation of the Gifted, Moderately Low-Adapted Achievers (Subgroup 2), it should be recalled that the adaptation mean of these girls *at age 13* was only one third of a standard deviation below the overall average.

We have demonstrated in chapter 3 that this subgroup formed a significant developmental stream with a subgroup characterized by a substantially lower relative adaptation mean at age 16. However, the effect that this decrease in school adaptation might eventually exert on aspiration was not apparent in early adolescence. Moreover, we know from the results in chapter 4 that the *specific* girls whose adaptation *decreased* over time did not display significantly lower aspiration at age 13 than did the moderately low-adapted girls whose adaptation *increased* by midadolescence. That both high- and somewhat low-adapted achievers would be characterized by the same pattern of choices and aspiration at age 13 was perhaps attributable to both subgroups' high achievement through Grade 6. In addition, it might be noted that the "theoretical" options offered in Grade 7 were still relatively easy, compared to the academic demands that theoretical choices would entail at a later stage in the education process.

The Ability-Underestimating Normals and the Moderately Low-Adapted Normals (Subgroups 5 and 6)

In contrast to the consistency between academically oriented choices and high aspiration displayed among the highest achievers, normal achievers who underestimated their ability and normal achievers who were moderately low-adapted were significantly overrepresented in patterns that reflected a certain *disparity* between choices and aspiration. Less than average self-perceived ability *or* school adaptation, when combined with normal but not outstanding performance, seemed to be associated, relatively *early* in girls' school careers, with somewhat low educational aspiration, even among girls whose actual *choices* were, to some extent, indistinguishable from those of their more academically able counterparts.

For example, the Ability-Underestimating Normals were overrepresented among girls characterized by a below-average aspiration mean, in combination with less than the most rigorous level of optional courses. Yet the members of this choices/aspiration subgroup were all enrolled in both high English and high math (the Hi Eng./Math, Moderately Low-Aspiring Mid-Theoreticals).

Reflecting a similar disparity, the Moderately Low-Adapted Normals were overrepresented among girls who unanimously chose the most academically oriented courses available (along with high English and high math) but displayed below-average aspiration (the Moderately Low-Aspiring Theoreticals). It might also be recalled from chapter 5 that the Moderately Low-Adapted Normals were significantly overrepresented among middle-class upwardly mobile families, whose aspiration for their daughters and evaluations of their daughters' capabilities reflected a parental value system oriented toward academic achievement. However, as suggested in the earlier discussion, the Moderately Low-Adapted Normals appeared to have rejected their parents' values.

The Low-Adapted, Realistic, Low-Achievers and the Low-Adapted, Low-Ability Non-Achievers (Subgroups 8 and 9)

Low-adapted low achievers were significantly characterized by patterns of choices and aspiration and that could be seen as limiting their potential for pursuing advanced academic work. Specifically, the Low-Adapted, Realistic, Low Achievers and the Low-Adapted, Low-Ability Non-Achievers were overrepresented among low-aspiring girls who chose low English and low math, in addition to less than the highest theoretical level of optional courses for Grade 7 (the Low Eng./Math, Low-Aspiring Mid-Theoreticals). This pattern of choices was consistent with these girls' low levels of achievement and school adaptation through Grade 6.

Additionally, the Low-Adapted, Low-Ability Non-Achievers, who displayed the lowest levels of intelligence and achievement of any of the girls at age 13, were also overrepresented among girls characterized by the lowest aspiration mean and the least academically oriented course selections available (the Unaspiring Non-Theoreticals). That such girls might be expected to leave school at the first opportunity is an assumption that is examined in later chapters.

SUMMARY OF ASPIRATION-RELATED ANALYSES

In summary, the relationship between girls' patterns of ability/adaptation and their patterns of educational choices and aspiration were generally consistent with the results observed when educational aspiration was treated as a single variable. That is, in early adolescence, intelligence and achievement were closely linked to aspiration, especially for girls who were at the high or the low end of the ability spectrum.

Nevertheless, our analysis of patterns that included both *future aspiration* and *present choices* provided information that complemented the results of the variable-oriented design. Specifically, the educational choices and aspiration patterns that characterized the girls at age 13 did not *solely* reflect academically oriented choices combined with high aspiration (or nonacademically oriented courses combined with low aspiration). The analysis also defined subgroups of individuals whose characteristic pattern exhibited a disparity between girls' choices and their aspiration. For example, all of the Moderately Low-Aspiring Theoreticals (Subgroup 2 in Table 7.2) chose high-level English and high-level math, in addition to selecting the highest level of optional courses; however, these girls had a *below-average* aspiration mean.

At age 13, some version of the disparity between "high choices" and low aspiration was significantly associated only with normal-ability girls who either underestimated their academic competence or who were not well-adapted to the school environment. We would expect that the eventual resolution of this disparity, which seemed to reflect a certain tension between external behavior and internal aspiration, would exert a powerful effect on these girls' educational outcomes in the long run. Furthermore, as the "theoretical" educational curriculum becomes more rigorous, we might expect the same disparity to become significantly manifested among *high*-ability girls who experience a poor adaptation to the academic aspects of school life.

DIFFERENTIAL PROCESSES UNDERLYING CHOICE

Sources of Influence

We knew from the previous analysis that girls' patterns of ability and school adaptation were differentially related to their actual choices of coursework in early adolescence, as well as to their aspiration toward future education. Our next analyses asked whether or not girls' *reasons* for selecting these courses would *also* be differentially associated with their ability/adaptation patterns at age 13.

Method

We first selected six possible *sources of influence* on which individuals might have differentially relied in deciding their optional curriculum for Grade 7—according to their own self reports:

1. previous grades,
2. interests,
3. parents' opinions,
4. teachers' opinions,
5. friends' opinions, and
6. subject's own opinions

The influence variables were single items taken from the Vocational Questionnaire administered in Grade 6.

The coding comprised a 4-point, Likert-type scale, which asked the respondent to indicate to what extent she agreed with the statement in question. A score of 1.00 reflected the lowest degree of agreement. Of the 403 girls who comprised the age-13 ability/adaptation subgroups (depicted in Table 3.1), no *fewer* than 374 (93%) had data on any of the items selected.

Results and Discussion

Grades As a Reason for Selecting Optional Courses. The first item asked girls to express the extent to which their previous grades had influenced their selection of optional courses for Grade 7. The results of an ANOVA showed that the subgroups differed significantly on this item [$F(8,367) = 5.97, p < .0001$].

The High-Ability, High-Adapted Achievers (Subgroup 1), reported that grades had influenced their decisions more strongly than was reported by any of the other subgroups. Duncan post hoc tests indicated that this subgroup's mean of 2.98 was significantly higher ($p < .05$) than that of five of the remaining eight subgroups. The Gifted, Moderately Low-Adapted Achievers (Subgroup 2), who were the *highest* achievers on standardized tests at age 13, reported deriving almost the same degree of influence from previous grades ($M = 2.97$).

In contrast, the lowest ability subgroups (Subgroups 7, 8, and 9) reported being the *least* influenced by past performance in their selection of optional courses for the next near ($M = 2.27$, 2.23, and 2.40, respectively). We have already demonstrated that the low-ability subgroups were associated with nontheoretical choices, whereas the high-ability subgroups were associated with academically oriented choices. Thus it would seem that, at age 13, *high* grades carried more influence in guiding girls' course selection than did *low* grades. Stated differently, those who had *good* grades reported these grades a more important factor in their decision to take the most rigorous course-work available than those who had *bad* grades reported their poor performance to have influenced their selection of a nonacademic curriculum.[1]

Interests As a Reason for Selecting Optional Courses. The second item asked to what extent the girls had followed their interests in choosing optional courses for Grade 7. The overall *F* test of mean *differences* was not significant. However, it might be noted that because all subgroups exhibited a mean score of above 3.00 on the scale of 1 to 4, (range = 3.24-3.71), interests seemed to provide an importance source of influence in terms of guiding high-ability girls toward further academic studies and low-ability girls in the opposite direction. Although the interests themselves obviously differed, given the systematic pattern of choices the various subgroups selected, virtually all the girls *followed* them. It might also be remembered from chapter 4 that the low-normal-ability girls who had become overachievers by age 16 had higher technical and verbal interests at age 13 than did their low-normal-ability counterparts whose performance remained consistent with their intelligence.

Others' Versus Self-Influence on Decisions. A further set of questions asked respondents to what extent they had relied on the opinions of (a) their parents, (b) their teachers, (c) their friends, or (d) themselves, in deciding their curriculum for Grade 7. The results demonstrated that the subgroups *differed* significantly with respect to only one of these areas.

Specifically, the overall test of mean differences in *parental* influence was significant [$F(8,374) = 2.19$, $p < .05$] Moreover, the *direction* of the subgroup mean scores was interesting: The *highest* degree of parental influence ($M = 2.62$) was reported by the *lowest* ability subgroup, the Low-Adapted,

---

[1]Our argument here assumed that achievement test scores, which were used as indicators in the age-13 ability/adaptation patterns, reflected the grades given by classroom teachers. This assumption was not without support. Among the 403 girls comprising the ability/adaptation subgroups at age 13, achievement in Swedish was positively and strongly correlated with grade in Swedish ($r = .83$). Likewise, achievement in mathematics was strongly and positively related to grade in mathematics ($r = .85$).

Low-Ability Achievers (Subgroup 9). In contrast, two of the three *lowest* parental influence means occurred for the two *highest* ability subgroups, the High-Ability, High-Adapted Achievers (Subgroup 1, $M = 2.33$) and the Gifted, Moderately Low-Adapted Achievers (Subgroup 2, $M = 2.13$). Duncan post hoc tests showed the difference in means between Subgroup 9 and both Subgroup 1 and Subgroup 2 to be significant ($p < .05$).

It might be recalled that our analyses in chapter 5 demonstrated that the Low-Adapted, Low-Ability Non-Achievers were significantly associated with low socioeconomic families characterized *either* by a lack of belief in their daughters' capabilities to pursue academic work despite the families' desire that they do so (the Low SES Pushers) *or* by both a lack of belief in their daughters' abilities *and* a lack of aspiration on their daughters' behalf (the Low SES Status Quos). Conversely, both the High-Ability, High-Adapted Achievers and the Gifted, Moderately Low-Adapted Achievers were significantly associated *only* with families who both valued education and believed in their daughters' academic capabilities. Thus, parents who might be assumed to have *discouraged* their daughters from selecting an academic curriculum appeared to exert a stronger impact on the girls' decisions at age 13 than did parents who could be assumed to have *encouraged* their daughters' selection of a theoretical course of study.

It happened to be the case that, out of 524 girls, 92% reported that they had discussed their choice of optional subjects with their parents to at least some extent. Therefore, the differential salience of parental influence we observed did not seem attributable to the high-ability girls' not talking about their plans. Rather, it might be more likely that the high-ability girls had internalized their parents' value system and thus did not perceive the parents' opinions as constituting an external source of influence. In contrast, the low-ability girls' parents' expressing *their* views on their daughters' realistic options had perhaps been less comfortable for the girls themselves, thereby increasing their perception that it had influenced their decisions. An alternate possibility, of course, is that the low-ability girls were seeking additional support for decisions that took them out of the educational "mainstream."

With regard to other sources of external influence, the subgroups did not differ significantly. The subgroup means ranged from 1.60 to 1.97 on the degree to which they had been affected by their *teachers'* opinions, indicating either that teachers *attempted* to exert little influence or that their students were largely impervious to their guidance. The girls' educational choices at age 13 appeared to have been even less influenced by their *friends*. On this item the means ranged from 1.03 to 1.26.

Finally, the age-13 ability/adaptation subgroups did not differ significantly in the extent to which they had relied on *themselves* in making their optional course decisions. However, because in this case all subgroup means were above 3.00 on the 1-4 scale (range = 3.05-3.35), it might be assumed that all the girls. despite the *differential* weight they gave to parental opinions and grades, perceived themselves as responsible for their own decisions. Although the overall F ratio was not significant, it was also noteworthy that the two subgroups who reported the highest sense of responsibility were the High-Ability, High-Adapted Achievers ($M = 3.35$) and the Gifted, Moderately Low-Adapted Achievers ($M = 3.34$).

CRYSTALLIZATION OF PLANS

Rationale

The next issue we considered was whether or not the girls in the various ability/adaptation subgroups would differ, in early adolescence, with respect to how definite or "crystallized" their future plans were. We knew from previous analyses in this chapter that high-ability girls had a high level of educational aspiration at age 13 and, as shown in chapter 3, that a pattern of high achievement combined with high adaptation to school was stable from age 13 to age 16. Therefore, our expectation was that among high-aspiring high achievers, whose performance matched the demands of the academic environment, plans to continue an academic education past compulsory school would stabilize early, particularly for girls who were well-adapted to this environment.

Data and Results

The item measuring crystallization of plans was taken from the Vocational Questionnaire administered in Grade 6. The item asked respondents to state, on a 5-point, Likert-type scale, how definite their plans were for the period following compulsory school. All of the 403 girls who comprised the age-13 ability/adaptation subgroups responded to this item.

Means on the crystallization item differed significantly among the ability/adaptation subgroups in a oneway ANOVA [$F(8,394) = 3.80$, $p < .001$]. Furthermore, the pattern of responses was similar to that observed for the single measure of educational aspiration.

Specifically, as was the case for educational aspiration, the highest means on the item measuring the definiteness of the girls' plans were exhibited by the two highest ability subgroups (Subgroup 1, $M = 3.78$ and Subgroup 2, $M = 3.63$). In contrast, the lowest degree of "definiteness" was expressed by the three lowest ability subgroups (Subgroup 8, $M = 3.17$; Subgroup 7, $M = 3.00$; and Subgroup 9, $M = 2.82$). Duncan post hoc tests revealed that the plans of the High-Ability, High-Adapted Achievers (Subgroup 1) were significantly more definite than those of all three low-ability subgroups, whereas the Gifted, Moderately Low-Adapted Achievers (Subgroup 2) were significantly more decided than were Subgroups 7 and 9 ($p < .05$ in both cases).

These results would seem to indicate that although aspiration, achievement, and choices were positively related to one another at age 13, especially for high and low performers, as was discussed earlier, the plans *themselves* were more *crystallized* at age 13 for high achievers, who intended to pursue advanced education past compulsory school, than for low achievers, who did not. In other words, the high achievers, for whom an established pathway toward gymnasium and university was a realistic option, appeared to find a "niche" more quickly than did their less able classmates. Whether or not this early crystallization remained stable for high-ability girls whose school adaptation decreased markedly by age 16 is an issue to be addressed in later chapters.

BIOLOGICAL MATURATION

Rationale

The final question raised in this series of analyses concerned the influence of biological maturation on the expression of ability and school adaptation at age 13. Stattin and Magnusson (1990) have presented evidence that early maturation in girls is associated with certain problems of school adjustment and that the earliest maturers attain a significantly lower level of adult education than do their later-maturing counterparts. However, because Stattin and Magnusson found that the deleterious effects of early maturation were not apparent until somewhat later than age 13, we would not *necessarily* expect the age-13 ability/adaptation subgroups to differ with respect to menarcheal age.

Method

The measure of biological maturation was taken from the Study of Symptoms Inventory administered to the female subjects during Grade 8. The item asked respondents to state at what age they had experienced their first menstrual period. In accordance with the method employed by Stattin and Magnusson (1990), the responses were coded on a 4-step scale: before age 11 = 1; between ages 11 and 12 = 2; between ages 12 and 13 = 3; and after age 13 or "haven't yet had" = 4. Biological maturation data were available for 327 (81%) of the 403 girls who comprised the age-13 ability/adaptation subgroups.

The associations between biological maturation and patterns of ability/ adaptation were assessed through the EXACON procedure described in chapter 2. The test assessed the significant overrepresentations (types) and underrepresentations (antitypes) of the nine ability/adaptation subgroups in the four levels of biological age described earlier.

Results

The results of the EXACON analysis yielded a veritable *coup* of nonsignificance. Of the 36 cells tested, *none* reflected a type (overrepresentation), and only one reflected an antitype (underrepresentation). Therefore, it seemed safe to assume that biological maturation, as such, was unrelated to the ability/adaptation patterns observed at age 13.

CONCLUDING REMARKS

The results presented in this chapter have allowed us to increase our understanding of girls' school ability and adaptation in early adolescence. We have demonstrated that when aspiration was investigated as a single variable, girls' patterns of ability/adaptation were differentially related to their future-oriented educational plans: In brief, the higher the past performance, the higher the aspiration. However, when aspiration was considered in interaction with actual choices for the following year, girls' short-term decisions were not always consistent with their long-term plans: Among certain normal-ability girls, academically oriented choices were paired with below-average aspiration.

Moreover, we have identified certain factors, such as previous grades and parental opinions, which seemed to exert a differential *influence* on the differential *choices* made by early adolescents, depending on their overall pattern of ability and school adaptation. Conversely, although the *extent* of their influence on girls' course decisions varied, early adolescents' own interests, their teachers' and friends' opinions, and their own sense of responsibility appeared to affect all girls in the same manner.

Additionally, we have shown that high-achieving and high-aspiring girls, especially those who also displayed a high adaptation to the academic environment, experienced an early crystallization of their plans to continue their education well beyond compulsory school. The issue of crystallization is addressed again in chapter 11.

Finally, we have demonstrated that, in early adolescence, biological maturation was not related to girls' patterns of ability and school adaptation. However, because we did not expect that significant relationships would necessarily be manifested by age 13, we examine the biological maturation issue again when our subjects are in midadolescence (chapter 9).

Chapter 8

The Relation of Family Background to Girls' Ability and School Adaptation in Midadolescence

In Chapter 5 we investigated family background factors associated with girls' intelligence, achievement, self-perceived ability, and school adaptation at age 13. This chapter focuses on the relations between family background and girls' educational experience 3 years later. In connection with this general issue, the chapter also addresses the manner in which parental values change or remain stable over time.

INTRODUCTION

Our previous results concerning the association between family background and girls' school performance in early adolescence provided considerable support for two overall conclusions: First, SES variables, such as family income and parents' level of education, do not necessarily represent the values parents express concerning their children's educational future. As discussed in detail in chapter 5, a great deal of previous research has been based on the implicit assumption that *high* parental SES connotes parents' placing a high *value* on their daughters' educational achievement, thereby influencing her own high aspiration and achievement. Conversely, if a linear relationship between parental SES and their offsprings' achievement is taken for granted, one implication is that *low* parental education connotes parents' placing a *low* value on their daughters' educational achievement.

However, when SES and values are considered together, as aspects of a *pattern* reflecting the home environment, parental aspirations that are oriented toward an advanced academic education for their daughters emerge across the entire SES spectrum. High aspirations are not restricted to families characterized by above-average levels of income and/or education.

Second, we demonstrated that it is the *value system* expressed in the home environment, *not* the household's socioeconomic level, that is associated with girls' performance in and adaptation to the academic demands of school life. If parents aspire to their daughter's pursuing an advanced education and exhibit confidence in their daughter's academic capability, family income and parents' own level of educational attainment appear to exert virtually no independent influence on females' school achievement. On the other hand, parental values that are directed *away* from long-term education for their daughter and reflect a low regard for their daughter's capability, appear to exert a powerfully negative influence on females' academic self-confidence and school adaptation, even among girls with average levels of intelligence and/or achievement.

Our present investigation was designed to determine to what extent these two conclusions were still supported after 3 additional years, during which parents' values and daughters' accomplishments had reciprocally influenced one another. To answer this question, we turned again to patterns.

As an initial step, we were interested in the associations and nonassociations between the patterns of family background we observed at age 13 and the patterns of girls' ability and adaptation we defined at age 16. We assumed at the outset that parents' aspiration for and evaluation of their daughter might well change over time, depending on their daughter's continuing response to academic demands. However, in this first analysis, we confined our predictions to those relationships in which we expected parental values *not* to have changed. We then investigated the family background patterns that characterized our subjects at age 16, in the expectation of observing more differentiated patterns of parental values than had emerged 3 years previously. Last, we assessed the associations between the patterns of family background we observed at age 16 and girls' ability/adaptation patterns at the same age.

FAMILY BACKGROUND AT AGE 13
AND ABILITY/ADAPTATION AT AGE 16

Method

Data and Analysis

The relation of girls' family background at age 13 to their ability and school adaptation at age 16 was analyzed through EXACON, which has been described in detail in chapter 2. The EXACON analysis assessed the overrepresentations (types) and underrepresentations (antitypes) between the eight family background subgroups described at age 13 (see Table 5.2) and the nine ability/adaptation subgroups described at age 16 (see Table 3.2). The 353 subjects who were represented among both sets of subgroups constituted the sample for the analysis.

Criteria for Significance

We have already emphasized the importance of establishing a priori expectations, to minimize the risk of "interpreting" Type 1 errors in a large contingency table. In chapter 7, where we conducted an EXACON analysis *without* constructing specific a priori expectations, we set as our significance criterion that a type would only be reported if the probability of its occurring by chance was less than or equal to .001. Because we *did* establish a priori expectations in the present analysis, our criterion was the traditional one of .05. However, to avoid over-interpreting spurious results, *unexpected* types and antitypes were reported only if their significance level met or exceeded a probability value of .01.

Results and Discussion

It is crucial to keep one important distinction in mind throughout the following discussion: When we refer to a *developmental stream* in support of an expectation, we are considering *only* those individuals, within a particular ability/adaptation subgroup at 13, who were significantly overrepresented among the members of another ability/adaptation subgroup at age 16. That is, we are focusing on the development of *specific individuals over time*, as predicted and verified in chapter 3 and as investigated in more detail in chapters 4 and 6. In contrast, when we discuss a subgroup's pattern per se, at either age, we are considering the possible consequences of subgroup membership for all members of that subgroup, including but not limited to the individuals whose developmental stream was identified in the earlier analysis.

In total, 13 expectations were specified regarding the associations or nonassociations between family background patterns at age 13 and girls' patterns of ability and school adaptation three years later. Of these expected relationships, 10 emerged as hypothesized. The results are depicted in Table 8.1 (For further clarification of the discussion that follows, the reader is also referred to Table 5.2, which describes the age-13 family patterns and to Tables 3.1 and 3.2, which describe the ability/adaptation subgroups defined at age 13 and at age 16, respectively. The subgroup numbers used here correspond to the numbers assigned to the subgroups in these previous tables.)

TABLE 8.1
Associations and Nonassociations Between Family Background Patterns
at Age 13 and Ability/Adaptation Patterns at Age 16

Family pattern at age 13	Ability pattern(s) at age 16	Overlap n
	Predicted types (p ≤ .05)	
1-High SES Brahmin	1-Gifted, High-Adapted Achievers	
(n = 24)#	(n = 64)	10**
	2-Gifted, Low-Adapted Achievers	
	(n = 33)	6*
2-High SES,	1-Gifted, High-Adapted	
High-Educated Fathers	Achievers	
(n = 50)#	(n = 64)	18***
	3-High-Adapted Overachievers	
	(n = 48)	8$^{n \cdot s \cdot}$
3-Middle-Class,	1-Gifted, High-Adapted	
High-Educated Mothers	Achievers	
(n = 37)	(n = 64)	10$^{n \cdot s \cdot}$
	3-High-Adapted Overachievers	
	(n = 48)	7$^{n \cdot s \cdot}$
8-Low SES Status Quos	4-Low-Adapted, Normal-	
(n = 85)	Ability Underachievers	
	(n = 34)	15**
	8-Moderately Adapted,	
	Realistic, Low Achievers	
	(n = 25)	16****
	9-Low-Adapted, Low-Ability	
	Non-Achievers	
	(n = 23)	13***
	Unpredicated types (p ≤ .01)	
7-Low SES Pushers#	7-Moderately Adapted,	
(n = 24)	Unrealistic, Low Achievers	
	(n = 35)	9****
8-Low SES Status Quos	7-Moderately Adapted,	
(n = 85)	Unrealistic, Low Achievers	
	(n = 35)	16**
	Predicted antitypes (p ≤ .05)	
7-Low SES Pushers	1-Gifted, High-Adapted Achievers	
(n = 24)	(n = 64)	0**
8-Low SES Status Quos	1-Gifted, High-Adapted Achievers	
(n = 85)	(n = 64)	2****
	2-Gifted, Low-Adapted Achievers	
	(n = 33)	1***
	3-High-Adapted Overachievers	
	(n = 48)	5**

(Continued)

TABLE 8.1 *(Continued)*

	Unpredicted antitypes (p ≤ .01)	
4-Middle-Class	8-Moderately Adapted,	
Upwardly Mobiles[#]	Realistic, Low Achievers	
(n = 66)	(n = 25)	0**
8-Low SES Status Quos	6-Moderately Able Normals	
(n = 85)	(n = 49)	4**

Note: Types and antitypes were derived, from exact tests of the single-cell frequency overlap between the two sets of patterns, for 353 subjects.

[#] = only significant type(s) or antitype(s) observed at the designated level of significance.

$*p < .05$; $**p \leq .01$; $***p < .001$; $****p < .0001$.

The High SES Brahmin (Subgroup 1)

Through their extremely high levels of education and income, in combination with their academically oriented values, the High SES Brahmin were expected to have continued to provide strong support for their daughter's advanced education. Moreover, this family background was significantly associated *at age 13* with high-ability, high-adapted, high-achieving individuals who subsequently formed a developmental stream with girls exhibiting a similar ability/adaptation pattern at age 16. Therefore, our *first* hypothesis was that the High SES Brahmin at age 13 would be significantly overrepresented among the Gifted, High-Adapted Achievers (Subgroup 1) at age 16. This type was observed ($p < .01$).

The second association we expected concerning the High SES Brahmin was that they would be overrepresented among the age-16 girls whose intelligence and achievement levels were quite high, but whose level of school adaptation was well below average (the Gifted, Low-Adapted Achievers, Subgroup 2). We had discovered in chapter 4 that the only discernible difference between the *age-13* high-ability, moderately low-adapted girls whose adaptation had *increased* by the age of 16 and those whose adaptation had *decreased* was that the "decreasers" appeared to come from higher SES backgrounds than did the "increasers."

The Brahmin family background was not significantly associated with the academically gifted girls whose school adaptation was only *moderately* low at age 13. However, it seemed possible that the value system and the high educational levels of the Brahmin might have exerted a stronger achievement-oriented influence on gifted girls characterized by *quite* low adaptation *at age 16*, especially because academic demands had increased over the intervening 3 years, thus making the whole issue of achievement more salient to both the girls and their parents.

This scenario received support from the present results. The High SES Brahmin formed a type ($p < .05$) with the Gifted, Low-Adapted Achievers (subgroup 2). Moreover, the Brahmin were the *only* families significantly associated with girls who, in midadolescence, combined high ability and performance with low adaptation to the school environment.

The High SES, High-Educated Fathers (Subgroup 2)

First, the High SES, High-Educated Fathers, whose characteristic pattern was similar to that of the Brahmin (except with regard to mothers' educational level, which was not high), were expected to be overrepresented among the high-ability, high-adapted, high-achieving girls who comprised the Gifted, High-Adapted Achievers (Subgroup 1) at age 16. This type was observed ($p < .001$). In line with our previous scenario, the High-Educated Fathers were not expected to form a type with the Gifted, *Low*-Adapted Achievers discussed above because we believed high education on the part of *both* parents to be a necessary condition for sustaining these girls' achievement levels in the face of their low level of school adaptation. This type did not emerge.

Second, we expected that the High SES, High-Educated Fathers might be overrepresented among the High-Adapted Overachievers (Subgroup 3), who were a particularly interesting subgroup in that no pattern of overachievement had emerged at age 13. The hypothesis was partially based on previous research showing that high fathers' education exerts a strong positive influence on daughters' educational aspirations and achievements (see Betz & Fitzgerald, 1987, for a review).

In addition, we had learned in chapter 4 that the age-13 high-adapted girls with low-normal intelligence *who formed a developmental stream with the overachievers* at age 16 came from families whose fathers were significantly more educated than were the fathers of girls characterized by the same high adaptation and low-normal intelligence at age 13, but who did not become overachievers at age 16. Because the High SES, High-Educated Father environments at age 13 reflected high parental aspiration concerning their daughters' education and high evaluation of their daughters' abilities, we considered that they might be associated with overachievement as the girls grew older and the fathers perhaps became more interested in their daughters' educational plans. Although this expectation was not supported by the EXACON analysis, the High-Adapted Overachievers are investigated further in chapter 9, to determine whether or not their *relationships* with their fathers were more positive than were the father–daughter relationships reported by other subgroups.

The Middle-Class, High-Educated Mothers (Subgroup 3)

On the basis of previous research concerning the positive effect of *mothers'* education on daughters' aspirations and achievements (see Betz & Fitzgerald, 1987, for a review), the Middle-Class, High-Educated Mothers were first expected to be overrepresented among the highly able and highly adapted girls who were the Gifted, High-Adapted Achievers (Subgroup 1). This family pattern, which was characterized by high parental aspiration and evaluation, as well as by the high mean on mothers' education for which it was named, had been expected to be overrepresented among *age-13* girls characterized by a similar pattern, who formed a developmental stream with the Gifted, High-Adapted Achievers at age 16. The type did not emerge in the earlier analysis.

Undaunted by the previous negative finding, we thought it possible that the influence of the High-Educated Mothers might be more evident 3 years later when the demands of a "theoretically oriented" curriculum were more difficult to meet and adolescents were making more far-ranging decisions than which optional courses to select for the following year. However, the association between the High-Educated Mothers at age 13 and the Gifted, High-Adapted Achievers at age 16 was not significant either.

Analogous to the reasoning we followed with the High-Educated Fathers, we expected, second, that the High-Educated Mothers might be associated with the overachievement pattern observed for the first time at age 16 (the High-Adapted Overachievers, Subgroup 3). The overrepresentation between these two subgroups was also nonsignificant.

The Low SES Status Quos (Subgroup 8)

Expected Associations.   Because the negative influence of low parental aspiration for their daughters and low evaluation of their daughters' capabilities was so pervasive at age 13, we expected the Low SES Status Quos to continue to be significantly associated with girls' demonstrating low achievement and/or low adaptation to school at age 16, even if, contrary to their parents' low evaluation of their academic capability, they had normal intelligence. It might be remembered that in chapter 6 we investigated rather closely those girls who, at age-13, expressed low self-perceived ability, despite their normal levels of intelligence and achievement, and who, by age 16, were underachievers. As we predicted then, the specific girls who formed this developmental stream were significantly overrepresented among the Low SES Status Quo families.

We now had the opportunity to demonstrate this deleterious influence process from a different angle. Specifically, we expected, first, that considering the *subgroup as a whole*, those age-16 girls characterized by a normal level of intelligence, but by below-average achievement, self-perceived ability, and adaptation means (i.e., the Low-Adapted, Normal-Ability Underachievers, Subgroup 4) would be overrepresented among the Low SES Status Quo families. This type was, indeed, observed ($p < .01$). In fact, *almost half* of the age-16 underachievers came from this family background.

Of course, it was also demonstrated in chapter 6 that, in certain cases, parents' low aspiration for their daughter and low evaluation of her capability constituted an *accurate* reflection of their daughter's academic potential. If, over 3 years' time, low-ability, low-achieving girls had incorporated their parents' low evaluations, we would expect that the Low SES Status Quos would be overrepresented, second, among the Moderately Adapted, Realistic, Low Achievers (Subgroup 8) and, third, among the Low-Adapted, Low-Ability Non-Achievers (Subgroup 9).

These low-ability subgroups were characterized by low achievement means, in addition to the lowest levels of perceived ability reported by any of the age-16 subgroups. Furthermore, both of these age-16 subgroups represented developmental streams from the age-13 Low-Adapted, Low-Ability Non-Achievers (Subgroup 9), who were significantly associated with the Low SES Status Quos in early adolescence. Each of our expectations yielded a type ($p < .0001$ for the Realistic, Low Achievers and $p < .001$ for the Non-Achievers).

Unexpected Associations.   With their lowest intelligence mean, the Moderately Adapted, *Unrealistic*, Low Achievers were also significantly associated with the Low SES Status Quos ($p < .01$) and with the Low SES Pushers ($p < .0001$), who also thought their daughters unsuited for academic studies. Neither association had been specified a priori.

As was mentioned in chapter 3, the Unrealistic, Low Achievers were moderately well-adapted to school at age 16, despite their low performance levels, perhaps because they had selected themselves out of an academically oriented curriculum by Grade 9, when the greatest freedom of course selection was available. (The achievement indicators for the age-16 ability/adaptation patterns, it should be remembered, reflected courses that *all* subjects were taking in Grade 8.) We investigate their choices in the next chapter. However, that the *Unrealistic* Low-Achievers *perceived* themselves as more capable than their intelligence and achievement means warranted, even though 25 out of 35 of these girls came from households in which the parents' evaluation did not concur with their daughters' perceptions, constituted somewhat of an anomaly.

Expected Nonassociations.   Several underrepresentations were also expected regarding the Low SES Status Quos. First, as further support for the presumed detrimental impact that low parental aspirations and evaluations may have on daughters' success in school, we hypothesized that the overachiever syndrome, a combination of high adaptation and higher achievement levels than intelligence alone seemed to warrant, would be incompatible with the parental values exemplified by the Low SES Status Quos. Thus, the Low SES Status Quos were expected to be *under*represented among the High-Adapted Overachievers (Subgroup 3). This underrepresentation was significant ($p = .01$).

Second, given the profound disparity between the Low SES Status Quos' noneducationally oriented values and the Gifted, High-Adapted Achievers' (Subgroup 1) high performance and high adaptation levels, an overlap between these two subgroups was expected to be virtually nonexistent. This antitype was also observed ($p < .0001$).

Third, because the Low SES Status Quo parents could not possibly function as personal examples for educational achievement, a process we considered essential for girls' continuing to exhibit high achievement in the face of low adaptation to the school environment, we expected the Low SES Status Quos to be underrepresented among the Gifted, Low-Adapted Achievers (Subgroup 2). This antitype ($p < .001$) emerged as well.

Unexpected Nonassociations

Finally, two unpredicted antitypes were observed across the entire analysis. From our perspective, both were reasonable. First, the Low SES Status Quos were significantly *under*represented ($p < .01$) among the Moderately Able Normals (Subgroup 6), again suggesting that this family pattern was not associated with parents' facilitating *normal* levels of achievement and adaptation in their daughters. Second, there was no overlap ($p < .01$) between the Middle-Class Upwardly Mobiles (Subgroup 4), who believed their daughters to be capable of pursuing academic coursework, and the Moderately Adapted, Realistic, Low Achievers (Subgroup 8), whose academic potential was quite low.

Summary Remarks

At first glance it might seem that these results argue as persuasively for an "SES" as for a "values" interpretation of family influence: The high SES families were associated with the highest achieving subgroups, whereas the Low SES Status Quos were associated with the lowest achievers. However, we would suggest that the influence process is a bit more subtle than the consideration of socioeconomic status *in isolation from values* can capture.

For example, it must be remembered that at age 13, only *one* family subgroup out of eight expressed *non*educationally oriented values. That these values were expressed among a subgroup of low-SES families (the Low SES Status Quos) should not be interpreted separately from the fact that the Low SES Upwardly Mobiles at age 13 were not characterized by noneducationally oriented values and were not associated with the low-achieving subgroups at age 16. Yet the Upwardly Mobiles' parental education means were as low as those of the Status Quos, and their income mean was even lower.

Thus, the *stability*, from age 13 to age 16, of parents' *high* aspirations and *high* evaluations' being associated with girls' high achievement, especially among the daughters of families in which the parents' own educational achievement provided an example for their daughter's high perform-ance, is not surprising. Nor is it a function of *social class per se* that par-ents' low aspiration and low evaluation continued to be associated with low performance, not only among low-ability girls but among underachievers as well.

ASSESSING SHIFTS IN PARENTAL VALUES

Our next analysis assessed the issue of *change*, rather than stability, in pa-rental values. We proposed that, as parents and their offspring interact with one another through the course of increasingly difficult academic demands, parental aspirations and evaluations would change to reflect more accu-rately their offsprings' actual potential. Moreover, because most parents of 13-year-old girls expressed values oriented towards their daughter's pursu-ing an academic education, these shifts were likely to constitute a *lowering* of parental aspirations and evaluations, in response to their daughter's dif-ficulty in meeting academic requirements.

Specifically, if parents' values shift downward over time, we should ob-serve that among patterns of home environments described when the girls are 16 years of age, low parental aspiration for their daughter, combined with low evaluation of her capability, will no longer be restricted to low SES families. Furthermore, such families, regardless of their socioeconomic status, should be associated with midadolescent patterns of low ability and low achievement.

Family Background Patterns at Age 16

Data and Method

The data used to characterize patterns of family backgrounds when the subjects were 16 years old once again comprised both SES and values mea-sures taken from the parents themselves, in this case from the Parents' Questionnaire administered during the subjects' last year in compulsory school (Grade 9). The pattern indicators of socioeconomic status, recoded as z scores, were (a) fathers' education and (b) mothers' education. Both in-dicators were measured on a 7-point scale, ranging from no education past compulsory school to at least 4 years of university. (No income measure was available.)

The indicators of parental values were again defined as (a) parents' aspi-ration for their daughter's education and (b) parents' evaluations of their daughter's academic capability. Although at age 13 each of these variables had comprised a two-step "continuous" scale constructed from a dichoto-mously scored item, the items available at age 16 provided data for a more

TABLE 8.2
Family Background Patterns at Age 16

Subgroup label	Standardized subgroup means			
	Fathers' ed.	Mothers' ed.	PAs[a]	PEv[b]
1-High-Educated Brahmin (n = 30)	1.80	2.56	.87	.72
2-High-Educated Fathers, High Expectations (n = 25)	1.84	.07	.54	.80
3-High-Educated Fathers, Low Expectations (n = 26)	1.02	−.44	−.44	−.68
4-Educated Fathers (n = 31)	.83	−.32	.53	.72
5-High-Educated Mothers (n = 26)	.13	1.63	.28	.44
6-Upwardly Mobiles (n = 86)	−.64	−.34	.69	.80
7-Low-Educated Pushers (n = 55)	−.69	−.38	.32	−.39
8-Low-Educated Status Quos (n = 45)	−.67	−.54	−.89	.02
9-Low-Educated, Low-Expectation Status Quos (n = 36)	−.71	−.51	−.68	−1.70

Note: In total, the family backgrounds of 360 subjects were clustered.
[a]Parents' aspiration for daughter's education.
[b]Parents' evaluation of daughter's capability.

fully continuous measure of parental values. These measures are described in detail in Appendix C.

Data on the four indicators (fathers' education, mothers' education, parents' aspiration, and parents' evaluation) were available for 376 of the age-16 subjects. The profiles of these subjects across the four variables were clustered in accordance with the techniques discussed in chapter 2.

Results

A nine-cluster solution was judged optimal. The family background clusters, depicted in Table 8.2, represented the assignment of each of 360 subjects to one of nine homogeneous subgroups. The solution, excluding a residual of 16 families (4.25%) whose profiles did not match the centroids of any of the derived clusters, accounted for a 75% reduction of error variance over considering the entire sample as a single cluster.

In assigning subgroup labels we used the term *expectations*, rather than *values*, to designate a configuration in which parents' aspiration for their daughter, whether high or low, was consistent with their evaluation of their daughter's capability. This designation was adopted to avoid denoting non-educationally oriented values as "low" values.

The overall characteristics of the family background subgroups supported the proposition that by the time the subjects were age 16, low parental expectations would no longer be circumscribed to low-SES families. For example, the High-Educated Fathers, *Low* Expectations subgroup (Subgroup 3) displayed relatively low mean levels of both aspiration and evaluation, despite its high mean level of fathers' education.

The age-16 family background analysis also yielded patterns in which parental aspiration for their daughter's educational future was inconsistent with their evaluation of her capability. For example, the "pusher" syndrome, whereby parents reported *above-average* aspiration for their daughter while expressing *below-average* confidence in her academic capability, was observed among the Low-Educated Pushers (Subgroup 7) at age 16. In addition, the age-16 patterns included a subgroup characterized by a *low* mean level of parental aspiration in combination with an *average* mean level of confidence in the daughter's capability to pursue academic work (the Low-Educated Status Quos, Subgroup 8). That such a subgroup was distinguishable from the Low-Educated, Low-Expectation Status Quos (Subgroup 9) might have been attributable, at least in part, to the increased sensitivity of the values measure available at age 16.

We might also note that an Upwardly Mobile subgroup (Subgroup 6), in which parents had high expectations for their daughter, despite their own relatively low levels of education, appeared at age 16 as it had at age 13. We were not able to designate this subgroup as lower or middle-class, however, because we had no measure of income when the girls were midadolescents. Last, a "Brahmin" subgroup (Subgroup 1), as well as a subgroup characterized by mothers whose education mean both relatively and absolutely exceeded that of fathers (the High-Educated Mothers, Subgroup 5) were again observed at age 16.

Age-13 Family Background Patterns Re-Visited

Issue

A supplementary EXACON analysis testing the associations between the eight family background subgroups at age 13 and the nine family background subgroups at age 16 ($N = 274$) was conducted to assure ourselves that the Upwardly Mobiles and the Brahmin at age 16 were essentially the same people who had comprised the similarly named subgroups at age 13. Because, at age 13, these subgroups had embodied educationally oriented parental values, and because they were significantly associated with girls' high achievement *in early adolescence* (see chapter 5), they were expected to remain stable over time. In other words, given that the performance of the girls from these backgrounds had matched their parents' aspirations and evaluations 3 years earlier, there was no reason to believe that the parents in these subgroups would alter their expectations. Nor, given that the measures of parental education were identical at the two ages, was there any reason to believe SES would change. Furthermore, demonstrating this stability would support the validity of the two-step, "continuous" measures we had used as indicators of parental values at age 13.

Results

Although the significant overrepresentations (types) observed through the EXACON analysis are depicted in their entirety in Table 8.3, we only discuss associations involving the subgroups we mentioned previously.

The Brahmin at Both Ages. Virtually all of the High SES Brahmin at age 13, for whom data were available 3 years later, were represented among the High-Educated Brahmin at age 16. Fully 20 out of a possible 22 families formed this significant overrepresentation ($p < .0001$).

The Upwardly Mobiles at Both Ages. The age-13 Middle-Class Upwardly Mobiles and Low SES Upwardly Mobiles were both overrepresented 3 years later among the Upwardly Mobiles ($p < .05$ and $p < .001$, respectively). The absence of an income indicator at age 16 prevented us from discriminating between middle- and lower class upward mobility; nonetheless, the pattern of parents' wanting their children to achieve more than they had achieved themselves was quite stable over time.

FAMILY BACKGROUND AND ABILITY/ADAPTATION AT AGE 16

Rationale

The last analysis in this chapter concerns the relation of family background to ability/adaptation when both domains are assessed in midadolescence. The associations are expected to yield support for two propositions.

First, 16-year-old girls characterized by either high or low ability and achievement should be associated with families in which

1. parents' expectations are internally consistent (high aspiration for the daughter paired with a high evaluation of her capability and vice versa) and
2. parents' expectations reflect their daughter's actual performance. The match between parental expectations and daughter's achievement,

TABLE 8.3
Associations Between Family Background Patterns at Age 13 and Family
Background Patterns at Age 16

Family pattern at age 13	Family pattern(s) at age 16	Overlap n
1-High SES Brahmin	1-High-Educated Brahmin	
(n = 22)	(n = 26)	20****
2-High SES,	2-High-Educated Fathers,	
High-Educated Fathers	High Expectations	
(n = 37)	(n = 20)	15****
3-Middle-Class,	5-High-Educated	
High-Educated Mothers	Mothers	
(n = 36)	(n = 19)	8***
4-Middle-Class	6-Upwardly	
Upwardly Mobiles	Mobiles	
(n = 60)	(n = 70)	21*
5-Middle-Class	3-High-Educated Fathers,	
Pushers	Low Expectations	
(n = 7)	(n = 18)	3**
6-Low SES Upwardly Mobiles	6-Upwardly Mobiles	
(n = 46)	(n = 70)	21***
	7-Low-Educated Pushers	
	(n = 48)	14**
7-Low SES	9-Low-Educated, Low-	
Pushers	Expectation Status Quos	
(n = 16)	(n = 23)	5**
8-Low SES Status Quos	7-Low-Educated Pushers	
(n = 50)	(n = 48)	15**
	8-Low-Educated Status Quos	
	(n = 27)	10**
	9-Low-Educated, Low-	
	Expectation Status Quos	
	(n = 23)	10**

Note: Types were derived, from exact tests of the single-cell frequency overlap between
the the two sets of patterns, for 274 subjects.
*$p < .05$; **$p \leq .01$; ***$p < .001$; ****$p < .0001$.

whether both are high or both are low, should be evident across all
levels of socioeconomic status.

Second, to the extent that parents' aspirations are higher (or lower) than
their evaluations of their daughters' capability, we should observe conditions under which these *inconsistent* parental expectations are associated
with underachievement among girls of normal ability.

Method

The method used to test these propositions was, once again, an EXACON
analysis. The test assessed the associations between the age-16 family back-

TABLE 8.4
Associations Between Family Background Patterns and Ability/Adaptation
Patterns at Age 16

Family pattern at age 16	Ability pattern(s) at age 16	Overlap n
1-High-Educated Brahmin	1-Gifted, High-Adapted Achievers	
($n = 28$)	($n = 59$)	11**
	2-Gifted, Low-Adapted Achievers	
	($n = 34$)	7*
2-High-Educated Fathers, High Expectations	1-Gifted, High-Adapted Achievers	
($n = 23$)	($n = 59$)	9*
3-High-Educated Fathers, Low Expectations	7-Moderately Adapted, Unrealistic, Low Achievers	
($n = 22$)	($n = 24$)	5*
4-Educated Fathers	6-Moderately Able Normals	
($n = 30$)	($n = 50$)	9*
6-Upwardly Mobiles	1-Gifted, High-Adapted Achievers	
($n = 78$)	($n = 59$)	22**
7-Low-Educated Pushers	4-Low-Adapted, Normal-Ability Underachievers	
($n = 46$)	($n = 34$)	11**
8-Low-Educated Status Quos	5-Ability-Underestimating, High-Adapted Normals	
($n = 39$)	($n = 43$)	12**
	8-Moderately Adapted, Realistic, Low Achievers	
	($n = 23$)	8**
9-Low-Educated, Low-Expectation Status Quos	8-Moderately Adapted, Realistic, Low Achievers	
($n = 29$)	($n = 23$)	7**
	9-Low-Adapted, Low-Ability Non-Achievers	
	($n = 8$)	5***

Note: Types were derived, from exact tests of the single-cell frequency overlap between the two sets of patterns, for 315 subjects.
$*p < .05$; $**p \leq .01$; $***p < .001$.

ground subgroups and the age-16 ability/adaptation subgroups. The EX-ACON sample comprised 315 subjects.

Results

The results of the analysis are depicted in Table 8.4. Because the general pattern of results was specified a priori, we reported all types for which the probability of chance occurrence was equal to or less than .05.

The results provided strong support for the two propositions outlined previously. With respect to the first hypothesis, the associations between the family background subgroups and the ability/adaptation subgroups at age

16 demonstrated that family patterns characterized by either high or low parental expectations were associated with girls' achieving at a level that matched their parents' expectations. Furthermore, this "match" occurred across the socioeconomic spectrum.

Specifically, the High-Educated Brahmin (Subgroup 1), the High-Educated Fathers with high expectations (Subgroup 2), and the Upwardly Mobiles (Subgroup 6) were all significantly associated with the highest achieving individuals at age 16 (i.e., the Gifted, High-Adapted Achievers). At the other end of the expectation continuum, the High-Educated Fathers with low expectations (Subgroup 3) and the Low-Educated, Low-Expectation Status Quos (Subgroup 9) were both significantly associated with one or more of the lowest achieving subgroups at age-16 (Subgroups 7, 8, and 9).

As an aside, it might be noted that the parents of only 8 of the original 37 lowest achievers at age 16 (i.e., the Low-Adapted, Low-Ability Non-Achievers, Subgroup 9) had returned the Parents' Questionnaire. This low return rate mirrored a problem endemic in longitudinal studies, namely, attrition of the most "risk-prone" subjects, in this case loss of data on the least academically successful students. That we were able, nevertheless, to demonstrate an expected relationship, at a high level of significance ($p < .001$), between this subgroup and a family background pattern characterized by low parental aspiration and by extremely low parental evaluation (i.e., the Low-Educated, Low-Expectation Status Quos, Subgroup 9) contributed to the generalizability of our findings across social strata.

The second hypothesis was that an *inconsistency* between parents' aspiration for their daughter and parents' evaluation of her capability would be related to underachievement. In support of this expectation we observed that the Low-Educated Pushers (Subgroup 7), whose above-average aspiration was inconsistent with their below-average evaluation, were significantly associated with the Low-Adapted, Normal-Ability Underachievers (Subgroup 4).

Moreover, the Low-Educated Status Quos (Subgroup 8), whose lowest aspiration was inconsistent with their average evaluation, were significantly overrepresented among the Ability-Underestimating, High-Adapted Normals (Subgroup 5). These girls also demonstrated achievement levels that were lower than warranted by their intelligence.

CONCLUDING DISCUSSION

At the beginning of this chapter we set out to investigate whether or not two conclusions drawn from the previous analyses concerning the associations between girls' family backgrounds and their ability and school adaptation at age 13 could be upheld with data collected 3 years later. Regarding the first of these conclusions, we have again demonstrated that socioeconomic status variables do not necessarily reflect parents' aspiration for their daughters' capability. Thus, it would seem inappropriate to use SES measures as indicators of parental values.

With respect to the second conclusion taken from the age-13 results, we have also shown that the parental value system composed of parents' aspiration and parents' evaluation continued to be related to offspring achievement in midadolescence. The mechanisms involved in the influence process, however, would seem to be more complex than the consideration of only the age-13 data would have allowed us to illustrate.

Specifically, parents' expectations appeared to shift downward over time, where necessary, to become consistent with their daughter's actual academic limitations, as exhibited through her low level of achievement. That these shifts reflected a *lowering* of parental expectations seemed to be a by-product of related factors: First, when the girls were in sixth grade (age 13) and all were enrolled in the same curriculum, only one subgroup of families expressed *low aspirations* concerning their daughter's educational future, although two other subgroups expressed low confidence in her academic capability. Therefore, if parental values shift in the direction of their daughter's "true" ability, the general optimism shared by most parents of young adolescents would be expected to change only if 3 years of continued interaction with their daughter's poor school performance had indicated that this optimism was unjustified. In contrast, high parental expectations, sustained by the high performance of their daughter over time, would be expected to be stable, irrespective of the family's socioeconomic level. This pattern of results was indeed observed in this chapter.

The general hypothesis that parental expectations would "match" the level of their daughter's achievement by midadolescence, whether both were high or both were low, further presupposed that the parents' value system would be internally *consistent*, that is, that high parental aspiration would be paired with high parental evaluation of daughter's capability and vice versa. At age 16, however, we observed certain family configurations in which the parental value system was not internally consistent. In support of our hypotheses concerning these subgroups, *inconsistency* between parental aspiration and parental evaluation was associated with midadolescents' not performing at the level of which they seemed capable, given their normal intelligence. These results perhaps suggest that "inconsistent" parents transmitted a "mixed message" that hindered the full expression of their daughters' potential.

It might be remembered at this point, that at age 13, such inconsistency was also evident in the two "Pusher" subgroups. The *difference* between the influence processes at the two ages appeared to be that while parental inconsistency at age 13 (the "Pusher" syndrome) was associated only with low-ability subgroups at age 13 and at age 16, parental inconsistency at age 16 was associated with underachievement.

These results also argue for the proposition that researchers interested in the relationship between parental values and offspring achievement should consider that these values *themselves* may, at different times, reflect different stages in a reciprocal process through which offspring and their parents influence one another. That the *reciprocal* nature of child–parent interactions has received too little attention in past research has been recently emphasized by Jacklin (1989).

Finally, despite the general *non*importance of socioeconomic status in interpreting the results of this chapter and of chapter 5 two exceptions should be noted. At age 13, as has been discussed, low SES did appear to constitute a limiting condition for low parental expectations, given that low aspiration and low evaluation were expressed only among one of the low socioeconomic status subgroups. High parental expectations, on the other hand, were characteristic of high-, middle-, and low-SES families. At age 16 low parental expectations were no longer circumscribed to low-SES families.

However, another potentially important SES phenomenon was observed with respect to girls' ability and adaptation at age 16: The "Brahmin" subgroup, characterized by the highest levels of parents' education, as well as by high parental expectations, was the only subgroup to be significantly associated with individuals who, in midadolescence, were intellectually gifted but not well-adapted to the school environment. Although the next chapter's analyses attempt to explicate this finding, it appeared that, in this particular case, high SES, reflected in the presence of two highly educated parents functioning as exemplars for their daughter's achievement (and perhaps exerting considerable pressure on their daughter to be successful in school), was a necessary condition for maintaining high performance among midadolescent girls who did not experience a "fit" with the academic aspects of the school environment.

As a final comment, we might mention that, in spite of the literature devoted in the past to the influence of *mothers*' education on daughters' achievement and aspiration (see introduction to chapter 5), the results of our investigations so far have demonstrated no such relationship. Aside from the significant association between the Middle-Class, High-Educated Mothers and a subgroup of normally intelligent individuals who did well in math but not in Swedish at age 13 (i.e., the Math-Oriented Verbal Underachievers), an anomaly that we commented on in chapter 5, no significant associations were observed between the high-educated mother pattern that emerged at each age and any of the ability/adaptation subgroups, within or across age. Although at first glance this lack of relationship might appear suspicious, it should be recalled, as we have discussed in chapter 5, that the *absolute* educational level of these women was not, in fact, very high, not nearly as high, for example, as the educational level of the Brahmin mothers.

Whether or not mothers' influence on daughters' achievement can be demonstrated through other means constitutes part of the next chapter's analyses. Following our previous strategy with the data gathered in early adolescence, chapter 9 concerns the possible influence of factors other than family background on girls' differential ability and school adaptation in midadolescence.

Aspiration and Choice as Related to Girls' Ability/Adaptation Patterns in Midadolescence

The analyses presented in this chapter focus primarily on the ability/adaptation subgroups defined at age 16. The chapter addresses factors, other than family environment, which are associated with the differential ability and school adaptation observed among our subjects in midadolescence.

INTRODUCTION

In chapter 7 we assessed the relationship between girls' educational aspiration and their patterns of intelligence, achievement, self-perceived ability, and school adaptation at age 13. One aspect of this assessment considered aspiration as part of an interacting pattern that also included the actual choices girls had made concerning their optional curriculum for the following year. The general finding of this investigation was that, in early adolescence, individuals characterized by patterns of academically oriented choices and high aspiration for further education were also characterized by patterns of high ability and high achievement (although not necessarily by high adaptation). The opposite scenario also held true to a certain extent: Individuals characterized by patterns of nonacademically oriented choices and low aspiration were also characterized by patterns of low ability, low achievement, and, in this case, low school adaptation.

However, certain of the age-13 girls were characterized by a disparity between their present choices, which were oriented toward an academic curriculum, and their aspiration for further education beyond compulsory school, which was below average. This disparity was significantly associated only with normal-ability girls who either underestimated their academic competence or were not well-adapted to the school environment. We suggested in chapter 7 that because academic demands would increase over time, the disparity observed at age 13 might, by age 16, become manifest among high-ability girls who experienced a low adaptation to the academic aspects of school life.

To test this proposition we turned once more to patterns. Analogous to our earlier strategy, we first described the *patterns of educational choices and aspiration* that characterized the subjects at age 16 when they were in their last year of compulsory school (Grade 9). In defining these patterns, we again relied on cluster analytic techniques. (See chapter 2 for a full explanation.)

GIRLS' PATTERNS OF EDUCATIONAL CHOICES AND ASPIRATION AT AGE 16

Pattern Indicators

Of the 485 subjects who comprised the age-16 ability/adaptation subgroups, 390 (80%) had complete data on the four indicators reflecting girls' choices and aspiration patterns in midadolescence. These indicators were:

1. curriculum chosen for Grade 9,
2. level of English course in Grade 8,
3. level of math course in Grade 8, and
4. educational aspiration

Measures of Choices

The three indicators of choices were measured as follows:

1. The measure of the girls' curriculum in Grade 9 (called a "line" in the Swedish system) was taken from an item on the Grade 9 Educational/Vocational Questionnaire. The item listed the options and asked the subjects to indicate the line in which they were enrolled. Our measure represented the classification of nine possible choices into three categories. The categories were coded, from 1 to 3, on the basis of their academic orientation:

- The four vocational or "practical" lines that involved no formal academic education past compulsory school were coded as 1.

- The technical, social, commercial, and humanities lines that led to 2-year gymnasium educations, from which students generally could *not* enter university directly, were coded as 2.
- The program of preparation for the theoretical, 3- to 4-year gymnasium education that would follow compulsory school and serve as a prerequisite for university was coded as 3.

2. The level of a girl's English course in Grade 8 was either high (scored as 2) or low (scored as 1).

3. The level of a girl's math course in Grade 8 was either high (scored as 2) or low (scored as 1).

The English and mathematics course selections were recorded for Grade 8 instead of for Grade 9 because students who selected a *practical* (vocational) line in Grade 9 no longer selected a high versus a low level of either math or English in this final year of compulsory school. The data concerning enrollment in these courses during Grade 8 was taken from the eighth-grade Educational/Vocational Questionnaire. All indicators were re-coded as z scores.

Measure of Educational Aspiration

The measure of education aspiration at age 16 was a composite score. The score was derived from five items, *two* selected from the Student Questionnaire administered to the subjects in Grade 9 and *three* selected from the Grade 9 Educational/Vocational Questionnaire.

The five items selected all assessed future-oriented issues concerning education or career. One item was identical to the single measure of aspiration employed at age 13: namely, "How many years of education can you accept, past compulsory school, in order to enter the occupation you would like?" The responses ranged from "no studies whatsoever" (1) to "more than 5 years" (5). Another item asked respondents to indicate, from "start work right away" (1) to "go into a 3- to 4-year gymnasium line" (5), what they "would do after compulsory school if they could do anything." The internal consistency of the five items was satisfactory ($\alpha = .71$).

Although all items were coded on 5-point scales, the response formats were different in content. Therefore, the items were all standardized before the composite score was formed. Last, the composite score was re-coded as a z score.

Overview of Results

For the cluster analysis performed with these four indicators, a seven-cluster solution was judged optimal, according to the criteria presented in chapter 2. These clusters, depicted in Table 9.1, represented the assignment of

TABLE 9.1
Educational Choices/Aspiration Patterns at Age 16

Subgroup label	Standardized subgroup means			
	Line chosen Grade 9[a]	Hi/Lo Eng. Grade 8[b]	Hi/Lo math Grade 8[c]	Ed. asp.
1-Super-Aspiring "Theoreticals" (n = 25)	.94	.58	.65	1.47
2-High-Aspiring "Theoreticals" (n = 89)	.94	.58	.65	.91
3-Moderately Aspiring "Theoreticals" (n = 69)	.94	.58	.65	.21
4-Low-Aspiring "Theoreticals" (n = 31)	.94	.58	.65	− .73
5-Moderately Aspiring "Mid-Theoreticals" (n = 38)	− .48	.58	.65	.47
6-Low-Aspiring "Mid-Theoreticals" (n = 31)	− .66	.58	.65	− .80
7-Low-Aspiring "Practicals" (n = 97)	− .96	− 1.73	− 1.53	− .44

Note: In total 380 subjects were clustered.

[a]Line selected for Grade 9, scored on a 3-point scale according to the degree of "theoretical" or academic orientation each reflected (z score of − 1.90 = raw score of 1, z score of − .48 = raw score of 2, and z score of .94 = raw score of 3).

[b]High-level versus low-level English course selected for Grade 8. A z score of .58 = raw score of 2 (more theoretical). A z score of − 1.73 = raw score of 1 (less theoretical).

[c]High-level versus low-level math course selected for Grade 8. A z score of .65 = raw score of 2 (more theoretical). A z score of − 1.53 = raw score of 1 (less theoretical).

each of 380 girls into one of seven characteristic subgroups. The seven-cluster solution, excluding a residual of 10 subjects (2.56%) whose profiles did not match the centroids of any of the derived clusters (see the discussion of residuals in chapter 2), accounted for an 87% reduction of error variance over considering the entire sample as a single cluster.

The seven choices/aspiration subgroups defined at age 16 differentiated among girls who were enrolled in

1. the single curriculum or "line" that was preparatory to a 3- to 4-year gymnasium program, as well as to university entrance (the "theoreticals");

2. one of the four lines that served as preparation for a 2-year gymnasium education (the "midtheoreticals"); and

3. one of the four vocational lines that signified an end to formal education after ninth grade (the "practicals").

From the raw-score equivalents of the standardized means, presented in the notes to Table 9.1, we observed that all the girls in Subgroups 1–4 were enrolled in the same gymnasium-preparatory program in Grade 9. However, despite the uniformity of *choice* apparent in the four "theoretical" subgroups, these girls differed markedly with respect to their *level of aspiration*. The Super-Aspiring Theoreticals (Subgroup 1) exhibited an aspiration mean far above the overall average, whereas the mean of the Low-Aspiring Theoreticals (Subgroup 4) was more than half a standard deviation *below* average.

Without a pattern that included aspiration, the four subgroups would have been indistinguishable from one another. With it, the patterns carried the potential of demonstrating strong differential associations with the ability/adaptation subgroups.

THE CONSTRAINING EFFECT OF EARLY CHOICES ON LATER OPTIONS

The Issue

The age-16 choices/aspiration patterns also revealed that all of the girls in Subgroups 1–6 had taken high-level English and high-level math in Grade 8. In contrast, all of the Low-Aspiring "Practicals" (Subgroup 7) had taken the low-level English and math courses in Grade 8 and, on the average, were enrolled in a ninth-grade curriculum that was not academically oriented.

In chapter 7 we speculated that having chosen, in Grade 6, to take low-level math and/or low-level English the following year might circumscribe girls' choices at a later date. If so, a further analysis should demonstrate that the age-16 Low-Aspiring "Practicals" included virtually all the girls who had selected one or both of the low-level offerings three years earlier. This expectation was also suggested by the fact that none of the age-16 choices and aspiration patterns combined high math with low English or vice versa.

The Test

The following analysis was designed to investigate the validity of the conjecture just outlined. Specifically, we used EXACON to test the associations between individuals' patterns of choices and aspiration at age 13 and their choices and aspiration patterns at age 16 ($N = 289$). (The EXACON test of single cell frequencies is discussed in detail in chapter 2.) In this analysis we were interested in the expected significant association between each of *three* subgroups of girls at age 13 and the Low-Aspiring "Practicals" (Subgroup 7) at age 16.

1. The first girls of interest were those who, at age 13, intended to take low-level English in Grade 7, despite their planning to enroll in the *most theoretical curriculum* that same year (i.e., Subgroup 4 in Table 7.2). The results showed that fully 16 out of the 18 girls who comprised the EXACON sample for this subgroup were Low-Aspiring "Practicals" at age 16 ($p < .0001$).

2. The second girls of interest were those who, at age 13, planned to combine low-level English *and* low-level math with a *mid-theoretical curriculum* in Grade 7 (i.e., Subgroup 6 in Table 7.2). Of the 24 girls who were included in the EXACON sample of this subgroup, 18 were Low-Aspiring "Practicals" at age 16 ($p < .0001$).

3. The third girls of interest were those whom, at age 13, planned to take low-levels of both English and math, combined with a *nontheoretical curriculum* in Grade 7 (i.e., Subgroup 7 in Table 7.2). Of the 20 girls who comprised the EXACON sample of this subgroup, all 20 were Low-Aspiring "Practicals" at age 16 ($p < .0001$).

The Implications

The results strongly supported our expectation that an early decision not to enroll in higher level academic electives, like English and math, constrained girls' later option to pursue the courses necessary for an academic gymnasium program and for direct university entrance after gymnasium. Moreover, the Low-Aspiring "Practicals" did not display the lowest or even the second lowest *aspiration* mean among the age-16 choices/aspiration subgroups. Thus, one might further speculate that not only did the decision to avoid one or two specific courses in Grade 7 carry long-range consequences, but these consequences might, in certain cases, have been borne by girls who were not as adverse to continued education as were some of their counterparts who had not circumscribed their options through early choices.

The issue of early, self-imposed limitations is somewhat reminiscent of Sells' (1973, as cited by Betz & Fitzgerald, 1987) study concerning first-year students at the University of California, Berkeley. Sells reported that only 8% of the female, as compared to 57% of the male, freshmen had completed 4 years of high school mathematics before entering university. Because 15 of the 20 academic programs available required 4 years of high school math as a prerequisite, fully 92% of the entering freshmen women were automatically relegated to the five programs that required little or no mathematical background. These programs were "traditional" female occupations, such as education, humanities, social work, library science, and social science.

In the present study, the limitation, to the extent that it existed, was the result of "opting out" of English as well as math; the resultant constraint prevented the girls affected from pursuing *any* university program immediately following gymnasium. Nonetheless, the general problem of foreclosing future opportunities at an early age might be considered comparable across the two cultures, especially because both Sells' and our subjects were from the same age cohort.

Finally, we know from the results of chapter 7 that our early adolescents' decisions regarding which optional curricula to select in Grade 7 were not strongly influenced by their sixth-grade teachers. We do not know, however, whether or not the teachers *attempted* to counsel their students. In any case, it would seem possible that certain girls may not have been fully aware of the long-term consequences likely to accompany their single decision to select low-level rather than high-level English in Grade 7.

ASSOCIATIONS BETWEEN PATTERNS OF ABILITY/ADAPTATION AND PATTERNS OF CHOICES/ASPIRATION

Rationale

Having derived the patterns that characterized girls' choices and aspiration at age 16, we next used an EXACON analysis to assess the association or nonassociation, in midadolescence, between individuals' patterns of ability/adaptation and their patterns of choices/aspiration ($N = 357$). Following the strategy adopted in chapter 7, no specific a priori hypotheses were set forth. Because we were interested in this analysis primarily as an illustration of the most *salient* relationships between the two domains, the only expectation was that the associations (types) and the nonassociations (antitypes) observed would be consistent with the results presented in earlier chapters.

To avoid spurious interpretations based on Type 1 errors, we set as a criterion that, in general, no type would be included in the table of results unless the probability of its occurring by chance were less than or equal to .001, the same criteria established for the parallel analysis at age 13 (see chapter 7). With respect to *antitypes*, however, we were again willing to mention certain zero-frequency cells that were part of an overall pattern of results, even if the cell was not statistically significant due to the small n's involved in the marginal frequencies.

TABLE 9.2
Associations Between Ability/Adaptation Patterns and Choices/Aspiration
Patterns at Age 16

Ability pattern at age 16	Choices/Aspiration pattern(s) at age 16	Overlap n
1-Gifted, High-Adapted Achievers ($n = 78$)	1-Super-Aspiring "Theoreticals" ($n = 25$)	14****
	2-High-Aspiring "Theoreticals" ($n = 87$)	42****
2-Gifted, Low-Adapted Achievers ($n = 35$)	4-Low-Aspiring "Theoreticals" ($n = 31$)	13****
3-High-Adapted Overachievers ($n = 48$)	5-Moderately Aspiring "Mid-Theoreticals" ($n = 36$)	12***
4-Low-Adapted, Normal-Ability Underachievers ($n = 38$)	6-Low-Aspiring "Mid-Theoreticals" ($n = 25$)	11****
6-Moderately Able Normals ($n = 53$)	3-Moderately Aspiring "Theoreticals" ($n = 66$)	20***
7-Moderately Adapted, Unrealistic, Low Achievers ($n = 29$)	7-Low-Aspiring "Practicals" ($n = 87$)	24****
8-Moderately Adapted, Realistic, Low Achievers ($n = 31$)	7-Low-Aspiring "Practicals" ($n = 87$)	25****
9-Low-Adapted, Low-Ability Non-Achievers ($n = 12$)	7-Low-Aspiring "Practicals" ($n = 87$)	10****

Note: Types were derived, from exact tests of the single-cell frequency overlap between
the two sets of patterns, for 357 subjects.
***$p < .001$; ****$p < .0001$.

Results

The associations that met the criterion of equaling or exceeding a probability of .001 are displayed in Table 9.2. The subgroup numbers for the
ability/adaptation subgroups correspond to the numbers used in Table 3.2.
The subgroup numbers for the choices/aspiration subgroups correspond to
those used in Table 9.1

The High Achievers

Associations.   First, it was noteworthy that *all* of the high-ability, high-
adapted girls (the Gifted, High-Adapted Achievers) and *all* of the high-ability, low-adapted girls (the Gifted, Low-Adapted Achievers) were enrolled in
the pre-gymnasium program that would prepare them for university. However, these two subgroups strongly differed with respect to their future-ori-

ented educational aspiration at age 16. The high-adapted achievers were associated with the Super- and the High-Aspiring Theoreticals, whereas the low-adapted achievers were associated with the Low-Aspiring Theoreticals.

Nonassociations.   In fact, despite their highest intelligence and their high achievement means, no Gifted, Low-Adapted Achievers appeared among the Super-Aspirers, although this antitype was not significant at the .05 level ($p = .06$). Moreover, as would be expected from their high levels of achievement into midadolescence, none of the gifted girls, high- or low-adapted, were represented among the Low-Aspiring Practicals ($p < .0001$, in both cases).

The Overachievers

The next result attested to the positive association between school adaptation and high aspiration: The High-Adapted Overachievers, those girls characterized by higher levels of achievement than would be expected given their below-average intelligence, were associated with the *Moderately*-Aspiring Mid-Theoreticals. It might also be noted that the highest *number* of age-16 Overachievers were represented among the *High-Aspiring Theoreticals* (overlap $n = 17$, $p < .05$), although this finding did not meet our rather stringent criterion of $p \leq .001$. This result connotes a long-term prognosis, tested in chapter 11, that girls who demonstrate overachievement and high adaptation to the school environment in midadolescence may, in adulthood, exhibit a significantly higher level of educational attainment than that achieved by their more intellectually gifted, but low-adapted, counterparts.

The Underachievers

The girls whose adaptation, self-perceived ability, and achievement were all below average, in spite of their normal intelligence (the Low-Adapted, Normal-Ability Underachievers), were associated with the *Low*-Aspiring Mid-Theoreticals. Furthermore, even though their intelligence appeared to qualify them for academically oriented coursework, the highest *number* of these girls were actually members of the vocationally oriented Low-Aspiring Practicals (overlap $n = 15$, $p < .05$).

It might be remembered from the results presented in chapters 6 and 8 that the Underachievers came from family backgrounds in which the parents did not aspire to their daughter's receiving an academic education and underestimated her academic capability. Additionally, as discussed in chapters 3 and 6, a significant number of these girls had displayed normal achievement and adaptation means at age 13, despite their low level of self-perceived ability. Adding the present results to the overall picture, it would appear that the educational aspiration and choices of these girls, as well as their academic achievement and adaptation, had suffered certain constraints across the adolescent period.

The Normals

In contrast to the Underachievers, girls who were characterized at age 16 by normal intelligence and achievement, average school adaptation, and above-average self-perceived ability (the Moderately Able Normals) were associated with the Moderately Aspiring Theoreticals. Moreover, none of them appeared among the Low-Aspiring Practicals ($p < .0001$).

The Low Achievers and the Non-Achievers

Last, we suggested in chapter 3 that, at age 16, *moderately high* school adaptation among girls who were low achievers might be accounted for by the girls' self-selection out of an academic and into a vocational curriculum by Grade 9. The results of the present analysis supported this conjecture: Both of the low-achiever ability/adaptation subgroups were associated with the vocationally oriented Low-Aspiring Practicals. Only five subjects from these two subgroups were represented among *any* of the other choices/aspiration subgroups. However, the *extremely* low achievement, self-perceived ability, and school adaptation that characterized the Low-Adapted, Low-Ability *Non-Achievers* might have prevented the girls in this final subgroup from adapting to even the least rigorous educational demands, although they, too, were almost unanimously represented among the Low-Aspiring Practicals.

Summary

We noted in chapter 7 that, in early adolescence, patterns characterized by a disparity between girls' choices and their aspiration, whereby academically oriented course selection was paired with below-average aspiration, were significantly associated only with *normal*-ability girls who displayed either below-average school adaptation or below-average self-perceived ability. We suggested that, as the demands of the academic environment increased, this disparity might also become evident among *high*-ability girls who were experiencing a poor adaptation to school.

In the present analysis, such a finding was observed among girls who were intellectually gifted, but not well-adapted to the school environment (i.e., among the Gifted, Low-Adapted Achievers). In midadolescence, these girls were pursuing the most rigorous academic program available, despite their low aspiration with regard to post-compulsory school education. Among other issues, the next analyses in this chapter addresses factors in these girls' lives that might be associated with the midadolescent disparity between their present choices and their future aspiration.

FAMILY PROCESSES ASSOCIATED WITH GIRLS' ABILITY/SCHOOL ADAPTATION AT AGE 16

Introduction

The next series of analyses explored the possible association between *processes of family interaction in midadolescence*, as seen from the girls' perspective, and girls' ability, achievement, and school adaptation at age 16. The processes considered were:

1. identification with mother,
2. identification with father,
3. relationship with mother,
4. relationship with father,
5. perceived parental approval, and
6. independence from parents.

Given the overall pattern of results to this point, we expected to observe strong differentiation among the ability/adaptation subgroups, based on their perceived interactions with their parents in these areas.

For example, identifying with (i.e., wanting to be "like") a parent might suggest that a girl identifies with the values her parents espouse concerning her educational future and/or with the examples her parents have set by their own levels of educational attainment. We demonstrated in chapter 8 that the age-16 high achievers in our sample, whether their adaptation to school was high or low, were significantly associated only with families in which the parents had a strong orientation toward their daughter's educational achievement. In addition to expressing educationally oriented values, the parents of the *low-adapted* achievers also had high educations themselves, although this was not necessarily the case for the high-adapted achievers.

Thus, for highly capable but low-adapted students, low adaptation may signal a rejection of parental examples and values. If so, we would expect these girls' identification with their parents to be less than that expressed by their highly adapted counterparts.

In addition, it seems reasonable to assume that this putative rejection might lead to disagreements between the low-adapted girls and their families and to low-adapted girls' experiencing parental disapproval. Therefore, we would also expect the relationships between parents and their gifted female offspring to be less harmonious for daughters who were not well-adapted to school (and, as we have seen, had low educational aspirations for themselves) than for daughters who appeared to have internalized parental expectations by demonstrating high adaptation to academic demands and high educational aspiration. To address these kinds of issues specifically, we have separated *identification* with parents from measures concerned more directly with parent–adolescent *relations*.

A growing sense of independence from parents may be another relevant component in midadolescent girls' differential achievement and school adaptation. An extensive body of literature has documented the positive relationship between parents' fostering independence in their children and their offspring's manifesting creativity (Cornelius & Yawkey, 1985; Datta, 1967; Getzels & Jackson, 1962; Hudson, 1968; Stein, 1968), although Rejskind (1982) has argued that the relationship between independence from parents and children's successful completion of creative endeavors is curvilinear, with the optimal degree of freedom's depending on task requirements.

With more particular reference to the area of the present investigation, Farmer (1980) reported that her measure of "early family socialization" comprised items assessing 15-year-old girls' perceptions that their parents encouraged independent behaviors, all of which were significantly positively correlated with items assessing girls' perceptions that their parents were strongly interested in their achievement. Therefore, we might expect that girls characterized by a high adaptation to school, which we have previously observed to be related to their own high educational aspiration and academically oriented choices, would express more independence from their parents than would girls characterized by low school adaptation and low aspiration.

Methods

Subjects

To facilitate tests of specific hypotheses concerning the manner in which these factors might affect midadolescent school achievement and adaptation, given the data we have already presented in this and in previous chapters, we decided to focus our investigation of the first six factors on *four* age-16 subgroups (see Fig. 3.2) whose differential ability/adaptation patterns formed a particularly interesting contrast with one another:

1. the high-ability girls who were highly adapted achievers (i.e., the Gifted, High-Adapted Achievers, Subgroup 1);
2. the high-ability and high-achieving girls who were *low*-adapted (i.e., the Gifted, Low-Adapted Achievers, Subgroup 2);
3. the high-adapted girls whose achievement levels were well above what would have been expected, given their below-average intelligence (i.e., the High-Adapted Overachievers, Subgroup 3); and
4. the low-adapted girls whose achievement and self-perceived ability were lower than what would have been expected, given their normal

intelligence (i.e., the Low-Adapted, Normal-Ability Underachievers, Subgroup 4).

These subgroups have been discussed rather extensively in previous chapters. For example, in our investigation of specific developmental streams in chapter 4, we attempted to determine factors in early adolescence that might influence the school adaptation of certain gifted girls to decrease substantially by midadolescence, whereas the adaptation of others increased. The only difference that emerged from our analyses with the age-13 data was that the socioeconomic status of the "decreasers" was higher than that of the "increasers." We referred to this result again in our chapter 8 discussion of the seeming importance of *both* parents' high education in maintaining high achievement among girls who did not report a "fit" to the school environment.

In chapter 4 we also investigated factors we believed might be associated with the developmental stream between high-adapted, low-normal-ability girls at age 13 and overachievers at age 16. We found that, in addition to having significantly more highly educated *fathers*, the girls who became overachievers had stronger technical and verbal interests in early adolescence than did their low-normal-ability counterparts who did *not* become overachievers.

Additionally, in chapter 3 we demonstrated that a significant number of the age-16 low-adapted girls whose achievement and self-perceived ability were lower than what would have been expected given their normal intelligence had, 3 years earlier, exhibited *normal* levels of achievement and adaptation. Furthermore, we demonstrated in chapter 6 that the girls who formed this developmental stream were significantly overrepresented among families who *inaccurately* assessed their academic capability as low.

Finally, we demonstrated in chapters 4 and 6 that the particular individuals who comprised these various developmental streams were representative of the ability/adaptation subgroups to which they belonged at age 13 and at age 16. Thus, the results of the following analyses can be said to apply to the *specific individuals* who constituted the developmental streams discussed previously, as well as to the full subgroups defined at age 16.

Analyses and Data

The analyses of mean differences between pairs of these four subgroups on all factors were conducted using one-tailed t tests. The specific hypotheses concerning predicted mean differences along with the results, are presented here.

The data assessing the girls' interactions with their parents were taken from the Study of Symptoms Inventory administered to all female subjects in Grade 8. The specific items, along with the number of subjects who had responded to each item, are detailed in Appendix D.

Results and Discussion

In line with the overview introduced earlier, we specified unidirectional hypotheses concerning expected mean differences between pairs of groups. Three contrasts were t tested for each factor. The specifications of these contrasts and the results of the one-tailed t tests associated with each are depicted in Table 9.3.

Identification and Relations with Parents

The High-Adapteds Versus the Low-Adapteds.   We have seen that both the Gifted, High-Adapted Achievers and the Gifted, Low-Adapted Achievers were significantly associated with families characterized by strong aspiration for their daughter's educational future and, in the case of the Low-Adapteds, by high levels of parental education. Our hypothesis was that given the difference between the school adaptation of these two groups, as well as the difference in their long-range educational aspiration for themselves, the High-Adapteds would identify more with their parents than would the Low-Adapteds. The observed differences were significant with respect to identification with mother ($p < .001$), but not with respect to identification with father.

Following the logic we outlined earlier, if greater acceptance of parental values characterized the Gifted High-Adapteds, their relationships with their mothers and fathers separately, as well as their sense of their parents' general approval of them, should be more positive than that experienced by the Gifted Low-Adapteds. Again, these hypotheses were supported for relations with mother ($p < .05$) and parental approval ($p < .01$). The mean difference between the groups on relationship with fathers was not significant.

Overachievers Versus Underachievers.   It also seemed reasonable to assume that the high achievement and adaptation of the High-Adapted Overachievers, relative to their intelligence, would be particularly likely to develop in a home environment that strongly reinforced achievement. If the high adaptation of the Overachievers was related to their having internalized parental values concerning education, the Overachievers' identification-with-mother and identification-with-father means should be higher than those of the Low-Adapted, Normal-Ability Underachievers (a significant number of whose parents did not, as we already know, express educationally oriented values). In addition, the Overachievers' means on relations with each parent and on perceived parental approval should be higher than those exhibited by the Underachievers (a significant number of whose parents underestimated their daughter's capability).

In making such hypotheses we were aware that we could not demonstrate directly that the Overachievers had, in fact, come from families espousing educationally oriented values. However, we had demonstrated (in chapter 8) that the Overachievers were significantly underrepresented ($p = .01$) among

TABLE 9.3
Planned Contrasts Between Age-16 Ability/Adaptation Subgroup Means
on Family Process Variables

Variable	Specified contrast	First mean	Second mean	t-value
Identification with mother	1-Gifted, High-Adapted Achievers (n = 78) >	3.21		
	2-Gifted, Low-Adapted Achievers (n = 39)		2.59	3.01***
	3-High-Adapted Overachievers (n = 50) >	3.02		
	4-Low-Adapted, Normal-Ability Underachievers (n = 48)		2.46	2.66**
	3-High-Adapted Overachievers (n = 50) >	3.02		
	2-Gifted, Low-Adapted Achievers (n = 39)		2.59	1.93*
Identification with father	1 (n = 74) > 2 (n = 37)	2.77	2.59	.80
	3 (n = 47) > 4 (n = 44)	2.96	2.14	3.60****
	3 (n = 47) > 2 (n = 37)	2.96	2.59	1.52
Relationship with mother	1 (n = 74) > 2 (n = 39)	3.35	3.07	1.77*
	3 (n = 50) > 4 (n = 49)	3.56	3.39	1.08
	3 (n = 50) > 2 (n = 39)	3.56	3.07	2.86**
Relationship with father	1 (n = 76) > 2 (n = 39)	3.82	3.71	.61
	3 (n = 49) > 4 (n = 42)	4.14	3.64	2.50**
	3 (n = 49) > 2 (n = 39)	4.14	3.71	2.12*
Perceived parental approval	1 (n = 79) > 2 (n = 39)	4.29	3.88	2.62**
	3 (n = 50) > 4 (n = 49)	4.21	3.90	1.97*
	3 (n = 50) > 2 (n = 39)	4.21	3.88	1.95*
Independence from parents	1 (n = 77) < 2 (n = 39)	3.80	4.20	−2.24**
	3 (n = 46) < 4 (n = 49)	3.63	4.08	−2.91**
	3 (n = 46) < 2 (n = 39)	3.63	4.20	−2.42**

Note: All p-values one-tailed.
*p < .05; **p < .01; ***p < .001; ****p < .0001

the Low SES Status Quo families described when the girls were age 13, families that did *not* hold educationally oriented values. Moreover, no Overachievers were represented among the Low-Educated, Low-Expectation Status Quos defined at age 16 ($p < .05$), a family pattern also characterized by nonacademically oriented parental values. Therefore, although we could not say exactly what sorts of parents these girls had, we could safely assert what sort they did not have.

The results of t tests comparing the means of these two groups on the parental identification and relations variables were largely supportive of our expectations. Compared to the Underachievers, the Overachievers were significantly more identified with their mothers ($p < .01$), significantly more identified with their fathers ($p < .0001$), had significantly better relationships with their fathers ($p < .01$), and experienced higher approval from their parents ($p < .05$).

The results concerning fathers were particularly noteworthy given our previous finding (in chapter 4) that the *developmental stream* to overachievement, observed among low-normal-ability girls who were highly adapted to school, was associated with family backgrounds characterized by a high level of fathers' education. It might also be noted that the *Underachievers'* identification-with-father mean was the *lowest* mean exhibited by any of the four groups on any of the identification and relationship variables.

Overachievers Versus Low-Adapteds. Last, we tested the hypotheses that the High-Adapted Overachievers would be significantly more identified with their parents, have more harmonious relations with them, and perceive a higher degree of parental approval than would the Gifted, *Low*-Adapted Achievers. Considering the large differences between the intelligence and achievement means of these two groups, these specified contrasts constituted a rather stringent test of our general framework. Nevertheless, the results were supportive. The High-Adapted Overachievers were significantly more identified with their mothers ($p < .05$), had significantly better relations with their mothers ($p < .01$) and with their fathers ($p < .05$), and perceived their parents as more approving ($p < .05$) than did the Gifted, Low-Adapted Achievers.

Independence from Parents

Our hypotheses with regard to the last family process-related variable were exactly the *opposite* of those just stated. Consistent with our earlier discussion of independence from parents as possibly comprising an important component of midadolescent females' high adaptation to the school environment and their high educational aspiration, we expected:

1. that the Gifted, Low-Adapteds, would be less independent (i.e., more dependent on their parents) than the Gifted, High-Adapteds;
2. that the Low-Adapted, Normal-Ability Underachievers would be less independent than the High-Adapted Overachievers; and
3. that the Gifted, Low-Adapteds would be less independent than the High-Adapted Overachievers.

The results supported all three hypotheses ($p < .01$ for each contrast).

These findings were especially interesting in terms of illustrating that the girls who were not well-adapted to the school environment were, nonetheless, more *dependent* on their parents than were the well-adapted girls. One might speculate that such dependence could have been particularly onerous to the Underachievers, a significant number of whose parents had underestimated their capability, thus contributing to the poor family relations experienced by this subgroup.

Similarly, *dependence* on parents whose educationally oriented values they did not appear to share (given their own low level of aspiration) might also have engendered or at least sustained the poor family relations experienced by the Gifted, Low-Adapted Achievers. These girls appeared to need their parents' direction, but not to emulate them.

DIFFERENTIAL PEER ASSOCIATIONS

Issue Addressed

Besides the differential relationships these four subgroups experienced within their families, another potentially important source of differences among them involves their social relationships. Gustafson et al. (1989) demonstrated that the life situations of adult females were influenced by whether or not they had associated, in midadolescence, with peer types that were presumed to direct their attention away from academic achievement (i.e., older peers, working peers, or a steady boyfriend): Among females who had associated with these types of peers in midadolescence, a higher percentage had borne at least one child by age 26, and a lower percentage had completed a post-compulsory school education, as compared to women who had not engaged with such peers. Although these long-term consequences were observed among both high- and low-aspiring females, they were most pronounced among subjects whose midadolescent aspiration had been low.

Similarly, Stattin and Magnusson (1990) have presented a comprehensive series of studies supporting the relation between females' early maturation and their engagement with these types of peers. Again, such adolescent peer associations were related to adult outcomes that were not oriented toward educational attainment.

With these former studies as background, we investigated the four subgroups of girls who were the focus of our previous analyses, to assess whether or not they could be differentiated on the basis of their peer associations in midadolescence. Our assumption was that high educational aspiration among girls who were well-adapted to the school environment (i.e., among the Gifted High-Adapteds and the Overachievers) was incompatible with these girls' associating with older peers, working peers, or steady boyfriends in midadolescence. Conversely, low aspirers who were not well-adapted to school (i.e., the Gifted Low-Adapteds and the Underachievers) were expected to have such peer associations. Of course, whether low aspiration and low adaptation occurred before, after, or in reciprocal interaction with the peer associations could not be determined.

Last, in theoretical connection with the "boyfriend" issue, we also tested whether or not these four subgroups could be differentiated in midadolescence on the extent to which they looked forward to having their own children. Again, our assumption was that any differences that emerged would reflect a stronger anticipation of childbearing on the part of the Gifted Low-Adapteds and the Underachievers, as compared to the anticipation reported by the other two subgroups.

Method

Data

The data on subjects' associations with older and working peers were taken from the Sociometric Questionnaire, administered to the girls in eighth grade (age 15). The girls were asked to state how many of their close friends were older than themselves and how many were working rather than attending school. The item asking whether or not the girl had a steady boyfriend was taken from the Study of Symptoms Inventory, also administered in Grade 8. The item asking the extent to which the subjects looked forward to bearing and raising their own children was also taken from the Study of Symptoms Inventory and was coded on a 5-point, Likert-type scale.

Analysis

Three EXACON analyses were used to test for differential peer associations among the four subgroups. The "older peer" variable in the first test was coded into three categories: (a) no older peer, (b) one older peer, and (c) two or more older peers. The same procedure was followed for the "working peer" variable in the second test. In the third test, the "boyfriend" variable was a dichotomy. In all three tests, the four selected ability/adaptation subgroups comprised the second variable.

The differential anticipation of bearing children was tested with an ANOVA. Post hoc significances were determined by the Duncan multiple-range procedure.

Results

Older Peers and Working Peers

The results of the EXACON tests concerning older peers ($N = 217$) and working peers ($N = 217$) partially supported our expectations. With regard to differential engagement with older peers, a significantly lower than expected number of the *Underachievers* had no older peers whom they considered to be close friends ($p < .05$). That is, the association between underachievement and not having older friends was less than would be expected given a random model. This "antitype" was the only cell that was significant at the .05 level.

Similarly, the results that were significant at the .05 level in the test concerning working peers also involved the Underachievers. Here, however, both an antitype and a type emerged: Not only did a significantly lower than expected number of Underachievers have no working peers ($p < .01$), but a significantly higher than expected number had two or more such peers among their close friends ($p < .01$).

Steady Boyfriend

In the EXACON test concerning boyfriends ($N = 212$), the significant results involved both the Underachievers and the Gifted High-Adapteds. A significantly higher than expected number of the Underachievers had boyfriends ($p < .05$), whereas a significantly lower than expected number of the Gifted High-Adapteds had them ($p < .01$). (Because there were only two categories on the "boyfriend" variable, the type and the antitype tests were not independent within a given subgroup category.)

Anticipation of Childbearing

Finally, the four subgroups did not differ significantly, at the conventional .05 level, in the degree to which they anticipated childbearing [$F(3,212) = 2.42$, $p = .07$]. Although, technically, one is not justified in considering post hoc tests in the absence of a significant F ratio, we relaxed the rule a bit in this case given that a p value of .07 is not unreasonably high. The post hoc tests ($p < .05$) revealed that, consistent with our general line of reasoning, the Underachievers anticipated having and raising their own children to a significantly greater extent than did the Gifted, High-Adapteds. However, the Underachievers also anticipated motherhood significantly more than did the Gifted Low-Adapteds, although we had not expected these two subgroups to differ from one another.

Comments

In conjunction with the information about family processes presented in the foregoing section, these results seemed helpful in creating an overall picture of differential development. For example, we already knew that the Underachievers were having considerable difficulty relating positively to their families and that they had low aspiration to continue school. At this point we may add that a significant number of these girls engaged with working peers and steady boyfriends. Such relationships might well have been associated with parental disapproval. Moreover, relationships with working peers and boyfriends might also have been associated with the Underachievers' orientation away from school achievement, especially considering that these girls looked forward to raising a family of their own.

Whether working peers and boyfriends preceded, followed, or interacted reciprocally with poor parental relations, low school aspiration, and high anticipation of motherhood is impossible to determine. However, the general pattern that has emerged here is consistent with the extensive literature concerning the negative impact of certain peer types, especially of boyfriends, on girls' educational ambitions. (See Stattin & Magnusson, 1990, for a review.)

Conversely, the exact opposite pattern emerged for the highly able, highly adapted subgroup of girls we have called the Gifted, High-Adapted Achievers. These girls got along well with their parents, had high aspiration for continued education, did not have boyfriends, and did not particularly look forward to becoming mothers.

BIOLOGICAL MATURATION AND SCHOOL PROBLEMS

Rationale

Finally, we reported in chapter 7 that biological maturation was not associated with the patterns that described our subjects' achievement and school adaptation in early adolescence. However, Stattin and Magnusson (1990) have observed that the period of highest risk for early maturers, in terms of their experiencing difficulty with various aspects of school adjustment, occurs in midadolescence. Therefore, we were interested in testing whether or not early maturers were overrepresented among any of the age-16 ability/adaptation subgroups whose patterns were characterized by adjustment problems, such as low school adaptation and/or inaccurately low self-perceived ability.

Method

The measure of biological maturation was taken from the Study of Symptoms Inventory administered to the female subjects during Grade 8. The item asked respondents to state at what age they had experienced their first menstrual period. In accordance with the method employed by Stattin and Magnusson, the responses were coded on a four-step scale: before age $11 = 1$, between ages 11 and $12 = 2$; between ages 12 and $13 = 3$; and after age 13 or "haven't yet had" $= 4$. Biological maturation data were available for 415 (86%) of the 485 girls who comprised the age-16 ability/adaptation subgroups.

The associations between biological maturation and all nine patterns of ability/adaptation were examined through an EXACON analysis. The analysis assessed the over- and underrepresentation of the age-16 ability/adaptation subgroups in the four levels of biological maturation.

Results

Of the 36 cells represented in the contingency table, only four yielded a significant ($p < .05$) type or antitype. Nevertheless, we observed tentative support for our proposition that, in line with Stattin and Magnusson's results, early maturation might be related to school adjustment problems in mid-adolescence.

Specifically, the cell yielding the lowest p value reflected the overrepresentation ($p < .001$) of the next-to-earliest maturers among the lowest achieving, lowest adapted subgroup of girls, who also had the lowest self-perceived ability (see Subgroup 9 in Table 3.2). Considering that there were only four subjects who belonged to the earliest maturing group, we were unable to draw any conclusions about the ability/adaptation patterns of these girls, who, in Stattin and Magnusson's investigation, were the most vulnerable to experiencing school-related difficulties.

CONCLUDING REMARKS

In conclusion, the most informative results of our variable-oriented analyses concerned differential processes that appeared to be operating in the home lives of the four groups of midadolescents we had selected for special investigation—and their differential association with specific types of peers. The highly adapted, highly intelligent, high achievers and the highly adapted overachievers systematically reported more identification and better relations with their parents, as well as experiencing a higher degree of parental approval, compared to the parental identification, relations, and approval reported by the intelligent high achievers whose school adaptation was low. In addition, a significant number of the high-adapted high achievers did not have a steady boyfriend.

The same basic pattern was observed when the highly adapted overachievers were compared to the low-adapted underachievers, a significant number of whom associated with working peers and had steady boyfriends. Yet the low-adapted girls, whether they were high achievers or underachievers, were more dependent on their parents to make decisions for them than were their high-adapted counterparts.

The combination of poor daughter–parent relations and strong daughterly dependence was particularly salient among the highly intelligent high achievers whose school adaptation was low. That this group exhibited the least independence of any of the four groups was noteworthy in terms of the family backgrounds with which these girls were associated. Because they were significantly associated only with families characterized by very high levels of education on the part of both parents and by high parental expectations (aspiration for their daughter's achievement and evaluation of her academic capability), one might conjecture that such families had exerted sustained pressure on their daughter to ensure her high performance and her selection of academically oriented curricula throughout compulsory school, even though these girls' school adaptation and their own educational aspiration were both quite low by midadolescence. One can thus imagine that high dependence on parents and poor relations with parents, as reported by the gifted girls with low school adaptation, might well be associated with ongoing issues concerning parental control.

This scenario is consistent with Spence, Pred, and Helmreich's (1989) observation that "the linkage between academic ability and achievement-related motives may in time become disconnected" among midadolescents who are capable of doing well in high school and of pursuing university studies (p. 187). Assuming that the low adaptation and the low aspiration of our gifted, low-adapted achievers might reflect this disconnection between ability and aspiration, we would surmise that these individuals would leave formal education as soon as they no longer felt obligated to live up to their parents' expectations. If so, we would expect that by young adulthood these women would not have reached a level of educational attainment consistent with their midadolescent intelligence and achievement, both of which were high. This expectation is tested in chapter 11.

One last issue perhaps deserves mention in relation to the low school adaptation of these particular individuals. In the early 1970s an influential and explicitly formulated position in the debate on education in Sweden was that teachers should devote their time to their poor students rather than to their good ones so that the gap between poor and good performers would not increase. It might be remembered that the patterns of the intellectually gifted but low-adapted midadolescent females we have investigated in such detail were defined with data collected in 1971.

We certainly do not intend to draw any causal inferences regarding the relationship between this widely held philosophy and these extremely intelligent girls' low adaptation to the academic aspects of the school environment. Nonetheless, it is theoretically possible that ignoring the needs of bright students who require special assistance to adapt to environmental demands—to the extent that such a strategy might have guided the daily behavior of classroom teachers—could have either influenced these girls' lack of "fit" or hindered their developing effective coping strategies. Such a suggestion carries further weight when we recall the difficulties these girls were experiencing in their home environments. In any case, one might argue that there are individuals for whom high intelligence does not automatically connote an easy adjustment to school and that such individuals require the support and encouragement of the educational system if they are to realize their full potential.

Chapter **10**

In Adulthood—Shared Life Experiences

Our final investigations consider the subjects nearly 11 years later. We first present an overview of the life experiences *shared* by a large proportion of our sample in 1982. Against this backdrop, we focus, in chapter 11, on those aspects that characterized female's *differential* life careers in early adulthood.

VALUING INTERPERSONAL RELATEDNESS

In chapter 1 we mentioned Carol Gilligan's (1982) documentation of interpersonal relatedness and commitment as elements crucial to a woman's worldview. Wood, Rhodes, and Whelan's (1989) findings have echoed what Gilligan called the feminine "voice." In their review of the literature concerning sex differences in feelings of positive well-being, Wood et al. found that women reported greater happiness and life satisfaction than did men. This difference, which was especially pronounced for married women, was largely attributable to women's greater orientation towards emotional responsiveness, compared to that of men (Wood et al., 1989).

With such studies in mind, our first question was whether or not the life situations of a representative sample of Swedish women might be said to connote a general orientation toward relatedness and commitment. We looked for evidence in both the personal and the work lives of our subjects.

The data were taken from the Adult Questionnaire, which was mailed to all subjects in 1982 when their mean age was 26 years and 10 months. The

TABLE 10.1
Subjects' Shared Life Experiences in Adulthood

Life experience	Percent of sample who shared the experience
Personal relations	
Being married	71
Having at least one child	46
Associating often with parents	80
Discussing problems with parents	68
Relying on parents in crisis	90
Associating often with friends	75
Discussing problems with friends	54
Relying on friends in crisis	43
Participation in workforce	
Working full time	46
Working part time	26
Being employed in "deep contact" occupations	35
Being employed in office occupations	20
Work values	
Valuing contact with others at work	87
Valuing helping others as a job component	72
Valuing job security	88
Valuing a healthy work environment	98
Valuing job clarity	71
Valuing high pay	82
Work satisfaction	
Feeling satisfied with relationships with co-workers	98
Feeling satisfied with relationship with supervisor	90
Feeling satisfied with work tasks	95
Feeling satisfied with work environment	90
Perception of own "agency"	
Feeling in control of own present life	83
Feeling in control of own future	72
Feeling responsible for own educational and career decisions	90
Feeling satisfied with own occupational choice	83

questionnaire was completed by 602 women, including 90% of the females from the original 1965 sample (Magnusson, 1988). The major findings of this first analysis, as well as those of the subsequent investigations that comprise this chapter, are presented in Table 10.1.

Personal Situation in Early Adulthood

Relatedness to Family

The female subjects' family lives at age 26 seemed to reflect a strong interpersonal orientation. Seventy-one percent were either married or living with a man, although only 46% had given birth to a child. The majority of adult women also appeared to maintain close ties with their parents. Eighty percent reported that they met their parents often, 68% reported that they could discuss their problems openly with their parents, and 90% reported that they could trust their parents to do everything possible to help them out of a really difficult situation.

Relatedness through Social Networks

In addition to their family contacts, the women participated in a variety of social networks composed of colleagues at school or work, neighbors, and/or other friends. Thirty-three percent associated frequently with their neighbors, and 52% often met with their colleagues from work or school. However, the most commonly reported social category was that of "other friends." Of the women, 75% engaged frequently with companions who were not part of their work, educational, or neighborhood environments. Finally, it was also of interest that not one woman out of 602 reported that she had no social contacts at all.

The picture changed somewhat when relationships were assessed at a deeper level. Although the majority still reported that they could discuss their problems openly with friends (54%), and 31% could talk to colleagues at school or work, only 9% confided their problems to their neighbors. Moreover, although the response was not common, 19 of the 602 women (3%) reported that they could not discuss their problems openly with anyone, although the item specifically excluded the subject's mate.

At the deepest level of connection, that of trusting someone (other than one's mate) to do everything possible to help one out of a difficult situation, the designation of the various social networks dropped even further. Of the women, 43% reported that they could rely on their friends, 21% reported that they could rely on school or work colleagues, and 6% designated their neighbors. Only eight women (1%) reported that they trusted no one to come to their aid in a time of trouble.

Summary

The results concerning subjects' families and friends suggested that, by and large, the women surveyed at age 26 valued interpersonal relationships. All of them socialized with people outside their immediate families, and almost all of them had someone, other than their mates, in whom they could confide and on whom they could rely when they needed help.

However, an interesting pattern emerged in these results. As the depth of the relationship being assessed increased, from meeting people socially to depending on someone to come to one's aid in a crisis, women's reliance on their social networks systematically decreased in favor of a reliance on their parents. A higher percentage of women confided in their parents, as compared to the percentages that confided in various categories of peers, and fully 90% of the women felt could rely on their parents when they really needed help. Thus, it would appear that "family" was an extremely important component of the relatedness that characterized our subjects' adult life situation.

Work Situation in Early Adulthood

We next looked at the women's work situations to see if the occupations the subjects chose and the job aspects they valued also indicated an orientation toward interpersonal relatedness. As background, we might first mention that out of 578 women who responded to the item, 46% were holding full-time and 26% were holding part-time jobs at the time of the adult survey. Thirteen percent reported that they were on some type of leave, and 13% said they were unemployed. Among the unemployed women, 61% were homemakers, and an additional 22% were seeking work. (The remainder were suffering from a long illness or were classified under a "miscellaneous" category.)

Thus, being employed outside the home, at least on a part-time basis, was a condition shared by 72% of our adult sample (not including employed women on leave). This figure is *identical* to the percentage of women, between the ages of 25 and 54, who were employed in the U.S. labor force in 1988 (Matthews & Rodin, 1989).

Relatedness and Job Choice

Moreover, the types of jobs held by the working women in our Swedish sample followed the same traditional lines as have been observed in the United States. Fitzgerald and Crites (1980) noted, for example, that female clients of career counselors, when asked what careers they have considered, frequently indicate a preference for social- or office-related occupations, "usually at the helper or assistant level" (p. 55). Similarly, in an earlier study of both the male and female adolescents in the present Swedish sample (Magnusson et al., 1975), girls' rankings of occupational domains reflected a first preference for social work (broadly defined as "deep contact" and including such fields as medicine and education, as well as "social work" per se), followed by a preference for office work. Although males preferred high status jobs in any area to middle- or low-status occupations, females exhausted the status categories within the social and office domains before they shifted their focus to other occupational fields (Magnusson et al., 1975).

Judging from the adult data, these early preferences appeared to be highly predictive of women's occupational decisions. More young adult women in our sample were employed in the domains designated as "deep contact" (35%) and office (20%) than were employed in any of the seven remaining domains. The most prevalent category, "deep contact," designated jobs that required prolonged interaction with others. Each job in this domain, from physician to hospital orderly, or from teacher to daycare helper, involved relating to other people on a continuing basis.

One might, of course, take Gottfredson's (1981) view that women gravitate toward deep contact occupations because they are influenced in their choice of employment more by sex-role identity, which develops early, than by interests and values, which develop later. Gottfredson further suggested that counseling women to pursue nontraditional careers may be of limited utility (and may be ethically wrong) because women, their destinies determined by the socialization process, want traditionally female jobs.

As one might surmise, this position has not gone unchallenged. Betz and Fitzgerald (1987) compared it to claiming that a slave would prefer slavery "over the vagaries and dangers of freedom if given the opportunity to do so" (p. 87). In addition, Fitzgerald and Crites (1980) pointed out that when females are encouraged to expand their career options beyond the traditional boundaries, they often do so (Fitzgerald & Crites, 1980).

However, we would like to argue an alternative viewpoint: It might be worth considering that the *value* "traditional" female occupations, particularly those involving healthcare, social service, and education, place on *relatedness* may, in its own right, provide an important source of fulfillment to many women, independent of, or even in spite of, the influence exerted by "social programming." Such a concept is consistent with the general perspective of interactionism, which stresses that individuals (including women) cognitively evaluate and actively select their environments, and with Holland's (1985) career development theory, which predicts that individuals will choose occupational environments that match their personal orientation.

After all, traditionally female occupations, unlike the "career" of slavery, are not without intrinsic merit. In fact, the functions they serve are essential. It is *society* that has given these occupations low prestige and its natural concomitant, low salary. And it is *because* occupations held primarily by women have low prestige and low salary that girls are frequently encouraged to seek elsewhere for career fulfillment. (No one, for example, urges boys to avoid traditionally "male" career paths.) Therefore, it would seem that, with respect to vocational choice, the "socialization process' *reciprocally interacts* with feminine values and, along the way, denigrates relatedness, a value that Gilligan's (1990) female subjects "voiced" clearly and consistently, well before the onset of puberty.

In support of the possibility that many women choose deep contact occupations because such vocations fulfill basic female values, we are reminded of Betz' (1982) own investigation of the differences in needs reported by employed women versus homemakers. In line with her hypothesis, Betz found that employed women reported a high need for self-esteem, whereas homemakers reported high social and safety-security needs. But the most interesting result was unexpected: The need that all groups of women ranked highest was the need for *self-actualization* (Betz, 1982).

In a similar vein, fully 83% of our adult female respondents reported that their present life situation was either primarily or entirely under their own control (total $N = 548$), and 72% felt that they exercised complete or nearly complete control over their future (total $N = 539$). Moreover, with respect to career development per se, 90% of the women said that they had been responsible for their own educational and career decisions (total $N = 587$), and 83% of the employed subjects were satisfied with their occupational choice (total $N = 522$).

If the need for self-actualization and the belief in oneself as the agent of one's own fate are as general among women as these results imply, and if these personal characteristics are expressed in vocational choice, as seems reasonable, then, logically, self-actualization and an internal locus of control may be represented in the choice of *traditional* as well as of *nontraditional* occupations, especially among women who have prepared themselves for full-time careers. Jenkins' (1987) longitudinal study strongly supports this view: Among women employed in what we designate as "deep contact" occupations, high need for *achievement*, as expressed during the senior year of college, was significantly associated, 14 years later, with their placing a high value on working with and helping people. Thus, females may not select deep contact professions only as a sort of "default option" dictated by cultural expectations.

In conclusion, we would concur with Betz and Fitzgerald (1987) that sexist stereotypes about which occupations are "appropriate" for females— and which are not—unconscionably constrain women's career opportunities. However, we would further argue that to *undervalue* occupations that are traditionally female, precisely because they are traditionally female, is to perpetuate an equally damaging disservice to women.

Relatedness and Job Values

The value women seemed to place on interpersonal relatedness at work was also evident in the job characteristics that they considered important to their liking a job, whether or not they were currently employed.[1] Of the adult sample, 87% reported that contact with people at work was "quite important" or "very important" to them. Similarly, 72% reported that having a job in which they could help others was "quite important" or "very important."

We might add that, in the main, the women who were actually employed

---

[1]Unless stated otherwise, the Ns for the items reported in the "Relatedness and Job Values" section ranged from 584 to 599.

were satisfied with the expression of these interpersonally oriented values in their current work environment. Of 487 respondents, 98% rated their relationships with co-workers as "quite good" or "very good," and 90% of 488 workers were equally positive about their supervisor.

In contrast, job characteristics that were geared toward hierarchy or autonomy, rather than toward relatedness, were valued less highly by a majority of the women, a result that Jenkins (1987) also observed in her U.S. sample, at least among high-need-for-achievement women employed in deep contact occupations. In accord with Fitzgerald and Crites' (1980) earlier cited statement that females frequently indicate a preference for subordinate or "assistant" positions, only 10% of our Swedish subjects reported that deciding what other people should do at work (i.e., performing a supervisory or management function) was "quite" or "very" important to their job satisfaction. And fewer than half of the respondents (40%) reported that setting their own time schedule for working hours was "quite" or "very" important.

VALUING BEING VALUED

The foregoing discussion is not meant to suggest that women's work values revolve *solely* around interpersonal relationships. The majority of adult women in our sample were as interested in *being valued*, in terms of having satisfactory working conditions and rewards, as they were in relating to others.[2]

With respect to working conditions, 88% of the sample stated that job security was a "quite" or a "very" important aspect of any employment situation. Additionally, 98% of the respondents stated that a healthy work environment was "quite important" or "very important" to their liking a job, and 71% responded that receiving clear and unambiguous work instructions was a "quite" or a "very" important facet of job satisfaction.

Again, the employed women expressed high satisfaction with their current work situation. Of 498 respondents, 95% were "quite" or "very" satisfied with their work tasks, and 90% expressed the same degree of satisfaction with their work environment.

Finally, despite the implications of the quotation we cited somewhat ironically in chapter 1, our subjects were not immune to monetary rewards. Among the female adult respondents, 82% considered high pay to be "quite important" or a "very important" job component.

---

[2]Unless stated otherwise, The *N*s for the items reported in the "Valuing Being Valued" section ranged from 590 to 596.

SUMMARY

In summary, our subjects' life experience in young adulthood was generally characterized by marriage or its equivalent, by close ties with parents, especially in times of trouble, by a variety of casual and more intimate social connections, and by paid employment. Within each of these domains, this representative sample of Swedish women expressed values that connoted a strong orientation toward establishing and maintaining interpersonal relations. However, with respect to work, they also valued high pay, job security, healthy working conditions, and clearly defined tasks.

Moreover, these women perceived themselves to be in control of their own lives. With regard to their working life per se, they had chosen their career paths themselves and were satisfied with the choices they had made. Their satisfaction was both general, in terms of believing they had selected the "right" occupation, and specific, in terms of being satisfied with the co-workers and supervisors with whom they interacted, the tasks that comprised their jobs, and the environments in which these tasks were performed.

This chapter has explored values and experiences that were *shared* by the women in our sample at age 26. Given this overall framework, the life experiences that *differentiate* women from one another in early adulthood provide the focus of our final empirical chapter.

Chapter 11

In Adulthood—Differential Life Experiences

The previous chapter addressed values and experiences that were *generally* characteristic of our subjects' lives in young adulthood. In this chapter we concentrate on those aspects of life that were *differentially* characteristic of the women in adulthood.

OVERALL STRATEGY

Rationale

The following analyses address the issue of individual differences in adult female careers. Our goal is to link what we have already learned concerning our subjects' divergent career paths across adolescence to their educations, their work, and their personal lives at age 26. The ability/adaptation subgroups defined at age 16—each with its characteristic pattern of intelligence, achievement, self-perceived ability, and school adaptation—comprise the "individuals" whom we expect to differ on the measures assessed in adulthood.

At this juncture, we know quite a bit about these girls. We know if and how their patterns of ability and adaptation changed from early adolescence to midadolescence. We know the economic circumstances and the educational values of the parents that raised them. We know how the

153

coursework they chose in early adolescence and in midadolescence limited or did not limit their future options. We know about their differing aspiration to continue school after they were no longer obligated to do so and whether or not their level of aspiration was stable over time. Moreover, for the four subgroups we examined in some detail in chapter 9, we know a fair amount about their relationships with their parents in midadolescence and something about their midadolescent social networks.

The associations between these facets of our subjects' lives and their patterns of ability and adaptation at age 16 provide us with a network of information on which to base the explorations and expectations we generate in this chapter. And, indeed, we do both—expect and explore. In these last analyses we *expect* an overall differential pattern of adult consequences that will demonstrate a lawful continuity with what we have already observed. However, because we do not expect all groups of individuals to be equally differentiated on all aspects we investigate, these final analyses are also exploratory. In a sense, they test the meaningfulness of the pattern approach we have employed throughout this volume, as well as the substantive framework we have constructed.

One last point should be noted in our presentation of the following results: In considering individuals' differential development from adolescence to early adulthood, we are, of course, increasing the "length" of the developmental streams we predicted and observed from early adolescence to midadolescence. In the interest of avoiding cumbersome repetition each time we wish to emphasize an adolescent developmental stream, our practice in this final empirical chapter is often to "collapse" developmental stream information into our discussions of the girls at age 16.

Therefore, the reader should remember that statements like "Girls who were underachievers in midadolescence had underestimated their ability in early adolescence" or "The Gifted, Low-Adapted Achievers' school adaptation had deteriorated substantially over time" are a sort of "shorthand," signifying that a significant number of the midadolescent underachievers or a significant number of the midadolescent Gifted Low-Adapteds had followed a predicted developmental path from age 13 to age 16. Similarly, when we characterize particular subjects in terms of factors *associated* with their ability/adaptation patterns, we are summarizing *significant* results observed in previous chapters.

Methods

To simplify further the presentation of results, we might do well to state our general methodology at the outset. The analyses conducted here were either EXACON tests of single-cell frequencies (as described in chapter 2), planned contrasts, or one-way analyses of variance (ANOVAs) with post hoc significances determined by the Duncan multiple-range procedure.

With respect to the EXACON tests, there were always, of course, two sets of categories. One set of categories comprised the nine age-16 ability/adaptation subgroups, whose mean profiles are given in Table 3.2, whereas the other set comprised the categories of whichever aspect we expected to differ across the subgroups. (As we move through the investigations, we define these categories for each test.) The test was to determine which homogeneous subgroups of individuals were significantly overrepresented (or underrepresented) within a particular category of the aspect being considered.

Predicted differences between certain pairs of subgroups were tested through planned contrasts, using one-tailed t tests. However, the ANOVAs employed all nine subgroups as the independent variable. Planned comparisons or ANOVAs were conducted when the dependent variable under investigation was most appropriately represented as a continuous variable.

Finally, unless noted otherwise, all the data for these analyses were taken from the Adult Questionnaire that was mailed to the subjects in 1982, when their average age was 26 years and 10 months. As reported earlier, 90% of the original sample of females (1965) had responded to this questionnaire.

EDUCATIONAL AND OCCUPATIONAL LEVEL IN ADULTHOOD

Between Specified Groups

Our first analysis was a series of t tests in which we predicted that certain individuals who were characterized by different patterns of ability and adaptation in midadolescence would differ significantly in adult educational and occupational level. Our concern was with the four subgroups who were the focus of our final investigations in chapter 9:

1. the high-ability girls who were highly adapted achievers (i.e., the Gifted, High-Adapted Achievers, Subgroup 1);
2. the high-ability and high-achieving girls who were *low*-adapted (i.e., the Gifted, Low-Adapted Achievers, Subgroup 2);
3. the high-adapted girls whose achievement levels were well above what would have been expected, given their below-average intelligence (i.e., the High-Adapted Overachievers, Subgroup 3); and
4. the low-adapted girls whose achievement and self-perceived ability were lower than what would have been expected, given their normal intelligence (i.e., the Low-Adapted, Normal-Ability Underachievers, Subgroup 4).

Data

Adult *educational* level was measured as an eight-step variable, ranging from no education past compulsory school to at least 4 years of an aca-

TABLE 11.1
Planned Contrasts Between Age-16 Ability/Adaptation Subgroup Means
on Adult Levels of Education and Occupation

Variable	Specified contrast	First mean	Second mean	t value
Adult education	1-Gifted, High-Adapted Achievers ($n = 79$) >	6.33		
	2-Gifted, Low-Adapted Achievers ($n = 35$)		5.40	3.71**
	3-High-Adapted Overachievers ($n = 54$) >	5.56		
	4-Low-Adapted, Normal-Ability Underachievers ($n = 50$)		3.98	6.52**
	3-High-Adapted Overachievers ($n = 54$) >	5.56		
	2-Gifted, Low-Adapted Achievers ($n = 35$)		5.40	.58
Adult occupation	1-Gifted, High-Adapted Achievers ($n = 69$) >	4.24		
	2-Gifted, Low-Adapted Achievers ($n = 29$)		3.07	3.60**
	3-High-Adapted Overachievers ($n = 46$) >	3.72		
	4-Low-Adapted, Normal-Ability Underachievers ($n = 42$)		2.45	4.01**
	3-High-Adapted Overachievers ($n = 46$) >	3.72		
	2-Gifted, Low-Adapted Achievers ($n = 29$)		3.07	1.85*

Note: All p values one tailed.
*$p < .05$; **$p < .01$.

demically oriented university education. The measure of *occupational* level
in adulthood was an identically coded item asking respondents to state the
educational level required for their current job.

Predictions and Results

The results of the planned contrasts are presented in Table 11.1.

The High-Adapteds Versus the Low-Adapteds.   The first contrast specified that, given their high performance and high adaptation across adolescence, the Gifted, High-Adapted Achievers, would, in adulthood, exhibit
higher levels of both education and occupation than would the Gifted,
Low-Adapted Achievers, whose school adaptation had deteriorated considerably over time and whose relative standing on achievement measures had

also diminished somewhat by age 16. The results, which yielded a *t* value that was significant at the .0001 level for both adult outcomes, strongly supported these expectations.

The Overachievers Versus the Underachievers.   Second, if high adaptation to the academic environment and high self-perceived ability facilitate long-term achievement, and, to a certain extent, even compensate for somewhat low intelligence, then the High-Adapted Overachievers should have higher levels of adult education and occupation than those achieved by the Low-Adapted, Normal-Ability Underachievers. Again, the results demonstrated that the mean differences for both adult outcomes were significant at the .0001 level.

The Overachievers Versus the Low-Adapteds.   The third contrast further tested the crucial influence of females' adaptation to the school environment on their future life course, over and above the influence exerted by intelligence and achievement. We hypothesized that the adult educational and vocational levels of the High-Adapted Overachievers, whose intelligence mean was half a standard deviation below average, would exceed even those of the Gifted, Low-Adapted Achievers, whose intelligence mean was the highest of any of the age-16 subgroups and whose school achievement means were considerably higher than those of the Overachievers.

These final hypotheses comprised an especially stringent test of the meaningfulness we had ascribed to these particular subgroups. At age 26, the mean difference between the two subgroups' occupational level was significant at the .05 level. However, although the mean difference was in the expected direction, the result concerning adult educational level was not significant.

Across the Entire Sample

Because the foregoing analyses were constructed as individual *t* tests, differences in adult educational and occupational levels had not yet been investigated for the other age-16 subgroups. The next analyses used ANOVAs to do so. Among the members of the nine ability/adaptation subgroups defined at age 16, 391 provided data concerning their level of education at adulthood; 324 responded to the item concerning adult occupational level.

For these analyses no contrasts were specified in advance. Nevertheless, it was expected that if the differential ability/adaptation patterns carried long-term implications regarding future education and working life and if these consequences followed lawfully from the developmental processes suggested through our interpretations of the previous results, then a certain overall pattern would emerge.

The results of the analyses are presented in Table 11.2 and 11.3. The *F* ratios of both ANOVAs exceeded the .0001 level of significance.

TABLE 11.2
Individual Differences in Adult Educational Level

Age-16 ability/adaptation subgroup	Subgroup mean	Post hoc tests[a]
1-Gifted, High-Adapted Achievers (n = 35)	6.33	1 > all other subgroups
3-High-Adapted Overachievers (n = 54)	5.56	3 > 9, 8, 7, 4, 5
2-Gifted, Low-Adapted Achievers (n = 35)	5.40	2 > 9, 8, 7, 4, 5
6-Moderately Able Normals (n = 60)	5.38	6 > 9, 8, 7, 4, 5
5-Ability-Underestimating, High-Adapted Normals (n = 51)	4.22	5 > 9, 8, 7
4-Low-Adapted, Normal-Ability Underachievers (n = 50)	3.98	4 > 9, 8, 7
7-Moderately Adapted, Unrealistic, Low Achievers (n = 39)	3.46	7 > 9
8-Moderately Adapted, Realistic, Low Achievers (n = 35)	3.09	
9-Low-Adapted, Low-Ability Non-Achievers (n = 32)	2.69	

Note: Grand mean = 4.72, $F (8, 426) = 50.48$, $p < .0001$.
[a]$p \leq .05$.

The Low Achievers and the Non-Achievers

We generally expected the three lowest ability subgroups (Subgroups 7, 8, and 9) to show the lowest levels of education and occupation in young adulthood. However, within these subgroups, we expected that school adaptation and perceived ability at age 16 would have continued to exert an influence on adult outcomes. Thus, the girls who had been lowest in these characteristics in midadolescence (i.e., the Low-Adapted, Low-Ability Non-Achievers, Subgroup 9) were expected to exhibit the lowest means on both these adult criteria. This expectation was further bolstered by our knowledge that these girls had had low aspiration for continued schooling from early adolescence on and had consistently selected vocational, rather than academic, coursework.

In contrast, the Moderately Adapted, Unrealistic, Low Achievers' (Subgroup 7) level of self-perceived ability was disproportionately high in midadolescence, considering their low intelligence and achievement. These girls' academic self-confidence, in combination with their above-average school

TABLE 11.3
Individual Differences in Adult Occupational Level

Age-16 ability/adaptation subgroup	Subgroup mean	Post hoc tests[a]
1-Gifted, High-Adapted Achievers (n = 29)	4.25	1 > 9, 8, 7, 4, 5, 2, 6
3-High-Adapted Overachievers (n = 46)	3.72	3 > 9, 8, 7, 4, 5, 6
6-Moderately Able Normals (n = 51)	3.08	6 > 9, 8, 7
2-Gifted, Low-Adapted Achievers (n = 29)	3.07	2 > , 9, 8, 7
5-Ability-Underestimating, High-Adapted Normals (n = 47)	2.53	5 > 9
4-Low-Adapted, Normal-Ability Underachievers (n = 42)	2.45	4 > 9
7-Moderately Adapted, Unrealistic, Low Achievers (n = 27)	2.22	
8-Moderately Adapted, Realistic, Low Achievers (n = 26)	1.92	
9-Low-Adapted, Low-Ability Non-Achievers (n = 27)	1.48	

Note: Grand mean = 2.97, $F (8, 355) = 15.04$, $p < .0001$.
[a]$p \leq .05$.

adaptation, connoted a certain perseverance, even though they, too, were enrolled in "practical" coursework by Grade 9. Thus, the Unrealistic Low Achievers were expected to have the highest adult educational and occupational levels among the three low-ability subgroups. As Table 11.2 and 11.3 demonstrate, these expectations were confirmed.

The Normals

We applied a similar logic to the normal-ability subgroups. The girls whose achievement and self-perceived ability were consistent with their average intelligence at age 16 (the Moderately Able Normals, Subgroup 6) were expected to have the highest educational and occupational levels among the normally able subgroups, with the exception of the High-Adapted Overachievers, who, we already knew, ranked even higher than the high-ability girls who were low-adapted.

On the other hand, we expected that the Low-Adapted, Normal-Ability Underachievers (Subgroup 4)—the underachieving and low-adapted girls who had already underestimated their ability in early adolescence and had had low aspiration by age 16, the girls whose parents (on whom they were dependent in midadolescence but from whom they experienced disapproval) had also underestimated them, the girls who had had working friends and boyfriends by age 15—would display the lowest levels of adult education and occupation observed among the normal-ability subgroups. As Tables 11.2 and 11.3 demonstrate, these expectations were also confirmed.

The High Achievers

In midadolescence the Gifted, High-Adapted Achievers (Subgroup 1) had had good relationships with their parents, had come from homes in which the parents had believed in their daughter's capability, had not had boyfriends, had consistently selected academic courses, and had exhibited the same high aspiration for continued schooling that had characterized them in early adolescence. Moreover, we knew from the previous analyses that these girls were more educated and had a higher level of employment in adulthood than did the Gifted, Low-Adapted Achievers (Subgroup 2), who, by midadolescence, had reported conflicted relations with their parents and had exhibited low aspiration for further schooling, even though they were also enrolled in an academic curriculum. The results of the present analyses served only to verify that the gifted, high-adapted girls had the highest levels of education and occupation at age 26.

Summary

Our expectations in these analyses were based on developmental processes assumed to underlie the differential ability/adaptation patterns that characterized our subjects in midadolescence. The results supported these expectations.

Post hoc tests revealed, overall, that the highest adolescent achievers displayed significantly higher means on the adult criteria than did the moderately achieving adolescents. In turn, the moderate achievers had significantly higher adult levels of education and occupation than did the lowest achievers.

However, within these categories, girls' adaptation to the academic environment and their self-perceived ability were important aspects of the patterns that carried differential implications for adult consequences. In fact, the high-adapted, low-normal intelligence girls who were overachievers in midadolescence surpassed their highly intelligent but low-adapted counterparts in both adult outcomes (significantly so on the occupational level when only these two groups were compared). Finally, the adult educational and occupational consequences observed here were consistent with the subjects' aspiration and educational choices in midadolescence and with the inferences we have drawn from their family and peer relationships.

The Issue of Underemployment

One final issue arising from these analyses deserves mention. The relationship between subjects' adult educational level and the level of education required for the jobs they actually held in adulthood was strongly positive ($r = .74$). Nevertheless, the grand mean of adult educational level, across the sample, was 4.72, whereas the grand mean of the educational level the adult subjects needed to qualify for their present jobs was only 2.97.

The educational mean of 4.72 corresponded to having completed between 2 and 3 years, beyond compulsory school, of a "theoretical" gymnasium education consisting of an economics, a social studies, or a technical course of study. In Sweden, such an education is frequently considered adequate for a professional level of employment. On the other hand, the mean of 2.97, reflected in the *actual employment* level of the adult subjects, corresponded approximately to having completed a 2-year, post-compulsory school vocational course. The difference between the women's attained level of education and the level of education that was required for their present jobs was significant at the .0001 level [paired sample t (363) = 27.52].

Thus, although the strong positive relationship between these two adult criteria demonstrated that the most highly educated women tended to hold the jobs that required the most education (and the lowest educated held those that required the least), the women, as a whole, were underemployed. This finding was, of course, not exactly astonishing. Similar results have been documented in the literature for decades (see Betz & Fitzgerald, 1987, for a review). Still, it is interesting to note that, in the present sample, underemployment characterized even the Gifted, High-Adapted Achievers. Although this subgroup's adult educational mean of 6.33 was somewhat higher than that associated with having completed 3 years of formal schooling *beyond the gymnasium*, their occupation mean of 4.25 reflected that, on the average, they held positions which required only two years of a theoretical gymnasium course. This difference was also significant at the .0001 level [paired sample t (68) = 13.54].

OCCUPATIONAL COMMITMENT

Overview

The underemployment of our subjects in adulthood might well have been related to the fact that 26% of the adult women were working part time rather than full time. In Sweden, as elsewhere, job levels that carry the most responsibility and require the highest educational preparation tend to be held by full-time employees. Thus, our next analysis was designed to assess individual differences in women's *occupational commitment*, defined, quite simply, as the time they actually devoted to the workplace.

The influence of occupational commitment on females' actualizing their career-achievement potential is *implied* by Card, Steel and Abeles' (1980) longitudinal investigation. Their study of high-ability males and females reported that 11 years after high school (when the subjects were about the same age as ours in adulthood), women were less likely than men to be employed full time. They also had less prestigious, lower paying jobs than the men did, but in light of our argument in chapter 10 concerning society's devaluation of traditional female careers, we would not interpret this finding as *necessarily* reflecting that women had not realized their potential.

In any case, one explanation that Card et al. (1980) suggested to account for women's lower occupational prestige is that women must juggle a variety of roles. And, indeed, it is almost a truism, in Sweden as in the United States, that when women attempt to combine family and employment, they often do so by working only part time. Thus, full-time employment might be said to connote a higher degree of commitment to occupational achievement.

Our definition of occupational commitment is somewhat reminiscent of Richardson's (1974) concept of career orientation. Richardson has distinguished between *career*-oriented women, who focus on achieving vocational goals, and *work*-oriented women, who seek to combine employment with family responsibilities. We have collapsed this distinction into a single measure of our subjects' actual work behavior in young adulthood. Specifically, we established three categories of occupational commitment: full-time employment, part-time employment, and no paid employment. Using an EXACON analysis ($N = 363$), we then tested for differential relationships between midadolescents' patterns of ability and adaptation and their commitment to working life.

It might be remembered that our measures of educational aspiration across adolescence focused on girls' indicating how much education they were willing to pursue in order to be accepted into an occupation they saw as desirable (see chapters 7 and 9). Therefore, our first assumption in the present analysis was that females whose career paths through midadolescence had reflected a strong aspiration toward advanced education, as well as the academic self-confidence and the adaptation to academic demands necessary to pursue such an education, would be more likely than other females to be employed full time in young adulthood. Conversely, we expected that girls who had not displayed these characteristics in adolescence were more likely to be employed part time or not at all at age 26.

Results and Discussion

Of the 27 cells in the EXACON contingency table (the nine age-16 ability/ adaptation subgroups X the three categories of occupational commitment), five were significant at the .05 level or higher. These five cells, all of which reflected our general assumptions, are depicted in Table 11.4.

TABLE 11.4
Significant Differences in Adult Occupational Commitment

Subgroup name	More than expected were	Fewer than expected were
1-Gifted, High-Adapted Achievers (n = 61)	Working full time* (n = 42, out of 209 full timers)	
3-High-Adapted Overachievers (n = 46)	Working full time** (n = 34, out of 209 full timers)	Working part time* (n = 7, out of 106 part timers)
4-Low-Adapted, Normal-Ability Underachievers (n = 40)	Working part time* (n = 17, out of 106 part timers)	
8-Moderately Adapted, Realistic, Low Achievers (n = 30)		Working full time** (n = 11, out of 209 full timers)

Note: The EXACON sample size was 363.
*p < .05; **p < .01.

Strong Occupational Commitment

First, with respect to females who had a full-time occupational commitment outside the home, a higher than expected number of Gifted, High-Adapted Achievers (Subgroup 1) and of High-Adapted Overachievers (Subgroup 3) were employed full time at age 26. Moreover, a lower than expected number of the High-Adapted Overachievers were working only part time.

These two subgroups of individuals had exhibited the highest levels of aspiration observed among the subjects at age 16. Their school adaptation and self-perceived ability were also higher than those of any of the other midadolescents, in spite of the fact that the intelligence and achievement levels of the Overachievers fell far below those of the Gifted High-Adapteds. Thus, the results once again demonstrated the substantial long-term positive impact of adolescent school adaptation, academic self-confidence, and aspiration on occupational commitment in adulthood.

Less Strong Occupational Commitment

The opposite outcome characterized women whose self-perceived ability had been low in early adolescence, despite their normal intelligence and achievement, and who, by midadolescence, had exhibited low achievement, low school adaptation, and low aspiration, as well as low self-perceived ability (i.e., the Low-Adapted, Normal-Ability Underachievers, Subgroup 4): A higher than expected number of the Underachievers were employed only part time. Everything we have mentioned previously concerning these individuals, from their parents' underestimating their academic capability in early adolescence to their associations with working friends and boy-friends at age 15, formed a lawful continuity with their not displaying strong occupational commitment in young adulthood.

Last, considering the low levels of aspiration and self-perceived ability exhibited by the Moderately Adapted, Realistic, Low Achievers (Subgroup 8) at age 16, it was also reasonable that a lower than expected number of these individuals were employed full time at age 26. As stated previously, the somewhat above-average school adaptation these subjects had exhibited in midadolescence might well have been due to their having enrolled in a nonacademic, vocational curriculum by age 16. In this case, ability, too, surely played a role in the adult outcome, given that these women had exhibited extremely low intelligence in midadolescence.

OCCUPATIONAL AREA

Question

The next question we asked was whether or not the subjects' midadolescent patterns of ability and adaptation were related to the occupational areas in which they were employed at age 26. We have already seen, from the results presented in chapter 10, that more of our total sample (35%) were employed in the area designated as "deep contact," which included the medical, educational, social science, and social work occupations, than in any of the other seven categories.[1] The second most popular area (20%) was office work, which included secretarial and clerical occupations. The question of differential selection of occupational areas was addressed through an EX-ACON ($N = 367$).

Our expectation in this analysis was fairly conservative. That is, given our knowledge of the women's employment as a whole, we did not expect many individual differences to emerge among subjects for whom we had both ability/adaptation data in midadolescence and occupational data in adulthood. However, we did predict that the high-ability girls who had exhibited the highest aspiration and school adaptation across adolescence, and had been enrolled in academic coursework throughout compulsory school (i.e., the Gifted, High-Adapted Achievers), would be the only female adults overrepresented among the *technical and natural science* occupations. This area included engineering, architecture, dentistry, natural science research, and technical support jobs, such as mechanical and electrical technician.

---

[1]The *nine* occupational areas coded for the sample were: deep contact; office; technical and natural science; industry (factory) and trades; business and accounting; communication and military; outdoor work, farming, and animal care; service contact; and creative, artistic.

TABLE 11.5
Significant Differences in Adult Occupational Area

Subgroup name	More than expected were employed in
1-Gifted, High-Adapted Achievers (n = 69)	Technical/natural science** (n = 7, out of 14 in technical jobs)
4-Low-Adapted, Normal-Ability Underachievers (n = 43)	Industry/trade* (n = 7, out of 27 in industry jobs)
9-Low-Adapted, Low-Ability Non-Achievers (n = 27)	Industry/trade*** (n = 8, out of 27 in industry jobs)

Note: The EXACON sample size was 367.
*$p < .05$; **$p < .01$; ***$p < .001$.

Results

The results justified our conservatism while supporting our single prediction. Among the 81 cells in the EXACON contingency table (nine subgroups X nine occupational areas), only 3 were significant at the .05 level or higher. These 3 cells are described in Table 11.5.

First, as predicted, the Gifted, High-Adapted Achievers (Subgroup 1) were significantly overrepresented among the occupations that comprised the *technical and natural science* area. In fact, half of all the women whose jobs fell into this category had been Gifted, High-Adapted Achievers in midadolescence.

Second, the *industry and trade area*, which was composed of factory jobs and trades such as carpentry, masonry, house-painting, and short-order cooking, employed a higher than expected number of women who, in midadolescence, had had low aspiration for continued schooling, low adaptation to academic demands, and low academic achievement. Specifically, both the Low-Adapted, Normal-Ability Underachievers (Subgroup 4) and the Low-Adapted, Low-Ability Non-Achievers (Subgroup 9) were overrepresented among these jobs, which required no academic education beyond compulsory school.

PROFESSIONAL STATUS

Issue

The next investigation of our subjects' occupations in adulthood considered the issue of *professional status*, defined in terms of the education required by different jobs. Knowing that the largest number of the adult women in our sample were employed in either deep contact or office occupations, we looked for differences in the status of jobs held by the individuals employed within these two areas.

We expected, generally, that the highest status jobs within the deep contact and the office areas would be held by women with strong occupational commitment (i.e., by women who were working full time). We refer, of course, to the individuals who had been Gifted, High-Adapted Achievers or High-Adapted Overachievers in midadolescence and displayed the highest levels of achievement across occupational areas in adulthood. (see Table 11.3).

As we have emphasized in previous discussions, these subjects' high self-perceived ability, their high aspiration, and their high adaptation to academic demands throughout adolescence all pointed to their achieving a high occupational status in adulthood. In addition, the Gifted, High-Adapted Achievers had exhibited high intelligence and high levels of achievement throughout adolescence. In contrast, we expected women who had been characterized by midadolescent patterns that did not incorporate these attributes to be significantly overrepresented in lower status occupations.

We assessed overrepresentations (and underrepresentations) of the nine age-16 ability/adaptation subgroups among nine occupational categories in the deep contact area through an EXACON analysis ($N = 157$). A second EXACON tested the nine ability/adaptation subgroups in relation to six categories of office occupations ($N = 90$).

Results and Discussion

No individual differences with respect to subjects' occupational status emerged within the office area. Among the 54 cells tested, none was significant at the .05 level. This lack of differentiation may have been due to the fact that none of the job categories included in this area (e.g., secretary, general office worker, telephone operator, custodian) required a high level of educational preparation.

Within the deep contact area, however, we observed individual differences that supported our expectations. Nine of the 81 cells tested were significant at the .05 level or higher. These cells are depicted in Table 11.6.

The Gifted, High-Adapted Achievers (Subgroup 1)

Overrepresentations. The High-Adapted Achievers, as adults, were overrepresented in occupations that required a university education and underrepresented in occupations that required no formal, academic schooling past compulsory school. That fully half of the teachers in the sample had belonged to this high-aspiring subgroup in midadolescence was reminiscent of Jenkins' (1987) U.S. finding that female college seniors' need for achievement was positively related, 14 years later, to their having pursued a career in teaching.

The other occupation in which the High-Adapted Achievers were over-

TABLE 11.6
Significant Differences in Adult Professional Status

Subgroup name	More than expected were employed as a	Fewer than expected were employed as a
1-Gifted, High-Adapted Achievers (n = 32)	Teacher** (n = 9, out of 18) Physical therapist** (n = 3, out of 3)	Hospital orderly*** (n = 4, out of 56) Day-care mother* (n = 1, out of 20)
2-Gifted, Low-Adapted Achievers (n = 11)	Social worker or psychologist* (n = 2, out of 5)	
3-High-Adapted Overachievers (n = 20)	Nurse* (n = 7, out of 27)	Day-care mother* (n = 0, out of 20)
8-Moderately Adapted, Realistic, Low Achievers (n = 15)	Hospital orderly* (n = 9, out of 56) Day-care mother* (n = 5, out of 20)	

Note: The EXACON sample size was 157.
$*p \leq .05$; $**p \leq .01$; $***p \leq .001$.

represented was that of physical therapist, which required the near equivalent of a university degree, although, in Sweden, the physical therapy education is offered in a special school. All three of the physical therapists in the adult sample had been Gifted High-Adapteds in midadolescence.

Last, we might note that there was one physician in the adult female sample. She, too, had been a Gifted, High-Adapted Achiever in midadolescence. The dearth of female physicians might have been attributable to the length of the education required for medical doctors. Because a medical education is especially long by Swedish standards (4 years of gymnasium, followed by more than 4 years of university), many students take time off to work during the course of their studies. Thus, age 26 may be too early to evaluate whether or not a significantly high number of Gifted, High-Adapted Achievers would eventually become physicians.

Underrepresentations. As also expected, in adulthood the Gifted, High-Adapted Achievers were underrepresented among occupations that required virtually no academic preparation. Specifically, they were underrepresented among hospital orderlies and day-care mothers.

The Gifted, Low-Adapted Achievers (Subgroup 2)

The Gifted, Low-Adapted Achievers were overrepresented among the social worker/psychologist occupation in adulthood. This result was rather surprising, considering that the education for these occupations required a university degree and that the Low-Adapteds had had low aspiration for continued schooling by age 16, despite their unanimous enrollment in the academic curriculum. However, given their high intelligence and their high academic achievement across adolescence, they were certainly capable of successfully completing the necessary preparation for these jobs.

The High-Adapted Overachievers (Subgroup 3)

In adulthood, the High-Adapted Overachievers were overrepresented among the nurses and underrepresented among the day-care mothers. Because nursing required the equivalent of a university degree from a hospital nursing school, whereas being a day-care mother required minimal training, these results were consistent with our expectations. In addition, we might mention that, although the cell did not reflect a significant overrepresentation, the second highest number of teachers were observed among the women who had been Overachievers in midadolescence ($n = 4$).

The Moderately Adapted, Realistic, Low Achievers (Subgroup 8)

Finally, in a lawful continuation of the low aspiration, low intelligence and achievement, and low self-perceived ability that characterized the Moderately Adapted, Realistic, Low Achievers in midadolescence, these individuals were overrepresented among the hospital orderlies and the day-care mothers in adulthood. In fact, 14 out of 15 women from this midadolescent subgroup were employed in one of these two occupations.

A RETROSPECTIVE LOOK AT LOW OCCUPATIONAL ACHIEVEMENT

Question

Before leaving the differential issues connected with our subjects' occupations in adulthood, we conducted a brief retrospective analysis aimed at identifying social factors in midadolescence that might have been associated with low occupational achievement in adulthood. We already knew that a significantly high number of the girls whose achievement had declined over the adolescent period, despite their normal intelligence (i.e., the age-16 Low-Adapted, Normal-Ability Underachievers, Subgroup 4), had had boyfriends and working peers at age 15. As discussed previously, association with such peers was assumed to have interacted with the Underachievers' low aspiration for continued education, thereby contributing to the various low educational and occupational outcomes we have observed for these girls in adulthood (see Tables 11.1–11.5)

We have now observed that other midadolescent girls characterized by low achievement, low self-perceived ability, and low aspiration (and, in this case, by low intelligence) also had low educational and occupational status in adulthood: specifically, the Moderately Adapted, Realistic, Low Achievers (Subgroup 8) and the Low-Adapted, Low-Ability Non-Achievers (Subgroup 9), virtually all of whom had been enrolled in a vocational curriculum by age 16. Therefore, it seemed reasonable to ask whether or not they, too, had had working (or older) friends—and boyfriends—in midadolescence.

This question was answered through three EXACONS. The ability/adaptation subgroups variable was collapsed into three categories: Subgroups 1–7, Subgroup 8, and Subgroup 9. The peer and boyfriend variables were coded as described in chapter 9.

Results

The EXACON tests regarding older peers ($N = 439$) and boyfriends ($N = 436$) yielded no cells that were significant at the .05 level. However, the results of the EXACON concerning working peers ($N = 439$) yielded significant results regarding the Low-Adapted, Low-Ability Non-Achievers (Subgroup 9):

1. A higher than expected number of the Low-Adapted, Low-Ability Non-Achievers had two or more working peers in midadolescence ($p < .001$).
2. A lower than expected number of the Low-Adapted, Low-Ability Non-Achievers had no working peers in midadolescence ($p = .0001$).

It might also be recalled here that, in chapter 9, the Non-Achievers were the only subgroup who demonstrated a noteworthy association with early biological maturation. Thus, these results replicate Stattin and Magnusson's (1990) findings regarding the peer networks that characterize girls who, biologically speaking, are "ahead of their time."

Aside from the issue of biological maturation, the results of the analysis involving working peers were the same for the Non-Achievers as they had previously been for the Underachievers. Therefore, we might conclude that association with working peers in midadolescence exerted the same negative influence on adult occupational outcomes for the lowest achievers in the sample as it did for the normally able girls who had "developed" a pattern of underachievement by age 16.

SOME CONCLUSIONS REGARDING WOMEN'S EMPLOYMENT

An Overall Pattern of Career Involvement

The foregoing results concerning individual differences in women's employment all supported the same overall conclusion: The developmental path to career investment begins early. A consistent configuration of high academic self-confidence, high adaptation to academic demands, and high aspiration to complete the schooling required for high-level jobs—across adolescence—appeared to constitute a *prerequisite* for individuals' high occupational achievement in adulthood. In our further discussions we refer to this configuration as an *overall pattern of career involvement*.

This basic finding held true regardless of the adult outcome being assessed, whether it was women's educational or occupational level, their occupational commitment, the areas in which they were employed, or their professional status within a given area. Although high intelligence and high academic achievement certainly played a positive role in adult career achievement when these attributes were *combined* with the prerequisite pattern, *in the absence of this pattern*, "intellectual giftedness" was significantly associated with high occupational achievement for only one result of one analysis (see the Gifted, *Low-Adapted* Achievers in Table 11.6)

An Overall Pattern of Noncareer Involvement

In contrast, midadolescents who had been characterized by an *opposite* configuration (i.e., by low academic self-confidence, low adaptation to academic demands, and low aspiration to complete the schooling required for high-level jobs), might be said to have exhibited an *overall pattern of noncareer involvement*. In adulthood, these individuals were not strongly committed to employment and had not achieved high job status. Moreover, generally speaking, such adult consequences were just as characteristic of normal-ability girls who had become underachievers by the end of compulsory school as they were of girls whose actual potential for academic success had been quite low in midadolescence. Finally, a retrospective look at these individuals' peer contacts in midadolescence further emphasized that their paths were unlikely to lead to professional careers.

ADULT EDUCATIONAL COMMITMENT

Expected Individual Differences

As we stated in connection with the observation that only one woman in our sample was employed as a physician, age 26 might be a bit early to judge females' differential occupational achievements. In Sweden it is not uncommon for young people to work for a few years after gymnasium or during university, before completing their university education. Furthermore, given that 71% of the entire sample of females were married or living with a man by age 26, it seemed possible that even the most career-involved females might have temporarily relaxed their occupational strivings at some point following compulsory school.

TABLE 11.7
Significant Differences in Adult Educational Commitment

Subgroup name	More than expected were	Fewer than expected were
1-Gifted, High-Adapted Achievers (n = 37)		Not studying* (n = 17, out of 116 nonstudents)
9-Low-Adapted, Low-Ability Non-Achievers (n = 13)	Not studying** (n = 13, out of 116 nonstudents)	Studying full time** (n = 0, out of 54 full-time students)

Note: The EXACON sample size was 185.
*$p < .05$; **$p < .01$.

If a certain rhythm between commitment to education and commitment to other areas of life *differentially* characterized our subjects in young adulthood, we would expect that women who had displayed an overall pattern of career involvement in adolescence might well have returned to their studies by the time the adult questionnaire was administered. Moreover, we would expect the *academic level* of their chosen curriculum to be quite high.

Conversely, we would expect that women who had displayed an overall pattern of noncareer involvement in midadolescence would not, by and large, be pursuing further education in young adulthood. However, among those who were, a significant number would be expected to be enrolled in low academic levels, because we know that the non career-involved individuals had selected themselves out of the most academically rigorous curricula during adolescence. In other words, it was unlikely that, in terms of education, these subjects would have matched their career-involved counterparts by age 26. We tested these expectations through EXACON analyses.

Results and Discussion

Studying Versus Not Studying

The first EXACON ($N = 185$) assessed the nine age-16 ability/adaptation subgroups' associations and nonassociations with three categories of educational commitment at age 26: (a) studying full time, (b) studying part time, and (c) not studying at all. The significant results ($p < .05$) of the first analysis are shown in Table 11.7.

The Students. The alert reader might have noted that a substantial number of adult respondents failed to complete the adult questionnaire item regarding their current educational commitment. Nevertheless, the results obtained from our most "conscientious" subjects were consistent with our expectations. A lower than expected number of the Gifted, High-Adapted Achievers (Subgroup 1), who had exhibited an overall pattern of career involvement across adolescence, were not enrolled in educational programs in adulthood.

More direct support for our expectation, in the form of a higher than expected number of these individuals' being enrolled in full-time study was also observed, although the result was not significant at the .05 level ($p = .07$). Still, it might be worth noting that 15 out of the 37 Gifted, High-Adapteds (40%) were studying full time at age 26 and that they accounted for 27% of the full-time students, the highest percentage contributed by any of the age-16 subgroups.

The Nonstudents.   In contrast, a higher than expected number of the Low-Adapted, Low-Ability Non-Achievers (Subgroup 9), who had exhibited an overall pattern of noncareer involvement across adolescence, were not pursuing further education in young adulthood. In fact, none of them was enrolled in an educational program, full or part time, at age 26.

This significant finding led us to explore one additional issue. Specifically, data from the Adult Questionnaire had provided information concerning the reasons women gave for not pursuing their studies in young adulthood. We surmised that, given their consistent pattern of noncareer involvement, in combination with their low intelligence and extremely low adolescent achievement, the Low-Adapted, Low-Ability Non-Achievers would be significantly overrepresented among one particular category of responses: namely, not thinking themselves capable of completing further academic requirements.

We tested this expectation with an EXACON ($N = 436$), in which the nine ability/adaptation subgroups comprised the first set of categories and agreement versus nonagreement with this reason comprised the second. (All of the women who *were* in school had *disagreed*, of course, as had nearly everyone else.)

The results supported our exploratory conjecture. Only 14 women gave low academic self-confidence, or low self-efficacy in Bandura's (1977, 1989) parlance, as a reason for not continuing their education. Among them, four had been Low-Adapted, Low-Ability Non-Achievers in midadolescence ($p = .01$). No other subgroup of midadolescents was significantly associated with this adult response.

Academic Level of Current Studies

The next EXACON ($N = 57$) tested our suggestion that, among the adults who were pursuing further studies, a significant number of individuals who in adolescence had exhibited an overall pattern of career involvement would be enrolled at high academic levels. Conversely, a significant

TABLE 11.8
Significant Differences in Academic Level of Adult Studies

Subgroup name	More than expected were enrolled in a
1-Gifted, High-Adapted Achievers (n = 19)	University course of 4 years or more* (n = 6, out of 9 such students) University course of 3 years** (n = 5, out of 6 such students)
4-Low-Adapted, Normal-Ability Underachievers (n = 6)	Two-year vocational course* (n = 3, out of 8 such students)

Note: The EXACON sample size was 57.
*p < .05; **p < .01.

number of individuals who had been noncareer-involved would be enrolled at low academic levels.

In this analysis we assessed the associations (but not the nonassociations) of the nine ability/adaptation subgroups with six academic levels—ranging from a 2-year "practical" or vocational course to a university course of 4 or more years. The significant results ($p < .05$) are presented in Table 11.8.

High-Academic Studies.   In line with our framework, a higher than expected number of Gifted, High-Adapted Achievers (Subgroup 1) were overrepresented among the young adult women who were enrolled in a university course of 4 or more years' duration and among women enrolled in a 3-year university program. Moreover, we might also note that the remaining three women who were enrolled in a university course of 4 or more years, were all High-Adapted Overachievers. This overrepresentation was not significant at the .05 level ($p = .10$); however, it did tend to support the validity of our overall-pattern-of-career-involvement concept because the Overachievers demonstrated this pattern across adolescence, without exhibiting the high intelligence and achievement that accompanied it for the Gifted High-Adapteds.

Low Academic Studies.   Last, an interesting result emerged concerning the girls who had underestimated their academic ability in early adolescence and had become underachievers by midadolescence (i.e., the Low-Adapted, Normal-Ability Underachievers, Subgroup 4). We have discussed previously that these girls' overall pattern of noncareer-involvement carried strong implications for their not exhibiting high educational or occupational status in adulthood, despite their normal intelligence. We have also discussed a variety of factors, from midadolescent peer contacts to conflicts with parents who had underestimated their capability, that were associated with these individuals' development across the time of our investigation.

From the results of the present analysis, we see that, by age 26, a few of the Underachievers had returned to school. But in lawful consequence of what had gone before, these young women were now in the position of having to play "catch up." They were significantly overrepresented only among the young women who were enrolled in a 2-year vocational program, and none of them was enrolled in any program higher than a 2-year academic gymnasium curriculum.

A LAST RETROSPECTIVE LOOK

With the lawful continuity of the adult occupational and educational results in mind, we addressed two final questions:

1. In adulthood, were our subjects' summary evaluations of their school experience consistent with their overall patterns of career (or noncareer) involvement in adolescence, especially with respect to their adolescent school adaptation?
2. Had the women who had exhibited an overall pattern of career involvement across adolescence firmly decided on their adult life course while they were in compulsory school, whereas the noncareer-involved adolescents had been less certain of their future plans?

Evaluation of School Experience

Method

The first question was answered through an ANOVA that tested the age-16 ability/adaptation subgroups' differential mean response to a single item on the Adult Questionnaire: "Did you like attending compulsory school?". The item was coded from "almost never" (1) to "almost always" (5).

Results and Discussion

The results, which are presented in Table 11.9, displayed significant individual differences [$F(8, 425) = 11.49$, $p < .0001$], although the grand mean of 3.93 reflected that, on the average, subjects recalled that they had liked school almost at the level of "for the most part" (coded as 4). Nonetheless, the individual differences that emerged were consistent with the subjects' differential school adaptation in midadolescence and with our definition of overall patterns of career and noncareer involvement that extended across adolescence.

Extreme Reactions and Highest Consistency.   Duncan post hoc tests showed that, in adulthood, individuals who had reported the highest levels of school adaptation across adolescence, as well as exhibiting an overall pattern of career involvement, reported the most favorable evaluations of their school experience. That is, the midadolescent Gifted, High-Adapted

TABLE 11.9
Individual Differences in Retrospective Evaluation of Compulsory School

Age-16 ability/adaptation subgroup	Subgroup mean	Post hoc tests[a]
1-Gifted, High-Adapted Achievers	4.48	1 > 9, 4, 8, 7, 2, 6, 5
3-High-Adapted Overachievers	4.28	3 > 9, 4, 8, 7
5-Ability-Underestimating, High-Adapted Normals	4.16	5 > 9, 4, 8
6-Moderately Able Normals	4.10	6 > 9, 4, 8
2-Gifted, Low-Adapted Achievers	4.09	2 > 9, 4, 8
7-Moderately Adapted, Unrealistic, Low Achievers	3.87	7 > 9
8-Moderately Adapted, Realistic, Low Achievers	3.58	
4-Low-Adapted, Normal-Ability Underachievers	3.54	
9-Low-Adapted, Low-Ability Non-Achievers	3.32	

Note: Grand mean = 3.93 $F (8, 425) = 11.49, p < .0001$.
[a]$p \leq .05$.

Achievers (Subgroup 1) evaluated their schooldays significantly more favorably than did any other subgroup except the High-Adapted Overachievers (Subgroup 3).

Moreover, in adulthood, both the Gifted High-Adapteds and the Overachievers had a significantly fonder memory of compulsory school than that reported by individuals who, in midadolescence, had exhibited an overall pattern of noncareer involvement. In fact, the most strikingly noncareer-involved midadolescents, namely, the Low-Adapted, Low-Ability Non-Achievers (Subgroup 9) and the Low-Adapted, Normal-Ability Underachievers (Subgroup 4), reported the least favorable evaluation of compulsory school. These results suggested that subjects who had experienced the most extreme reactions to their years of compulsory schooling—whether these reactions were positive or negative—gave retrospective evaluations of their experience that were the most consistent with the evaluations they had made when they were in the actual school environment.

Less Extreme Reactions and Lower Consistency.   For other individuals, the retrospective accounts were not quite so consistent with the school adaptation these subjects had reported in midadolescence. Among the Gifted, *Low-Adapted* Achievers (Subgroup 2), for example, high ability might have offset low school adaptation in midadolescence, with respect to the overall memory these women retained concerning their school experience—a sort of "I got through it okay, so how bad could it have been?" strategy for encoding one's "personal story" of school life. Thus, their recollection was that, for the most part, they had liked school fine.

On the other hand, individuals who had exhibited relatively positive school adaptation in midadolescence, despite their low ability (i.e., the Moderately Adapted, Realistic, Low Achievers, Subgroup 8, and the Moderately Adapted, Unrealistic, Low Achievers, Subgroup 7), reported relatively negative recollections in adulthood, compared to the recollections reported by other subgroups. We have suggested elsewhere that the moderately positive school adaptation these subjects displayed in midadolescence might have been due to their having selected themselves out of an academic curriculum by age 16, rather than to their having experienced a "fit" to academic demands per se. If so, it was not unreasonable that, as adults, they would report a less favorable than average *summary* evaluation of the 9 years they had spent in compulsory school.

Comments.   What we imply through this discussion is that the consistency between subjects' current and retrospective evaluations of an experience, to the extent that such consistency can be demonstrated, is moderated by the *salience* the individual attaches to the experience: Consistency will be higher when the experience was especially salient than when it was not. However, in the interest of a preserving a healthy skepticism, we might also note that second author of this volume has been heard to remark, on occasion, that the only retrospective item on which subjects' responses are free from selective memory is the question, "How many times have you been married?"

Early Crystallization of the Career-Involvement Pattern

In chapter 7 we observed that the post-compulsory school plans of girls characterized by high intelligence and high achievement at age 13 were significantly more definite (i.e., more crystallized) than the plans of their less intelligent and low-achieving counterparts. In the following analysis we addressed the issue of early crystallization again, this time in relation to individuals' overall pattern of career involvement, as we defined it earlier. Although this pattern is certainly not antithetical to high intelligence and high achievement, we have seen from the adult career achievements of the High-Adapted Overachievers that high ability per se was less important to achievement by age 16 than it had been at age 13.

We expected that women who, past age 13, had fit comfortably into the first developmental program that society encourages, that of succeeding in the academic environment, would have firmly decided, during their compulsory school years, that they would continue their education. In other words, having been presented, early on, with an option that was acceptable, career-involved girls would, in fact accept it. However, for women who had been noncareer-involved in midadolescence, this first option had not been

TABLE 11.10
Individual Differences in Early Crystallization of
Post-Compulsory-School Plans

Age-16 ability/adaptation subgroup	Subgroup mean	Post hoc tests[a]
1-Gifted, High-Adapted Achievers	3.97	1 > 9, 7, 4, 6
2-Gifted, Low-Adapted Achievers	3.91	2 > 9, 7
3-High-Adapted Overachievers	3.83	3 > 9, 7
5-Ability-Underestimating, High-Adapted Normals	3.78	5 > 9, 7
8-Moderately Adapted, Realistic, Low Achievers	3.56	
6-Moderately Able Normals	3.55	6 > 9
4-Low-Adapted, Normal-Ability Underachievers	3.42	
7 Moderately Adapted, Unrealistic, Low Achievers	3.24	
9-Low-Adapted, Low-Ability Non-Achievers	3.00	

Note: Grand mean = 3.58 F (8, 425) = 3.95, $p < .001$.
[a]$p \leq .05$.

acceptable. Thus, in adulthood, they would report that their future plans had still been uncertain at the end of compulsory school.

Method

These expectations were tested through an ANOVA that assessed the age-16 ability/adaptation subgroups' differential mean response on another item from the Adult Questionnaire: "By the time you completed compulsory school, did you have definite plans about what to do after Grade 9?". The item was coded from "no plans at all" (1) to "quite definite plans" (5).

We should note that the item asked the extent to which plans had been decided by the end of compulsory school, not what the plans actually were. However, because we now knew the differential paths chosen by the individuals who had been career-involved versus noncareer-involved at age 16, the wording of the item posed no problem.

Results and Discussion

An overall examination of the means indicated that, in adulthood, *none* of the subgroups reported having been less than "somewhat uncertain" (coded as 3) concerning their future plans while they were in compulsory school. Nonetheless, the results, shown in Table 11.10, again displayed a significant differential pattern that reflected our expectations [F(8, 425) = 3.95, $p < .001$].

In this analysis, we were primarily interested in *four* subgroups of individuals:

1. the individuals who had exhibited an overall pattern of career involvement across adolescence and had continued their education well past compulsory school (i.e., the Gifted, High-Adapted Achievers, Subgroup 1, and the High-Adapted Overachievers, Subgroup 3), and
2. the individuals who had exhibited an overall pattern of non-career involvement and had not pursued advanced academic coursework (i.e., the Low-Adapted, Normal-Ability Underachievers, Subgroup 4, and the Low-Adapted, Low-Ability Non-Achievers, Subgroup 9).

In line with our predictions, both the Gifted High-Adapteds and the Overachievers reported, in adulthood, that their plans (to pursue further education) had been well-established by the end of compulsory school. In contrast, post hoc tests revealed that the adults who had been Non-Achievers and Underachievers (and had not pursued an education) had, at age 16, been significantly less certain of their plans than their career-involved counterparts had been. Thus, early crystallization of plans characterized the career-involved individuals significantly more than it did the noncareer-involved subjects.

Nevertheless, we should note that firmly decided plans in midadolescence were also reported by the Gifted, *Low-Adapted* Achievers (Subgroup 2) in adulthood. This result constituted something of an anomaly: These women had had high self-perceived ability across adolescence. Moreover, as discussed in chapter 7, they had had high *aspiration* and firmly decided plans at *age 13*. Yet, by age 16 they had lacked both the high adaptation and the high aspiration that were integral components of the *overall pattern of career involvement*. Furthermore, their levels of adult educational and occupational achievement were lower than those of the Overachievers.

Further, we know that in midadolescence these subjects had been quite dependent on (although not in harmony with) their parents, who, in turn, were highly educated and had placed a high value on their daughter's education. Perhaps as a result of parental pressure, the Gifted Low-Adapteds had all been enrolled in a pre-academic-gymnasium curriculum in Grade 9. With this background in mind, it might therefore be reasonable to assume that the Gifted Low-Adapteds had, in fact, been prepared to continue school at age 16, despite their apparent disinclination to do so, and that their plans had shifted subsequently—for example, after they had left home. (An alternative explanation, of course, is that by age 16 they had firmly decided on a specific plan that did not include an academic education, parental expectations and early adolescent aspiration notwithstanding.)

PERSONAL LIVES IN ADULTHOOD—MARRIAGE AND CHILDREN

The next series of analyses concerns individual differences in our subjects' personal life situations at age 26. Our purpose was to investigate personal domains in which individuals might differ in adulthood, depending on their overall pattern of career involvement or noncareer involvement in adolescence. (As defined earlier, individuals who had displayed *an overall pattern of career involvement* had, across adolescence, exhibited high academic self-confidence, high adaptation to academic demands, and high aspiration to complete the schooling required for high-level jobs—with or without high levels of intelligence and achievement. The opposite configuration characterized individuals whom we have designated as having exhibited an *overall pattern of noncareer involvement.*)

Marriage

Expected Individual Differences

We know from chapter 10 that 71% of our adult sample were either married or living with a man by age 26. This statistic reflected the women's general orientation toward relatedness, an issue we have discussed in the previous chapter. Nevertheless, we expected that subjects who had been career-involved in adolescence would constitute a higher than expected number of the women who were not committed to a live-in relationship in young adulthood. Conversely, we predicted that a higher than expected number of noncareer involved subjects *would* have such relationships.

Observed Individual Differences

The results of an EXACON ($N = 435$) partially supported our predictions. The two significant cells are presented in Table 11.11

The individuals who comprised one of the subgroups that had been particularly noncareer-involved across adolescence (i.e., the Low-Adapted, Low-Ability Non-Achievers, Subgroup 9) were significantly overrepresented among the married women. In addition, if one accepts our earlier argument that the somewhat positive school adaptation exhibited by the Moderately Adapted, Realistic, Low Achievers (Subgroup 8) reflected their successful avoidance of an academic curriculum by age 16, rather than their "fit" to academic requirements per se, these subjects, too, had exhibited an overall pattern of noncareer involvement. In adulthood, they were also overrepresented among the married subjects.

TABLE 11.11
Significant Differences in Adult Marital Status

Subgroup name	More than expected were
8-Moderately-Adapted, Realistic, Low Achievers (n = 36)	Married** (n = 32, out of 303 married subjects)
9-Low-Adapted, Low-Ability Non-Achievers (n = 31)	Married* (n = 17, out of 303 married subjects)

Note: The EXACON sample size was 435.
*p = .05; **p < .01.

Children

Expected Individual Differences

Although the previous analysis showed no significant association between having exhibited an overall pattern of career involvement in adolescence and being single in young adulthood, we knew from the results of chapter 10 that 54% of our adult sample had not yet given birth by age 26. Therefore, we expected pronounced individual differences to emerge with respect to childbearing. Our predictions were consistent with those stated earlier: A higher than expected number of career-involved adolescents would have no children in adulthood, whereas a higher than expected number of noncareer-involved adolescents would have given birth to at least one child by age 26.

Observed Individual Differences

In Adulthood.   The EXACON ($N = 435$) testing these predictions assessed five categories of childbearing, from having no children at age 26 to having four children. The significant results are shown in Table 11.12

It might be noted, first, that the individuals who were significantly over- or underrepresented in the various categories of adult childbearing were, to a great extent, the same individuals who displayed differences in adult occupational commitment (see Table 11.4). Moreover, the patterns of differences observed in the two analyses were complementary. Thus, the present analysis supported our definition of occupational commitment as the actual time spent in the workplace while offering additional evidence for the proposition that occupational commitment, and the career achievement with which it was associated, did not mesh well with the commitment to raise a family.

From the results in Table 11.12, we see that, as expected, individuals with a strong overall pattern of career involvement in adolescence (i.e., the

TABLE 11.12
Significant Differences in Adult Childbearing

Subgroup name	More than expected had	Fewer than expected had
1-Gifted, High-Adapted Achievers (n = 79)	No children**** (n = 60, out of 248 with no children)	
3-High-Adapted Overachievers (n = 54)	No children** (n = 39, out of 248 with no children)	
4-Low-Adapted, Normal-Ability Underachievers (n = 50)	Two children* (n = 11, out of 55 with two children)	No children** (n = 20, out of 248 with no children)
6-Moderately Able Normals (n = 60)		Two children** (n = 2, out of 55 with two children)
8-Moderately Adapted, Realistic, Low Achievers (n = 36)	Two children** (n = 10, out of 55 with two children)	No children** (n = 12, out of 248 with no children)
9-Low-Adapted, Low-Ability, Non-Achievers (n = 31)	Two children* (n = 8, out of 55 with two children)	No children** (n = 11, out of 248 with no children)

Note: The total EXACON sample size was 435.
*p < .05; **p < 01; ****p < .0001.

Gifted, High-Adapted Achievers, Subgroup 1, and the High-Adapted Over-achievers, Subgroup 3) appeared to have deferred childbearing. In contrast, a significant number of individuals who had displayed an overall pattern of non-career involvement in their earlier lives, (i.e., the Low-Adapted, Nor-mal-Ability Underachievers, Subgroup 4, and the Low-Adapted, Low-Ability Non-Achievers, Subgroup 9) had given birth to two children by age 26. The Moderately Adapted, Realistic, Low Achievers (Subgroup 8), whose overall pattern in midadolescence was likewise oriented away from career achievement, as evidenced by their withdrawal from academic studies to vo-cational courses, were also overrepresented among the women who had two children.

We might again emphasize that the individual differences observed in this analysis had very little to do with "ability" per se. The adolescent Overachievers had not been nearly as "able," intellectually speaking, as the Gifted High-Adapteds had been in adolescence. Yet, in adulthood, both subgroups were invested in careers. Similarly, in adolescence the "ability" of the Underachievers had been nowhere near as low as that of the Realistic Low Achievers or the Non-Achievers. Yet, as young adults, all three subgroups were significantly characterized by the same orientation towards raising a family.

In Adolescence. Having observed the preceding results, we undertook one further analysis concerning childbearing. We have reported in chapter 9 that, in midadolescence, the Underachievers anticipated raising a family more than the Gifted High-Adapteds did. This analysis, however, had addressed differences among only four of the nine age-16 ability/adaptation subgroups.

Therefore, we conducted a second ANOVA, in the expectation that when all nine subgroups were considered, we might find individual differences that would reflect actual childbearing at age 26. However, because the overall F ratio was not significant ($p = .26$), we were unable to demonstrate that noncareer-involved girls who later became mothers were fulfilling an ambition they had held since midadolescence.

PERSONAL LIVES IN ADULTHOOD—LIFE QUALITY

Rationale

The last adult area we investigated was concerned with life *quality*. We did not expect that our subjects' adult life quality would be associated with their overall patterns of career or non-career involvement in adolescence in the same manner as we had predicted adult outcomes from adolescent orientations in previous analyses. Rather, in line with our statement in chapter 1, that adult career achievement is not the *sine qua non* of life satisfaction, we expected a somewhat different pattern of results to emerge.

The results we expected draw on Garmezy's (1990) concept of "competence." Like Garmezy, we view competence as reflecting a general adaptation that extends across environmental domains, what we might denote as a *skill at living*. The females whose developmental paths we have followed from early adolescence through early adulthood might well differ in this skill. However, we would not expect the differences to be associated with their overall patterns of career or noncareer involvement in adolescence, defined as their high (or low) self-perceived ability, their high (or low) adaptation to academic demands, and their high (or low) aspiration for further education—except in two cases.

Specifically, everything we have observed up to now points to two subgroups of individuals who seemed to have lacked a generalized skill at living, who seemed most "at risk" for not experiencing a high quality of life. The first are the Low-Adapted, Normal-Ability Underachievers (Subgroup 4)—who came from families who underestimated their capability (as they themselves did as early as age 13), who engaged with working peers and boyfriends by age 15, whose school achievement had dropped far below their capability by midadolescence, and who lacked independence from their parents in midadolescence, even though they did not experience their parents as approving of them. The overall life-course of these individuals, up to age 26, connoted a certain absence of fulfillment, a certain lack of general reinforcement that might not have been wholly mitigated by their having had children.

The second subgroup of individuals whom we would consider "at risk" are the Low-Adapted, Low-Ability Non-Achievers (Subgroup 9), who were associated with low socioeconomic status homes in which parents neither aspired on their daughter's behalf nor thought her capable of academic achievement. The low intelligence and extremely low achievement, self-perceived ability, and school adaptation of these individuals across adolescence, even after they had selected themselves out of an academic curriculum, combined with their early engagement with working peers who might be assumed to have reinforced their negative adaptation to school, all suggested that they, too, might have failed to acquire the overall competence necessary for successful living in adulthood.

Of course, both these subgroups *did*, in adolescence, exhibit an overall pattern of noncareer involvement, as we have defined it here. Moreover, the Non-Achievers had the lowest levels of adult education and occupation in the entire sample (see Table 11.2 and 11.3). But the feeling we were trying to capture is that, given a series of negative environmental interactions, from lack of parental support to lack of success at school, these subjects simply might not enjoy their adult lives to the same extent that other women did.

Enjoyment of Leisure-Time Activities

Analysis

We first examined this proposition by investigating individual differences in the extent to which the adult women enjoyed their leisure time. The item, "Can you use your leisure time in a manner that you find satisfying?", was scored on a 5-point scale, from "yes, for the most part" (5) to "no, almost never" (1). The ANOVA included all nine age-16 ability/adaptation subgroups.

Results and Discussion

The ANOVA results, depicted in Table 11.13, yielded significant individual differences [$F(8, 419) = 2.16, p < .05$)], although not nearly as many as we have observed in the earlier analyses. While supporting our "risk group" expectations, the results also demonstrated that, in the main, adult enjoyment of leisure time was *not* systematically related to patterns of abil-

TABLE 11.13
Individual Differences in Adult Enjoyment of Leisure Time

Age-16 ability/adaptation subgroup	Subgroup mean	Post hoc tests[a]
5-Ability-Underestimating, High-Adapted Normals	4.56	5 > 4, 2, 9
7-Moderately Adapted, Unrealistic, Low Achievers	4.42	
8-Moderately Adapted, Realistic, Low Achievers	4.42	
1-Gifted, High-Adapted Achievers	4.31	
3-High-Adapted Overachievers	4.23	
6-Moderately Able Normals	4.22	
9-Low-Adapted, Low-Ability Non-Achievers	4.00	
2-Gifted, Low-Adapted Achievers	4.00	
4-Low-Adapted, Normal-Ability Underachievers	3.96	

Note: Grand mean = 4.23 F (8, 419) = 2.16, $p < .05$.
[a]$p \leq .05$.

ity and school adaptation in adolescence or to an overall pattern of career involvement.

The grand mean of 4.23 indicated that, as one would hope, our adult women felt that they could enjoy their leisure time somewhere between "often" (coded as 4) and "for the most part" (coded as 5), whether or not their nonleisure time was invested in a career. In fact, such enjoyment was reported most strongly, not by the Gifted, High-Adapted Achievers (Subgroup 1), who had so persistently "headed the list" on the adult criteria related to career achievement, but by the Ability-Underestimating, High-Adapted Normals (Subgroup 5), who had not been differentiated in previous adult outcomes.

The other subgroup means were uninterpretable, with respect to leisure-time enjoyment in adulthood's being associated with female adolescents' career involvement versus noncareer involvement, or with their intelligence and past academic achievement—*until* we came to the two "risk" subgroups. Both the Underachievers and the Non-Achievers (Subgroups 4 and 9) were significantly less able to use their leisure time in a satisfying manner than were the highest scoring Ability-Underestimating, High-Adapted Normals. These results suggested that the individuals we had targeted as lacking a certain "skill at living" or "generalized competence" did, in fact, seem to enjoy life somewhat less than did their more "skillful" counterparts.

Nevertheless, we must note that the women who had been Gifted, *Low*-Adapted Achievers (Subgroup 2) in midadolescence had exactly the same adult "enjoyment" mean as the Non-Achievers did. We knew that, across adolescence, the school adaptation of these girls had dropped substantially, relative to the adaptation of other girls at each age, and that they had come from high-educated families in which the parents had wanted their daughter to pursue an academic education and had believed her capable of doing so. As we have noted in previous chapters, these girls' family background was the mirror-opposite of the Non-Achievers'.

However, despite the difference in their family backgrounds, the two subgroups had shared one characteristic in midadolescence: low aspiration for an advanced education. Thus, although we certainly would not have expected that, as adults, the highly intelligent, high-achieving Gifted Low-Adapteds would demonstrate a significantly lower than average ability to enjoy their leisure time, the result was not totally inexplicable.

Reliance on Friends

Given the suggestion that the Underachievers and the Non-Achievers were at risk for experiencing a less than optimal quality of life in adulthood, another area we investigated was adult relationships with friends. We know from chapter 10 that 54% of the adult women stated that they could rely on their friends to help them in a crisis. Our question, very simply, was, "Did the Underachievers and the Non-Achievers share this confidence about relationships?"

The results of an EXACON ($N = 436$) indicated that the Low-Adapted, Low-Ability Non-Achievers (Subgroup 9) did not. Out of 32 Non-Achievers, 24 *disagreed* with the statement ($p < .05$). This result, which was the only significant individual difference observed, supported our suggestion that the life quality of these individuals had been curtailed by a long history of less than successful environmental transactions.

Abortions

Our next investigation of "risk" involved the issue of abortion. Until our subjects were 19 years old, Swedish law required that permission for an abortion could be granted only after a woman had consulted a psychiatrist. Because we had access to data concerning the reasons subjects sought psychiatric help (coded by the psychiatrist consulted), we were able to determine that 49 of the young women who had been represented in one of the 9 age-16 ability/adaptation subgroups had had at least one abortion by the age of 19.

Our prediction, tested through an EXACON ($N = 485$), was that one or both of the two subgroups we considered most susceptible to negative environmental events (i.e., the Low-Adapted, Normal-Ability Underachievers and/or the Low-Adapted, Low-Ability Non-Achievers) would be overrepresented among these 49 individuals. The results showed that the Under-achievers comprised 10 of them ($p < .01$). No other cell was significant.

Criminality

Our final analysis of the "risk" groups investigated criminality. We were able to ascertain that, through the *age of 29*, a total of 33 subjects who had been represented in one of the age-16 ability/adaptation subgroups had established a criminal record. Again, we expected that the Underachievers and/or the Non-Achievers would be overrepresented among this total.

The results of an EXACON ($N = 485$) supported this prediction for the Low-Adapted, Low-Ability Non-Achievers (Subgroup 9). Eight of the 37 Non-Achievers were represented among the adult women who had committed at least one crime by age 29 ($p < .01$). No other significant differential results were observed.

Summary

The findings regarding life *quality*, taken altogether, provided at least tentative evidence that the Low-Adapted, Normal-Ability Underachievers and the Low-Adapted, Low-Ability Non-Achievers to some extent lacked a generalized skill at living. Although "career achievement" is not the sole criterion of successful adult adjustment, the lives of these women, viewed from an overall perspective, seemed to reflect a less than optimal developmental path.

As we have stressed again and again throughout this and previous chapters, the life course of these individuals had been problematic from early adolescence on. In interaction with both their home environment and their school environment, they had experienced certain reinforcement deficits as early as age 13. By age 15 they had had peer associations that could be assumed to direct their attention further away from career involvement. By age 19 a significant number of the Underachievers had had an abortion, and by age 29 a significant number of the Non-Achievers had established a criminal record. In young adulthood, both the Underachievers and the Non-Achievers were significantly overrepresented among women who held low-level jobs that required minimal training. Moreover, both subgroups expressed a significantly low degree of satisfaction with their leisure activities.

The low intellectual ability of the Non-Achievers might certainly have contributed to the difficulties these individuals had experienced over time. However, the lives of the Underachievers appeared to have followed an essentially similar developmental pattern, despite their quite normal intelligence. These latter individuals emerged, more saliently than any of the other subjects, as women who had neither realized their achievement potential nor maintained their options for the future.

CONCLUDING REMARKS

The analyses discussed in this chapter conclude our empirical investigation. In the final chapter we briefly summarize several of the other developmental paths we have traced from early adolescence to early adulthood. In addition, we address certain issues concerning the generalizability of the results we have presented.

Chapter 12

Summary and Implications

In this final chapter we first present an abbreviated summary of the female career paths we have followed most closely from early adolescence through early adulthood. We then discuss certain methodological, substantive, and cross-cultural implications of the pattern approach that has informed our overall investigation.

PRECURSORS OF ADULT CAREER ACHIEVEMENT

Parental Values

At the conclusion of chapter 11, we described, in some detail, the career paths of two groups of individuals whose development had been characterized by adjustment problems—including abortion or criminal activity—from early adolescence through young adulthood: (a) low-ability, non-achieving girls who had not been well-adapted to the academic aspects of the school environment since early adolescence; and (b) normal-ability girls who had expressed low self-perceived ability in early adolescence and, by midadolescence, combined this low perception of their own academic capability with low achievement and low adaptation to school. In young adulthood both groups were significantly overrepresented among women who had two children and among women who held part-time jobs requiring minimal educational preparation. Moreover, as emphasized in our previous

188

discussions, both the low-ability subjects and the subjects who became un-derachievers were significantly associated with family backgrounds in which the parents neither aspired to their daughter's pursuing an education past the 9 years of compulsory school nor believed her capable of doing so.

The issue of parents' values concerning their daughters' education—that is, parents' aspiration for their daughters' academic future and parents' evaluation of their daughters' academic capability—has received considera-ble attention throughout this volume.

Our results have consistently indicated that parental values exert a strong influence on females' educational and occupational outcomes, *independent* of parents' socioeconomic status. Just as values directed away from aca-demic achievement were associated with underachievement among normal-ability adolescents, so, too, values directed toward achievement carried long-range consequences.

Specifically, the highest adolescent and adult achievers in our sample, fe-males who had been well-adapted to the school environment and had had an accurate perception of their own high ability, came only from families in which the parents placed a high value on educational achievement and believed in their daughter's capability. Furthermore, both low SES and high SES families were included among the home backgrounds that were signifi-cantly associated with these girls' high educational and occupational achievement across 13 years.

The highest achievers were also very bright, although they were not the brightest group in the sample. However, similar adult outcomes character-ized a group of girls whose adolescent intelligence was below average. Al-though it is reasonable to assume that the processes through which the adult outcomes were achieved were somewhat different, virtually none of these latter girls, whom we have called overachievers, came from homes in which educationally oriented values were *not* expressed. In addition, like the highest achievers, the overachievers had been well-adapted to the school environment and had expressed high confidence in their own academic ca-pability and high aspiration for advanced education. In adulthood, they at-tained significantly higher levels of education and occupation than did the average-intelligence underachievers and a significantly higher occupational level than that achieved by the most intelligent group of girls, whose mida-dolescent school adaptation had been quite low.

An Overall Pattern of Career Involvement

Although cognitive ability was certainly not irrelevant to adult career achieve-ment, the developmental course of the overachievers led us to define an over-all pattern of career involvement, comprising high self-perceived ability, high adaption to academic demands, and high aspiration. Individuals who had sustained this pattern across adolescence demonstrated stronger occupational commitment and higher professional status in adulthood than those who did not.

When we examined the family processes operating in the homes of girls who had exhibited an overall pattern of career involvement, it appeared that these girls had internalized the achievement-oriented values expressed by their parents. In midadolescence the highest *achievers*, in comparison with the *low-adapted* girls who exhibited the highest *intelligence* of any individuals in the sample, reported stronger identification with their mothers, better relations with their mothers, higher perceived approval from their parents, and less dependence on their parents to make decisions for them. In comparison with the same group of intellectually gifted but low-adapted girls, the overachievers exhibited an identical pattern of significant results; in addition, the overachievers reported significantly better relations with their fathers.

A Caveat Concerning Parental SES

We have observed throughout our investigation that educationally oriented parental values, in interaction with girls' own high aspiration, positive self-evaluation, and high adaptation to academic demands, were generally associated with adult career achievement, *irrespective* of parental education or income. However, one important caveat needs to be addressed.

Among our subjects in midadolescence we observed a group of individuals whom we designated as the Gifted, Low-Adapted Achievers. These girls were the most intelligent subjects in the sample; nevertheless, their levels of achievement had dropped somewhat from early adolescence, although their performance was still well above average, and their school adaptation had decreased substantially from age 13 to age 16. The only families with which these girls were significantly associated were families in which parental SES (i.e., fathers' education, mothers' education, and family income) was extremely high.

The parents of the Gifted Low-Adapteds had expressed exactly the same educationally oriented values that characterized the parents of the highest achievers, whom we discussed earlier. In fact, a significant proportion of the highest achievers had come from the same subgroup of families that was also associated with the Gifted Low-Adapteds. The difference was that although the highest achievers exhibited an overall pattern of career involvement, the Gifted Low-Adapteds, despite their high intelligence, lacked both the high aspiration and high adaptation to academic demands that were integral aspects of the career-involvement pattern.

As reflected in our previous discussion, these were also the girls whose midadolescent relations with their parents were conflicted, compared to the family relations reported by the highest achievers or the overachievers. Yet, in comparison with the self-reports of either of the other two groups, the Gifted Low-Adapteds were *more* dependent on their parents to make decisions for them. Thus, it would appear that a strong influence toward educational achievement, operating within families in which both parents were themselves highly educated, might well be experienced as achievement pressure by girls who were academically capable but not academically motivated.

In any case, we may infer from their low aspiration that, unlike the highest achievers and the overachievers, the Gifted Low-Adapteds had not internalized the values their parents had espoused on their behalf—even though, as late as the final year of compulsory school, they were unanimously enrolled in the most academically rigorous curriculum available. Moreover, as we noted earlier, not only were the adult educational and occupational levels of the Gifted Low-Adapteds significantly lower than those of the highest achievers, but the Gifted Low-Adapteds were significantly surpassed in adult occupational level by the overachievers.

In summary, it appeared that high SES, in the form of high educational attainment on the part of both parents, was a crucial element in maintaining high academic performance among intellectually gifted females who did not experience a "fit" with the school environment and had little aspiration to continue their studies beyond the obligatory nine years. Given this finding, it would seem that a particularly important area for future research might be to investigate more fully the processes that differentiate gifted girls who experience a decline in school adaptation across adolescence and, as adults, have failed to realize their achievement potential from gifted girls from the same type of family environment who maintain high adaptation and high achievement all the way to young adulthood.

We have commented on these results extensively in earlier chapters, especially in terms of their compatibility with recent U.S. findings concerning high-ability girls whose performance deteriorates over short periods of time (Dweck, 1986; Leggett, 1985; Licht & Dweck, 1984; Stipek & Hoffman, 1980). However, to our knowledge, no previous research has linked a high-ability/long-term-deteriorating-achievement syndrome among females to a particular family background configuration.

The patterns that differentiated between the high-adapted, highest achievers and the Gifted, Low-Adapted Achievers in our sample, along with the patterns that differentiated between high SES families and low SES families, all of whom shared the same educationally oriented values, allowed us to separate conditions under which parental SES was not relevant to long-term career aspiration and achievement from the one condition under which high parental SES seemed to be a necessary component of high performance in adolescence, although not in adulthood. Such developmental differences, in addition to those involving the underachievers and the overachievers, would very likely have been masked by traditional linear-model analyses.

IMPLICATIONS OF THE PATTERN APPROACH

As presented in chapters 1 and 2, we view the pattern approach, and its accompanying methodology, as a natural consequence of modern interactionism. We have argued throughout this volume that a research strategy oriented toward defining patterns that characterize individuals in a particular domain and testing the associations among individuals' patterns across domains and across time reveals individual differences that are generally obscured in studies of linear relationships among variables.

Our investigation of individual differences in female career development is intended to illustrate this overall strategy, as well as to contribute to a substantive research area. Because, to our knowledge, this volume represents the first systematic attempt to apply a pattern approach to a comprehensive longitudinal investigation, the empirical results we have presented should be validated through further research.

Moreover, we should emphasize that any results gleaned from analyzing patterns are inextricably linked to the variables initially selected as pattern indicators. As demonstrated through the rationales we have presented to introduce each pattern domain, our pattern indicators were theoretically derived from an examination of previous research. The assumption that guided our interpretations of the patterns we observed and our expectations concerning relationships among patterns was that differences among patterns reflected differences in developmental processes. Nonetheless, a different selection of indicators in a given domain might well have illuminated developmental processes that we have not addressed.

Finally, the pattern approach carries what might be viewed as an "aesthetic" implication worth noting: As our networks of interacting patterns widened, we increasingly found ourselves thinking in terms of individuals. For us, the Gifted, High-Adapted Achievers, the Gifted, Low-Adapted Achievers, the High-Adapted Overachievers, and the Low-Adapted, Normal-Ability Underachievers became holistic persons. In a manner that is perhaps similar to that experienced by researchers who focus on case studies, we felt we "knew" these girls. By forming homogeneous subgroups of individuals, based on the similarity of their functioning across a specific domain, we were able to analyze quantitative data concerning several hundred subjects. Yet we were also able to retain a qualitative appreciation of the girls whose life careers we were tracing. Thus, the pattern approach, which allowed us to see which individuals followed which developmental paths, yielded findings that were both statistically significant and substantively "accessible," in terms of their relevance to people rather than to variables.

CROSS-CULTURAL GENERALIZABILITY

Our last issue concerns the generalizability of our findings across cultures. Although our investigation encompassed a representative sample of Swedish females, the extent to which similar findings would emerge elsewhere remains an empirical question.

The issue of cross-cultural validation, in terms of a pattern-oriented research strategy, raises two central questions that future research might address: "Will similar patterns emerge from one culture to another?" and "Will similar patterns carry similar developmental implications, regardless of the culture in which they are observed?" Although we have no definitive answers to these questions, we would like to offer certain suggestions.

With respect to the first question, we would suggest that, at least within Western cultures that expressly value individual achievement among females, we might continue to observe the patterns that have yielded the most robust differential findings in the present investigation—that is, the patterns of high-adapted high achievement, high-adapted overachievement, and low-adapted underachievement. Furthermore, because the pattern of our Gifted, Low-Adapted Achievers seems so consistent with the earlier cited U.S. research on deteriorating performance among bright girls, we might also expect this pattern to emerge in cultures other than Sweden.

Nevertheless, we must also acknowledge that Swedish society from 1968 to 1982 was not nearly as heterogeneous as U.S. society was during the same time period. As a simple example, our sample, although it represented a wide spectrum of socioeconomic status, included virtually no non-Caucasian subjects. Thus, a more heterogeneous society might well give rise to differential patterns that we did not observe in Sweden.

With regard to the second question, we would propose that, once activated, the differential developmental processes that underlie the networks of interacting patterns we have observed will operate with a great deal of generality across cultural boundaries. In support of this proposition, we might note that the previous research on which we based our selection of relevant pattern indicators and our expectations concerning pattern associations had been conducted primarily in the United States. Although we are not arguing that U.S.- generated hypotheses, combined with Swedish data, constitute a "cross-cultural" study, we would suggest that the overall support our expectations received speaks to the generalizability of certain psychological dynamics, once these dynamics are manifest in an individual's interaction with the environment.

For example, we have observed that once normal-ability girls doubt their own academic competence, and this process of doubt is reinforced by their parents' low evaluation of their capability, the girls' achievement and school adaptation declines substantially. In contrast, we have also observed that among high achievers who are well-adapted to the school environment, high performance and high adaptation reinforce one another over time, a process that is facilitated by these girls' internalization of parental values oriented towards achievement. Unless one were conducting research in an Alice-in-Wonderland culture that reserved its highest approbation for its lowest achievers, it seems reasonable to envision that the differential processes underlying these interacting individual and environmental patterns would exhibit a marked degree of cross-cultural correspondence.

FINAL REMARKS

The primary purpose of our investigation has been to illustrate a pattern approach to the exploration of individual differences in female career development. Our specific findings must await confirmation from future research; however, we believe the pattern strategy, especially in conjunction with a longitudinal research design, offers exciting possibilities for the investigation of individual differences across a wide variety of psychological domains.

Appendix A:
Measures of Ability
and School Adaptation
at Ages 13 and 16

INTELLIGENCE INDICATORS

Intelligence at Age 13

At age 13 the girls' intelligence was measured through the Härnqvist (1961) Differential Intelligence Analysis (DIA). The test, which was developed in Sweden and was administered in Grade 6 as part of the ongoing school program, is a battery of six subtests: Similarities and Opposites (a two-test Verbal Ability composite); Groups of Letters and Number Series (a two-test Logical Inductive Ability composite); and Cube Counting and Metal Folding (a two-test Spatial Ability composite). In accordance with Härnqvist's recommendation, a total intelligence measure, labeled General Study Aptitude, was derived from the sum of the stanine scores on each of the six subtests. The reliability of the total score, as calculated from the reliability of the subtests, is estimated to be .95 (Härnqvist, 1961). This total score, restandardized as a z score, served as the intelligence indicator for the ability/adaptation patterns in early adolescence.

Intelligence at Age 15–16

At age 15, in Grade 8, the subjects were administered the Wechsler Intelligence Test III as part of the general educational program. The test, translated into Swedish by Westrin (1967), consists of four subtests: Analogies, a measure of verbal inductive ability; Opposites, a measure of verbal comprehension; Number Combinations, a measure of deductive ability; and Puzzle, a measure of spatial ability. The split-half reliability of the total score, which was transformed into a z score to comprise the intelligence indicator for the ability/adaptation patterns at age 16, is estimated to be .93 (Westrin, 1967).

ACHIEVEMENT INDICATORS

Achievement at Age 13

Nationally standardized achievement tests were also administered by the various schools as part of the ordinary Swedish educational program in Grade 6. The total score on the achievement test in Swedish and the total score on the achievement test in mathematics, both represented as z scores, comprised the two achievement indicators used for the ability/adaptation patterns at age 13 (Grade 6). The internal consistency of each measure is estimated to be .90 (Magnusson et al., 1975).

Achievement at Age 15–16

At Age 15 (Grade 8) achievement tests were again administered as part of the educational program. However, the achievement test in mathematics was not equivalent for all subjects because students had opted for one of two levels of mathematics courses offered in Grade 7. Thus, to define a uniform measure of achievement that would reflect, insofar as possible, subjects' competence in manipulating mathematics-related concepts at age 15–16, a composite was formed, using students' final eighth grade marks in chemistry and physics. These mandatory courses were the same, regardless of a student's chosen curriculum in mathematics.

The composite of two grades was used to increase the measure's reliability, both through minimizing the potential effect of an individual teacher's systematic bias in awarding grades and through considering more than one "subtest" of math-related achievement. The correlation between the two grades was substantial ($r = .74$). Grades were given on a scale of 1–5, and the composite score was represented as a z score.

Although a standardized Swedish test, analogous to the test used in Grade 6, had been administered in Grade 8, the subjects who took this later test were fewer in number ($n = 497$) than those for whom eighth-grade marks in Swedish were available ($n = 573$). Because there was a strong correlation between the standardized test scores and the grades ($r = .79$), the final eighth-grade mark in Swedish was selected as the second achievement indicator for the ability/adaptation patterns at age 15–16. As before, the grades were given on a 1–5 scale, and the indicator was represented as a z score.

SELF-PERCEIVED ABILITY INDICATORS

Self-Perceived Ability at Age 13

At age 13 subjects' self-perceived ability was assessed in terms of optional courses available in the following grade, a context that was considered appropriate, given their limited exposure to making independent decisions concerning their educational future. The measure was taken from the Educational and Vocational Choice Questionnaire administered to all subjects during Grade 6.

The item from which the measure was derived listed the five groups of *optional* courses that were available in Grade 7 and asked the respondent to indicate whether or not she believed herself capable of handling each of these subject combinations. The content of the various combinations differed with respect to the degree of "theoretical" or "academic" emphasis it entailed, from five classes per week in handicrafts (reflecting the lowest emphasis on an academically oriented curriculum) to five classes per week in German or French (reflecting the highest emphasis on academically oriented subjects).

The five course combinations were first grouped to form a 3-point scale, ranging from the lowest to the highest level of theoretical emphasis:

1: the two optional combinations that contained no foreign language instruction;

2: the two choices that included three classes in foreign language per week, combined with two classes in other subjects; and

3: the choice of five classes in foreign language per week.

This grouping formed the basis for the self-perceived ability scale, which was coded from 1 to 3, according to the most theoretical combination of optional courses the respondent had indicated she could handle. Finally, the self-perceived ability scores were re-calculated as z scores.

Self-Perceived Ability at Age 16

At age 16 the subjects were in the process of completing their last year of compulsory schooling (Grade 9) in one of nine divergent lines of study. Because the intervening 3 years had provided them considerable opportunity to form judgments of their own competence in the academic arena, a somewhat more broadly based measure than that used at age 13 comprised the indicator of self-perceived ability.

The indicator was drawn from three items administered during Grade 9 as part of the Educational and Vocational Choice Questionnaire. Each item asked respondents to state, on a 4-point, Likert-type scale, the extent to which they believed they could successfully complete the program of post-compulsory education designated by the item. The single measure of self-perceived ability was the *highest* level of education which the girl stated she was "certain" or "quite certain" she could attain. The resulting scale, which was standardized as a z score, ranged from 1 to 4 as follows:

1—no further education past compulsory school;

2—pursuing a 2-year gymnasium (secondary school) curriculum in any area except economics, social studies, or technical studies;

3—pursuing a 2-year gymnasium curriculum in economics, social studies, or technical studies; and

4—pursuing a 3- or a 4-year gymnasium education.

SCHOOL ADAPTATION INDICATORS

School Adaptation at Age 13

At age 13 the measure of adaptation to the academic aspects of school life constituted the composite score of 10 items taken from the Student Questionnaire administered to subjects during Grade 6. The scale formed from these items was designated to reflect the extent to which sixth-grade subjects experienced a comfortable "fit" with their current academic environment.

The response format for each item was a 5-point, Likert-type scale, ranging from "almost always" (1) to "almost never" (5). The composite, which was not assumed to be unidimensional (Lord & Novick, 1968), demonstrated a high level of internal consistency ($\alpha = .82$). It included such items as, "Do you have to work very hard in school?", "Are you afraid of getting bad grades on tests and examinations at school?", "Do you find it difficult to keep up with the working pace at school?", "Do you find the lessons at school interesting and varied?" (reversed), and "Do you like being at school?" (reversed). The composite score on the 10 items was standardized as a z score.

Finally, a series of t tests was conducted to ascertain whether or not subjects with and without data on all 10 of the school adaptation items differed significantly from one another on any of the single items used to form the composite. In these analyses, the item mean scores of two groups were compared: Group 1 comprised the subjects who had responded to all 10 items ($n = 518$); Group 2 consisted of the subjects who had answered the item in question but had not completed at least one other item in the composite and thus had no composite score. Except that Group 2 reported significantly more anxiety than Group 1 over receiving bad grades on tests $[t(522) = 2.25, p < .05]$, no significant differences were observed.

School Adaptation at Age 15–16

The same basic procedure was followed in defining a comparable indicator of school adaptation for the ability/adaptation patterns at age 15–16. A total of six items was drawn from three separate self-report inventories: two items from the Educational and Vocational Choice Questionnaire administered to all subjects during the eighth grade, one item from the Study of Symptoms Inventory administered only to females during the eighth grade, and three items from the Student Questionnaire administered to all subjects in the ninth grade. All items were answered on 5-point, Likert-type response formats, with a score of 5 indicating high adaptation. Sample items were "Do you like being at school?", "Do you try to do your best at school?", and "Do you think it's important to have good test grades?".

Because the items comprising the adaptation scale at age 15–16 were taken from several inventories administered over a 1-year period, the final composite score was subjected to a further modification to ensure that the loss of subjects due to incomplete data would be minimal. Given the relatively high internal consistency of the six-item index ($\alpha = .79$), it was decided to include all subjects who had responded to at least four of the items. The procedure was to calculate the mean of the z scores for the number of items answered, re-standardize this mean, and use the resulting z score as the indicator of school adaptation in the ability/adaptation patterns at age 16.

Last, to assure ourselves that the subjects with sufficient data to be included in the school adaptation composite were representative of the whole sample, another series of t tests was conducted. For each item, a t test compared the item mean of subjects with complete data across all items (Group 1, $n = 437$) to the item mean of subjects with incomplete data on the total of composite (Group 2).

Significant differences were found for three of the six items: Group 2 reported doing well in school to be less important to them than did Group 1 $[t(513) = 1.94, p = .05]$; Group 2 reported liking school less, compared to Group 1 $[t(522) = -2.22, p < .05]$; and Group 2 agreed less than Group 1 with the statement that they did their best at school $[t(519) = -4.76, p < .001]$. This systematic loss of subjects whose adaptation appeared to be somewhat lower than that of subjects with complete data, at least with regard to these specific items, might have been problematic. However, the previously discussed decision that subjects needed to have answered only four of the six items to be included in the composite resulted in 58 of the various Group 2 members' being restored to the final sample of 495.

Appendix B:
A Note About the
Average Coefficient

For every subgroup derived through our cluster analyses, the results of the RELOCATE procedure, conducted with CLUSTAN to confirm the assignment of subjects to their respective clusters and to remove a residual (see chapter 2), included the calculation of a statistic called the *average coefficient*. The average coefficient is the average squared Euclidian distance (average D^2) between each member of the cluster, across all variables, and the means of the cluster as a whole. It can be interpreted as a sort of generalized within-cluster variance. Obviously, the smaller the average coefficient, the tighter and more homogeneous the subgroup.

Although the average coefficient associated with each subgroup was not reported, our inspection of these coefficients after each RELOCATE procedure (along with our ascertaining that the variance on each indicator *within* a subgroup was substantially less than its variance in the sample as a whole) led us to conclude that the subgroups were homogeneous enough to allow us to test meaningful hypotheses concerning differences *among* them. The average coefficients for the age-13 and the age-16 ability/adaptation subgroups ranged from a minimum of .19 to a maximum of .48, with 15 of the 18 clusters yielding an average coefficient between .19 and .35.

The rather large average coefficient of .48 characterized the age-16 Low-Adapted, Low-Ability Non-Achievers (Subgroup 9 in Table 3.2). However, the means of the Non-Achievers on four of the five indicators were *so* low, relative to the means of the other subgroups at age 16, that their within-cluster dissimilarity was unlikely to reflect any theoretically meaningful differences among them, at least with respect to comparing the subgroup as a whole to other subgroups.

Appendix C:
Measures of Parental Values
When Girls Were Age 16

PARENTAL ASPIRATION

Three items, taken from the Parents' Questionnaire administered to the subjects' parents when the girls were age 16, comprised the parental aspiration scale:

1. The first item, coded from 1 to 3, according to the strength of parents' educationally oriented aspiration for their daughter, asked parents if they wanted their daughter to "go into vocational training immediately after compulsory school" (coded as 1), to "continue an academic education as long as she likes" (coded as 2), or to "continue an academic education as long as possible" (coded as 3).

2. The second item, which asked parents what they thought their daughter should do after compulsory school, was coded from 1 ("get a job") to 5 ("enroll in a 3-year 'theoretical' gymnasium curriculum").

3. The third item asked parents whether or not they thought it best for their daughter to choose a post-compulsory school curriculum that was as long and as "theoretical" as possible, in preparation for her future occupation. The response format for this item ranged from 1 ("definitely not") to 5 ("yes, definitely").

The internal consistency of these items (assessed after the responses were standardized) was satisfactory, given that only three items were involved

(α = .68). The mean z score of the items was used as the single indicator of parental aspirations.

PARENTAL EVALUATION

The measure of parents' evaluation of their daughter's academic capability was also drawn from three items in the Parents' Questionnaire. Each item asked parents to state, on a 4-point, Likert-type scale, the extent to which they believed their daughter capable of completing the program of post-compulsory designated by the item.

The items were ordered on a continuum reflecting a low to high emphasis on theoretical, or academically oriented, education:

1. Pursuing no education past compulsory school was coded as 1.
2. Pursuing any of the 2-year gymnasium (secondary school) curricula, *except* economics, social studies, or technical studies was coded as 2.
3. Pursuing a 2-year gymnasium in economics, social studies, or technical studies was coded as 3.
4. Pursuing a 3-year or a 4-year gymnasium education was coded as 4.

The single measure of parents' evaluation was then defined as the highest academic level the parents stated they were "certain" or "quite certain" their daughter could attain. Finally, the parental evaluation indicator was standardized as a z score.

Appendix D: Measures of Girls' Interactions with Their Parents in Midadolescence

The six measures of girls' interactions with their parents, as assessed by the girls themselves, were taken from the Study of Symptoms Inventory administered to all females in the eighth grade. The specific measures were as follows:

1. Identification with mother—a single item asking, "How much do you, as an adult, want to be like your mother?" The response was coded from "not at all" (1) to "very much" (5) Of the 236 girls who were represented among the four subgroups tested (see chapter 9), 215 (91%) had responded to this item.

2. Identification with father—a single item asking, "How much do you, as an adult, want to be like your father?" The response was coded from "not at all" (1) to "very much" (5). Of the 236 girls who were represented among the four subgroups tested, 202 (86%) had responded to this item.

3. Relationship with mother—a three-item composite, with each item coded on a 5-point, Likert-type scale from "never or hardly ever" (5) to "very often" (1). The items were

   - "Are you often disappointed in your mother?",
   - "Do you wish your mother were different from the way that she is?", and
   - "Are you often irritated with your mother?"

Because the internal consistency of these three items was high ($\alpha = .79$) and the coefficient alpha dropped only to a minimum of .70 when any one of the items was removed, we included all subjects who had answered either two or all three of the questions. The composite score was computed as the mean of the two or three responses. Of the 236 girls who were represented among the four subgroups considered in the analysis, 212 (90%) furnished data on the composite.

4. Relationship with father—a three-item composite, with each item co-ded on a 5-point, Likert-type scale from "never or hardly ever" (5) to "very often" (1). The items were

   • "Are you often disappointed in your father?",
   • "Are you often irritated with your father?", and
   • "Do you and your father understand each other?" (reverse-coded).

Because the internal consistency of these three items was also high ($\alpha = .83$) and the coefficient alpha dropped only to a minimum of .76 when any one of the items was removed, we again included all subjects who had answered either two or all three of the questions. The composite score was computed as the mean of the two or three responses. Of the 236 girls who were represented among the four subgroups considered in the analysis, 206 (87%) furnished data on the composite.

5. Perceived parental approval—a three-item composite, with each item coded on a 5-point, Likert-type scale from "never or hardly ever" (5) to "very often" (1). The items were

   • "Do you think your parents are disappointed in you?",
   • "Do you think your parents are irritated with you?", and
   • "Do your parents criticize you?"

Since the internal consistency of these three items was high ($\alpha = .81$) and the coefficient alpha dropped only to a minimum of .72 when any one of the items was removed, we included all subjects who had answered either two or all three of the questions. The composite score was computed as the mean of the two or three responses. Of the 236 girls who were represented among the four subgroups tested, 217 (92%) furnished data on the composite.

6. Independence from parents—a single item asking, "How much do you want your parents to make decisions for you about clothes, make-up, leisure time activities, choice of friends, plans for summer, plans for profession, etc.?" The response was coded from "very

much" (1) to "very little" (5), with higher scores connoting more independence. Of the 236 girls who were represented among the four subgroups tested, 211 (89%) had responded to this item.

References

Anastasi, A. (1958). *Differential psychology* (3rd ed.). New York: Macmillan.

Anastasi, A. (1982). *Psychological testing* (5th ed.). New York: Macmillan.

Anderberg, M. R. (1973). *Cluster analysis for applications*. New York: Academic Press.

Astin, H. S., & Myint, T. (1971). Career development of young women during the post high school years. *Journal of Counseling Psychology Monographs, 18*, 369–393.

Bandura, A. (1977). Self-efficacy: Toward a unifying theory of behavioral change. *Psychological Review, 84*, 191–215.

Bandura, A. (1986). *Social foundations of thought and action: A social cognitive theory.* Englewood Cliffs, NJ: Prentice-Hall.

Bandura, A. (1989). Human agency in cognitive theory. *American Psychologist, 44*, 1175–1184.

Baron, R. M., & Boudreau, L. A. (1987). An ecological perspective on integrating personality and social psychology. *Journal of Personality and Social Psychology, 53*, 1222–1228.

Bergman, L. R. (1973). Parent's education and mean change in intelligence. *Scandinavian Journal of Psychology, 14*, 273–281.

Bergman, L. R. (1988). You can't classify all of the people all of the time. *Multivariate Behavioral Research, 23*, 425–441.

Bergman, L. R., & El-Khouri, B. (1987). EXACON: A FORTRAN 77 program for the exact analysis of single cells in a contingency table. *Educational and Psychological Measurement, 47*, 155–161.

Bergman, L., & Magnusson, D. (1987). A person approach to the study of the development of adjustment problems: An empirical example and some research strategy considerations. In D. Magnusson & A. Öhman (Eds.), *Psychopathology: An interactional perspective* (pp. 383–401). New York: Academic Press.

Berry, C. (1981). The Nobel scientists and the origins of scientific achievement. *British Journal of Sociology, 32*, 381–391.

Betz, E. L. (1982). Need fulfillment in the career development of women. *Journal of Vocational Behavior, 20*, 53–66.

Betz, E. L., & Fitzgerald, L. F. (1987). *The career psychology of women*. New York: Academic Press.

Betz, N. E., & Hackett, G. (1981). The relationship of career-oriented self-efficacy expectations to perceived career options in college women and men. *Journal of Counseling Psychology, 28*, 399–410.

Blashfield, R. K. (1976). Mixture model tests of cluster analysis: Accuracy of four agglomerative hierarchical models. *Psychological Bulletin, 83*, 377–388.

Blashfield, R. K., & Aldenderfer, M. S. (1978). The literature on cluster analysis. *Multivariate Behavioral Research, 13*, 271–295.

Bowers, K. S. (1973). Situationism in psychology: An analysis and a critique. *Psychological Review, 80*, 307–336.

Bradway, K. P., Thompson, C. W., & Cravens, R. B. (1958). Preschool IQ's after twenty-five years. *Journal of Educational Psychology, 49*, 278–281.

Burlin, F. (1976). The relationship of parental education and maternal work and occupational status to occupational aspiration in adolescent females. *Journal of Vocational Behavior, 9*, 99–104.

Camarena, P., Petersen, A., & Seidensticker, R. (1990, March). *Gender, academic achievement, and emotional well-being as predictors of adolescent career paths*. In J. Eccles (Chair), The development of career and family values and aspirations: Longitudinal perspectives on the influence of gender roles. Symposium conducted at the meeting of the Society for Research on Adolescence, Atlanta, GA.

Campbell, P. B. (1976). Adolescent intellectual decline. *Adolescence, 11*, 629–635.

Card, J. J., Steel, L., & Abeles, R. P. (1980). Sex differences in realization of individual potential for achievement. *Journal of Vocational Behavior, 17*, 1–21.

Chipman, S. F., & Thomas, V. G. (1985). Women's participation in mathematics: Outlining the problem. In S. F. Chipman, L. R. Brush, & D. M. Wilson (Eds.), *Women and mathematics* (pp. 1–24). Hillsdale, NJ: Lawrence Erlbaum Associates.

Cohen, J., & Cohen, P. (1983). *Applied multiple regression/correlation analysis for the behavioral sciences* (2nd ed.). Hillsdale, NJ: Lawrence Erlbaum Associates.

Conley, J. J. (1984). The hierarchy of consistency: A review and model of longitudinal findings on adult individual differences in intelligence, personality and self-opinion. *Personality and Individual Differences, 5*, 11–25.

Cornelius, G. M., & Yawkey, T. D. (1985). Imaginativeness in pre-school and single-parent families. *Journal of Creative Behavior, 19*, 56–66.

Crandall, V,. Dewey, R., Katkovsky, W., & Preston, A. (1964). Parents' attitudes and behaviors and grade school children's academic achievements. *Journal of Genetic Psychology, 104*, 53–66.

Cronbach, L. J., & Gleser, G. C. (1953). Assessing similarity between profiles. *Psychological Bulletin, 50*, 456–473.

Datta, C. E. (1967). Family religious background and early scientific creativity. *American Sociological Review, 32*, 626–635.

Dweck, C. S. (1986). Motivational processes affecting learning. *American Psychologist, 41*, 1040–1048.

Dweck, C. S., & Henderson, V. L. (1989, April). *Theories of intelligence: Background and measures*. Paper presented at the meeting of the Society for Research in Child Development, Kansas City, MO.

Dweck, C. S., & Leggett, E. L. (1988). A social-cognitive approach to motivation and personality. *Psychological Review, 95*, 256–273.

Eccles, J. (1983). Sex differences in mathematics participation. In M. Steinkamp & M. Maehr (Eds.), *Women in science* (pp. 80–110). Greenwich, CT: JAI Press.

Eccles, J. E., Adler, T. F., Futterman, R., Goff, S. B., Kaczala, C. M., Meece, J. I., & Midgley, C. (1983). Expectations, values, and academic behaviors. In J. T. Spence (Ed.), *Achievement and achievement motives* (pp. 75–145). San Francisco: Freeman.

Eccles, J., Adler, T. F., & Meece, J. L. (1984). Sex differences in achievement: A test of alternate theories. *Journal of Personality and Social Psychology, 46*, 26–43.

Eiduson, B. T. (1962). *Scientists: Their psychological world*. New York: Basic Books.

Ekehammar, B. (1974). Interactionism in personality from a historical perspective. *Psychological Bulletin, 81*, 1026–1048.

Endler, N. S. (1975). A person-situation interaction model for anxiety. In C. D. Spielberger & I. G. Sarason (Eds.), *Stress and anxiety in modern life*. Washington, DC: V. H. Winston.

Endler, N. S., & Hunt, J. McV. (1966). Sources of behavioral variance as measured by the S-R Inventory of Anxiousness. *Psychological Bulletin, 65*, 338–346.

Endler, N. S., & Hunt, J. McV. (1968). S-R inventories of hostility and comparisons of the proportions of variance from persons, responses, and situations for hostility and anxiousness. *Journal of Personality and Social Psychology, 9*, 309–315.

Endler, N. S., & Magnusson, D. (1976). Toward an interactional psychology of personality. *Psychological Bulletin, 83*, 956–974.

Ernest, J. (1976). Mathematics and sex. *The American Mathematical Monthly, 83*, 595–614.

Everitt, B. (1974). *Cluster analysis*. London: Heinemann Educational Books.

Falkowski, C. K., & Falk, W. W. (1983). Homemaking as an occupational plan: Evidence from a national longitudinal study. *Journal of Vocational Behavior, 22*, 227–242.

Farmer, H. S. (1980). Environmental, background, and psychological variables related to optimizing achievement and career motivation for high school girls. *Journal of Vocational Behavior, 17*, 58–70.

Fassinger, R. E. (1985). A causal model of college women's career choice. *Journal of Vocational Behavior Monograph, 27*, 123–153

Feldman, J. (1986). A note on the statistical correction of halo error. *Journal of Applied Psychology, 71*, 173–176.

Fisher, R. A. (1934). *Statistical methods for research workers* (5th ed.). Edinburgh: Oliver and Boyd.

Fitzgerald, L. F., & Crites, J. O. (1980). Toward a career psychology of woman: What do we know? What do we need to know? *Journal of Counseling Psychology, 27*, 44–62.

Flynn, F. R. (1987). Massive IQ gains in 14 nations: What IQ tests really measure. *Psychological Bulletin, 101*, 171–191.

Garmezy, N. (1990, March). *Resilience, competence, and development in adolescence*. Invited address presented at the Society for Research on Adolescence meeting, Atlanta, GA.

Getzels, J. W., & Jackson, P. W. (1962). *Creativity and intelligence: Explorations with gifted students*. New York: Wiley.

Gilligan, C. (1982). *In a different voice*. Cambridge, MA: Harvard University Press.

Gilligan, C. (1990, March). *The psychology of women and the development of girls*. Invited address presented at the Society for Research on Adolescence meeting, Atlanta, GA.

Ginzberg, E., Ginsburg, S. W., Axelrad, S., & Herma, J. L. (1951). *Occupational choice: An approach to a general theory*. New York: Columbia University Press.

Gold, A. R., Brush, L. R., & Sprotzer, E. R. (1980). Developmental changes in self-perceptions of intelligence and self-confidence. *Psychology of Women Quarterly, 5*, 231–239.

Gottfredson, L. S. (1981). Circumspection and compromise: A development theory of occupational aspirations. *Journal of Counseling Psychology, 28*, 545–579.

Green, D. R. (1974). *The aptitude-achievement distinction*. New York: McGraw-Hill.

Greenwald, A. G., Pratkanis, A. R., Leippe, M. R., & Baumgardner, M. (1986). Under what conditions does theory obstruct research progress? *Psychological Review, 93*, 216–229.

Gustafson, S. B., Stattin, H., & Magnusson, D. (1989). *Aspects of the development and moderation of sex role orientation among females: A longitudinal study* (Tech. Rep. No. 694). Stockholm, Sweden: Department of Psychology, Stockholm University.

Hackett, G., & Betz, N. E. (1981). A self-efficacy approach to the career development of women. *Journal of Vocational Behavior, 18*, 326–339.

Härnqvist, K. (1961). *Manual till DBA-differentiell begåvningsanalys* [Manual to DIA-differential intelligence analysis]. Stockholm: Skandinaviska Testförlaget.

Härnqvist, K. (1968). Relative changes in intelligence from 13 to 18. *Scandinavian Journal of Psychology, 9,* 50–82.

Holland, J. L. (1985). *Making vocational choices* (2nd ed.). New York: Prentice-Hall.

Hollinger, C. L. (1983). Self-perception and the career aspirations of mathematically talented female adolescents. *Journal of Vocational Behavior, 22,* 49–62.

Hudson, L. (1968). *Frames of mind.* London: Methuen.

Husén, T. (1951). The influence of schooling on IQ. *Theoria, 17,* 61–88.

Jacklin, C. N. (1989, April). *Discussant.* In H. Lytton (Chair), Parents' differential socialization of boys and girls—revisited. Symposium conducted at the meeting of the Society for Research in Child Development, Kansas City, MO.

Jenkins, S. R. (1987). Need for achievement and women's careers over 14 years: Evidence for occupational structure effects. *Journal of Personality and Social Psychology, 53,* 922–932.

Kirk, R. E. (1968). *Experimental design: Procedures for the behavioral sciences.* Belmont, CA: Brooks/Cole.

Kuhl, J. (1978). Standard setting and risk preference: An elaboration of the theory of achievement motivation and an empirical test. *Psychological Review, 85,* 239–248.

Leggett, E. (1985, March). *Children's entity and incremental theories of intelligence: Relationships to achievement behavior.* Paper presented at the meeting of the Eastern Psychological Association, Boston, MA.

Lent, R. W., Brown, S. D., & Larkin, K. C. (1986). Self-efficacy in the prediction of academic performance and perceived career options. *Journal of Counseling Psychology, 33,* 265–269.

Lerner, R. M. (1983). A "goodness of fit" model of person-context interaction. In D. Magnusson & V. L. Allen (Eds.), *Human development: An interactional perspective* (pp. 279–294). New York: Academic Press.

Licht, B. G., & Dweck, C. S. (1984). Determinants of academic achievement: The interaction of children's achievement orientation with skill area. *Developmental Psychology, 20,* 628–636.

Lindgren, B. W. (1965). *Statistical theory* (3rd ed.). New York: Macmillan.

Lord, F. M., & Novick, M. R. (1968). *Statistical theories of mental test scores.* Reading, MA: Addison-Wesley.

Maccoby, E. E., & Jacklin, C. N. (1974). *The psychology of sex differences.* Stanford, CA: Stanford University Press.

MacKinnon, D. W. (1962). The nature and nurture of creative talent. *American Psychologist, 17,* 484–495.

Magnusson, D. (1985). Implications of an interactional paradigm for research on human development. *International Journal of Behavioral Development, 8,* 115–137.

Magnusson, D. (1988). *Individual development from an interactional perspective: A longitudinal study* (Vol. 1). Hillsdale, NJ: Lawrence Erlbaum Associates.

Magnusson, D. (1990). Personality development from an interactional perspective. In L. Pervin (Ed.), *Handbook of personality theory and research* (pp. 193–222). New York: Guilford.

Magnusson, D., Dunér, A., & Zetterblom, G. (1975). *Adjustment: A longitudinal study.* New York: Wiley.

Magnusson, D., & Endler, N. S. (1977). Interactional psychology: Present status and future prospects. In D. Magnusson & N. S. Endler (Eds.), *Personality at the crossroads: Current issues in interactional psychology* (pp. 3–31). Hillsdale, NJ: Lawrence Erlbaum Associates.

Magnusson, D., & Törestad, B. (in press). The individual as an interactive agent in the environment. In W. B. Walsh (Ed.), *Person environment psychology: Models and perspectives.* New York: McGraw-Hill.

Marini, M. M. (1978). Sex differences in the determination of adolescent aspirations: A review of research. *Sex Roles, 4,* 723–753.

Matthews, K. A., & Rodin, J. (1989). Women's changing work roles. *American Psychologist, 44,* 1389–1393.

McCauley, C. M. (1989, April). *Influential factors on educational aspirations.* Paper presented at the meeting of the Society for Research in Child Development, Kansas City, MO.

Meece, J. L., Parsons, J. E., Kaczala, C. M., Goff, S. B., & Futterman, R. (1982). Sex differences in math achievement: Toward a model of academic choice. *Psychological Bulletin, 91,* 324–348.

Mischel, W. (1973). Toward a cognitive social learning reconceptualization of personality. *Psychological Review, 80,* 252–283.

Morey, L. C., Blashfield, R. K., & Skinner, H. A. (1983). A comparison of cluster analysis techniques within a sequential validation framework. *Multivariate Behavioral Research, 18,* 309–329.

Mulvey, M. C. (1963). Psychological and sociological factors in prediction of career patterns of women. *Genetic Psychology Monographs, 68,* 309–386.

Mumford, M. D., & Owens, W. A. (1984). Individuality in a developmental context: Some empirical and theoretical considerations. *Human Development, 27,* 84–108.

Pedro, J. O., Wolleat, P., Fennema, E., & Becker, A. D. (1981). Election of high school mathematics by females and males: Attributions and attitudes. *American Educational Research Journal, 18,* 207–218.

Pervin, L. A. (1968). Performance and satisfaction as a function of individual-environment fit. *Psychological Bulletin, 69,* 56–68.

Rejskind, F. G. (1982). Autonomy and creativity in children. *Journal of Creative Behavior, 16,* 58–67.

Revelle, W., & Michaels, E. J. (1976). The theory of achievement motivation revisited: The implications of inertial tendencies. *Psychological Review, 83,* 394–404.

Richardson, M. S. (1974). The dimensions of career and work orientation in college women. *Journal of Vocational Behavior, 5,* 161–172.

Roe A. (1949). Psychological examinations of eminent biologists. *Journal of Consulting Psychology, 13,* 225–246.

Roe, A. (1951). A psychological study of physical scientists. *Genetic Psychology Monographs, 43,* 121–235.

Roe, A. (1953). *The making of a scientist.* New York: Dodd Mead.

Roe, A. (1956). *The psychology of occupations.* New York: Wiley.

Rooney, G. (1983). Distinguishing characteristics of the life roles of worker, student, and homemaker for young adults. *Journal of Vocational Behavior, 22,* 324–342.

Schiamberg, L. B. (1989, April). *Family influence on occupational and educational attainment of rural/urban, low-income adolescents: Some racial comparisons.* Paper presented at the meeting of the Society for Research in Child Development, Kansas City, MO.

Sells, L. W. (1982). Leverage for equal opportunity through mastery of mathematics. In S. M. Humphreys (Ed.), *Women and minorities in science* (pp. 7–26). Boulder, CO: Westview Press.

Silver, H. R. (1983). Scientific achievement and the concept of risk. *British Journal of Sociology, 34,* 39–43.

Smith, E. R. (1980). Desiring and expecting to work among high school girls: Some determinants and consequences. *Journal of Vocational Behavior, 17,* 218–230.

Sokal, R. R., & Sneath, P. H. A. (1963). *Principles of numerical taxonomy.* London: Freeman.

Spence, J. T., Pred, R. S., & Helmreich, R. L. (1989). Achievement strivings, scholastic aptitude, and academic performance: A follow-up to "Impatience versus achievement strivings in the Type A pattern." *Journal of Applied Psychology, 74*, 176–178.

Stake, J. E. (1979). The ability/performance dimension of self-esteem: Implications for women's achievement behavior. *Psychology of Women Quarterly, 3*, 365–377.

Stattin, H., & Magnusson, D. (1990). Pubertal maturation in female development (Vol. 2). Hillsdale, NJ: Lawrence Erlbaum Associates.

Stein, M. I. (1968). Creativity. In F. Bogarta & W. W. Lambert (Eds.), *Handbook of personality theory and research* (pp. 67–89). Chicago: Rand McNally.

Sternberg, R. J. (1977). *Intelligence, information processing, and analogical reasoning: The componential analysis of human abilities*. Hillsdale, NJ: Lawrence Erlbaum Associates.

Sternberg, R. J. (1979). The nature of mental abilities. *American Psychologist, 34*, 214–230.

Sternberg, R. J., & Detterman, D. K. (Eds.). (1979). *Human intelligence: Perspectives on its theory and measurement*. Norwood, NJ: Ablex.

Stevenson, H. W., Lee, S. Y., & Stigler, J. W. (1986). Mathematics achievement of Chinese, Japanese, and American Children. *Science, 231*, 693–699.

Stipeck, D. J., & Hoffman, J. (1980). Development of children's performance-related judgments. *Child Development, 51*, 912–914.

Super, D. E. (1953). A theory of vocational development. *American Psychologist, 8*, 185–190.

Super, D. E. (1963). Vocational development in adolescence and early childhood: Tasks and behaviors. In D. E. Super, R. Starishevsky, N. Matlin, & J. P. Jordaan (Eds.), *Career development: Self-concept theory* (pp. 79–95). New York: College Entrance Examination Board, Research Monograph No. 4.

Super, D. E. (1980). A life-span, life-space approach to career development. *Journal of Vocational Behavior, 16*, 282–298.

Tinsley, D. J., & Faunce, P. S. (1980). Enabling, facilitating, and precipitating factors associated with women's career orientation. *Journal of Vocational Behavior, 17*, 183–194.

Tittle, C. K. (1983). Studies of the effects of career interest inventories: Expounding outcome criteria to include women's experiences. *Journal of Vocational Behavior, 22*, 148–158.

Uttal, D. H. (1986). *The relation between parental beliefs and school achievement in Japanese, Taiwanese, and American elementary school children*. Paper presented at the annual meeting of the American Education Research Association, San Francisco, CA.

Uttal, D. H., Miller, K. J., & Stevenson, H. W. (1985). *Correlates of poor and excellent performance in mathematics in Japanese, Taiwanese, and American children*. Paper presented at the biennial meeting of the Society for Research in Child Development, Toronto.

Walsh, W. B., & Betz, N. E. (1985). *Tests and assessment*. New York: Prentice-Hall.

Ward, J. H., Jr. (1963). Hierarchical grouping to optimize an objective function. *Journal of the American Statistical Association, 58*, 236–244.

Weinberg, R. A. (1989). Intelligence and IQ: Landmark issues and great debates. *American Psychologist, 44*, 98–104.

Weiner, B. (1978). Achievement strivings. In H. London & J. E. Exner, Jr. (Eds.), *Dimensions of personality* (pp. 1–36). New York: Wiley.

Weiner, B. (1985). An attributional theory of achievement motivation and emotion. *Psychological Review, 92*, 548–573.

Westrin, P. A. (1967). *WIT III Manual*. Stockholm: Skandinaviska Testförlaget.

Wishart, D. (1982). *User manual and supplement* (3rd ed.). Edinburgh: Edinburgh University, Program Library Unit.

Wood, W., Rhodes, N., & Whelan, M. (1989). Sex differences in positive well-being: A consideration of emotional style and marital status. *Psychological Bulletin, 106*, 249–264.

Yuen, R. K., Tinsley, D. J., & Tinsley, H. E. (1980). The vocational needs and background characteristics of homemaker-oriented women and career-oriented women. *Vocational Guidance Quarterly, 28*, 250–256.

Zimmerman, R., Jacobs, R., & Farr, J. (1982). A comparison of the accuracy of four methods for clustering jobs. *Applied Psychological Measurement, 6,* 353–366.

Zuckerman, D. M. (1980). Self-esteem, personal traits, and college women's life goals. *Journal of Vocational Behavior, 17,* 310–319.

Author Index

214

Subject Index

A

Ability, 68, 181

Ability/Adaptation Pattern Indicators, 15–16, 18–21, 195–199

Ability/Adaptation Patterns, Age 13, 21–24
See also Ability-Underestimating Normals; Gifted, Moderately Low-Adapted Achievers; High-Ability, High-Adapted Achievers; High-Adapted Normals; Low-Adapted, Low-Ability Nonachievers; Low-Adapted, Realistic, Low Achievers; Low-Adapted, Unrealistic, Low Achievers; Math-Oriented Verbal Underachievers; Moderately Low-Adapted Normals

Ability/Adaptation Patterns, Age 16, 25–30
See also Ability-Underestimating, High-Adapted Normals; Gifted, High-Adapted Achievers; Gifted, Low-Adapted Achievers; High-Adapted Overachievers; Low-Adapted, Normal-Ability Underachievers; Low-Adapted, Low-Ability Nonachievers; Moderately Able Normals; Moderately Adapted, Realistic, Low Achievers; Moderately Adapted, Unrealistic, Low Achievers

Ability-Underestimating, High-Adapted Normals, 39, 45–47, 51–53, 159–160, 184
See also Ability/Adaptation Patterns, Age 16

Ability-Underestimating Normals, 24, 34–35, 75, 83–84, 87, 91, 96
See also Ability/Adaptation Patterns, Age 13

Accurates v. Inaccurates, 83–87

Achievement, 16–17, 19, 52–53, 79–80, 82–83

Achievement Indicators, 196–197

Adaptation, School, 17, 20, 28, 49–50, 79–80, 82, 133–134, 138–139, 142–143, 157, 160, 163–164

Adaptation Indicators, 198–199

Aspiration, 50, 52, 56–57, 63, 89–90, 95, 123–125

Associations/Nonassociations, 5–6
See also Type/Antitype

B

Biological Maturation, 102–103, 139, 142–143

Boyfriends, 139–142

217

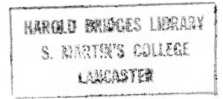

HAROLD BRIDGES LIBRARY
S. MARTIN'S COLLEGE
LANCASTER